BOOKS BY THOMAS HANNA
The Body of Life (1980)
The End of Tyranny: An Essay on the Possibility of America (1976)
Bodies in Revolt: A Primer in Somatic Thinking (1970; 2nd edition, 1985)
The Lyrical Existentialists (1963; 2nd edition, 1985)
The Thought and Art of Albert Camus (1958)

BOOKS EDITED BY THOMAS HANNA
Explorers of Humankind (1979)
The Bergsonian Heritage (1963)

THE
LYRICAL
EXISTENTIALISTS

Thomas Hanna

THE
LYRICAL
EXISTENTIALISTS

F
P
FREEPERSON PRESS
NOVATO, CALIFORNIA

The author is grateful to Princeton University Press for permission to reprint excerpts from the following books by Søren Kierkegaard: *Attack upon Christendom*; *The Concept of Dread*; *Concluding Unscientific Postscript*; *Either/Or*; *Philosophical Fragments*; *Repetition*; *Sickness unto Death*; *Stages on Life's Way*.

Library of Congress Catalogue Card Number: 62-7933

Second Edition

Designer: Harry Ford
ISBN: 0-918236-02-9
Printed in the United States of America

For My Mother

PREFACE

WHAT FOLLOWS is not a general introduction to the works of three modern thinkers. It is not intended to be. If the Reader seeks an exposition of the total range of Kierkegaard's, Nietzsche's, and Camus' literature, it will be better for him to seek elsewhere; there are numerous expository works of this kind in any number of languages, which will serve his purpose excellently. *The Lyrical Existentialists*, on the other hand, is primarily a work of interpretation, an attempt to sum up the religious and moral import in the thought of three of the most compelling and controversial thinkers of the modern era. But lest even this be misunderstood, I should hasten to add that this study is in no way a grouping of three isolated essays on three men; rather, it is an integrated interpretation, which sees all three of these thinkers united under a common viewpoint. This is the viewpoint that I have termed "Lyrical Existentialism," and each of the three men is treated as a representative of this larger moral-religious attitude. When this study focuses upon one of these thinkers, it does so only in continual reference to the other two. They speak as a group, and they find their common voice in Lyrical Existentialism.

This is not to say that with this study I am attempting to found a new "school" of philosophy. Existential philosophy—if it be a "school"—is already well founded with a tradition behind it. But it must be admitted that within this tradition of existential thought, I have made the attempt to single out three men who are in a distinct sense the most authentic sources of this tradition and, in a sense, the fountainheads of this way of thinking. If Kierkegaard, Nietzsche, and Camus stand at dead center of this tradition, then other representatives of existentialism (e.g., Sartre, Heidegger, Marcel, Bultmann, etc.) appear to be on the periphery of the circle, following up special concerns in terms of special points of view. The Lyrical Existentialists are thus seen to be the controlling and authentic thinkers within this broad circle. So then, even though a new school of thought is not defined, a claim of similar importance is made to the effect that Kierkegaard, Nietzsche, and Camus are the essential spokesmen for the existential viewpoint, and that once we come to understand their common voice, we shall be in possession of the fundamentals of existential philosophy. For those who become increasingly confused by the amorphous catchall, "existential," this may serve as a step toward clarifying the nature of what is certainly one of the most influential and far-reaching developments in modern philosophical history.

I must confess that another reason for this study was my frequent perplexity—and often irritation—with presumably serious works on existential philosophy that lightly pass over men such as Kierkegaard and Nietzsche as "precursors" of this tradition, so that they might come to what they feel are the more "substantial" and "philosophical" representatives of this way of thinking. Apparently, the conviction behind this is that Kierkegaard and Nietzsche are somewhat vague and unsystematic, and that the more important men are those whom one can get his teeth into. This is, I am persuaded, good evidence of what bad teeth many of our philosophical analysts have. The normal prejudice in favor of more consistent and unequivocal modes of thinking is all too frequently evidence of the inability of some present-day philosophers to digest anything that is not presented to them cleaned, baked, and quartered. This is not at all to disparage the traditional concern for systematic statement of thought; it is only to point up the inability of too many academically trained scholars to do serious and original analysis of new ideas, which are burgeoning in the modern world. Kierkegaard and Nietzsche must be given this kind of attention, and if they have lacked it in the past, the responsibility is not theirs but falls in the laps of their interpreters.

There are other purposes which I had in mind in writing this study, some of which I am aware of, and others, surely, that have not occurred to me, but none of these need be mentioned here; they will become apparent in the course of the reading and, in part, will be summed up in the concluding chapter. Whatever else of interest the Reader may find in this work, one obvious fact is the inclusion of Albert Camus, a contemporary writer, with Søren Kierkegaard and Friedrich Nietzsche. If the latter two thinkers have received less than their due from their interpreters, Camus has, at times, been almost punished by his critical authors. All three men stand together as Lyrical Existentialists and must be treated with equal seriousness. The inclusion of Camus in this group is witness to the fact that Lyrical Existentialism is not the precursor of a later development but is a continuing tradition, still bearing its fruits.

About the translations. All the translations from German and French in the Nietzsche and Camus sections are my own responsibility. For the translations from Kierkegaard I am indebted—as are all English readers —to Messrs. Lowrie, Swenson, and yet others.

There are other debts. These are to my friends at the Divinity School of the University of Chicago. The school itself, through a generous grant, made possible a year's stay in Germany, where the Nietzsche section was completed. And my debts to various men at the Divinity School far outnumber those of which I am presently aware. I have an especial feeling of gratitude to such men as Dean Jerald Brauer, Bernard M. Loomer, Bernard E. Meland, and Preston T. Roberts. I thank them for feeling, as I felt, that it was not our answers that drew us together, but, rather, our questions.

THOMAS HANNA

Hollins College, Virginia

PREFACE
TO THE FREEPERSON PRESS EDITION

In preparing this second edition of The Lyrical Existentialists I have had the impressive experience of carefully re-reading a book that I wrote 23 years ago—almost the time-span of a generation. The distance created by that great length of time has afforded me a sharper perspective on the nature of what I had produced so long ago: its outline and its shadows stand out in clear detail. In re-experiencing the book with such a sharper focus I have been impressed with two of its features.

The first impression is of its quality as a scholarly work. I am delighted and only moderately embarrassed to observe that The Lyrical Existentialists *is somewhat of a* tour de force. *The complexity of the thought of these three men is a hairy challenge to philosophical scholarship. And I can happily see, in retrospect of these twenty-odd years, that I brought to this challenge the thorough preparation and the clear-headedness their complex works demand of the scholar.*

So my first impression has been a glow of happiness that I have done justice to the remarkable accomplishment of these three wonderful thinkers. The Lyrical Existentialists *is one of the better ways of obtaining a grasp of the* whole *of the thinking of these writers.*

My second impression has been the reaffirmation of my feeling of comradeship with Søren Kierkegaard, Frederick Nietzsche and Albert Camus. I knew the latter, and it is almost as if I knew the other two: they are, all three, like my older brothers — I identify with their spirit and I admire their labors.

What is singularly impressive about them is their intensity and their tenacity in holding on to a point of view that not only lacked public sympathy and support but which went strongly against the grain of their times. There is a courage and steadfastness in their lives that I find deeply moving. The roots of their thinking plunged deeply into the waters of their times and they held resolutely to these roots despite the onrush of superficial waves and currents that stormed about them throughout their careers. Shallowness may be lacking in substance but it does not lack in power when it is represented by the bulk of one's contemporaries. One can be easily destroyed by superficiality. That is why steadfastness and strength are prerequisites of the philosopher: if you wish to sink your roots deeply, you must be ready to pay the price.

The lyrical existentialists sank their roots in a conception of the world and of the human individual whose upshot was not simply a way of thinking but was a way of existing.

*These men are not thinking academically; they are think-
ing in a genuinely philosophical manner: i.e., they are rig-
orously committed to tracing out a way of living that has
wisdom.*

*This "way" to which they point is what I have called their
"existential admonition": because of the way the world ultimately is and because of the way the human being ultimately is, we must live in a certain way. All three of these
thinkers see that the very nature of the cosmos and the very
nature of self-conscious humankind sets up ground-rules for
existence. If we look carefully, they say, we shall see that human life is not uncharted but has a certain directionality.*

*What they are telling us is that, even though human life
may not have a* given *direction—a goal or* telos *or fixed
destiny—it does have a* given *sense of directing: that is, an
internal ability to sense and control and shape our lives.
When these three men speak of human freedom, they are
speaking of the practical ability given to all humans to be
wholly responsible for themselves. And by "wholly" they
mean responsibility not simply of our minds or our souls but
also of our bodies. Their existential admonition is that if
we have the wisdom and fortitude to sink our roots deeply
enough we shall discover that we, by the genetic gifts of our
humanity, have the capacity for knowing and directing our
spirits and our living bodies in the ways that are wisest.*

*What is so strikingly different about their philosophies is
that they are not simply speaking of the "true" life, or the
"good" life or even the "beautiful" life—all of which are
traditional philosophical interests—rather, the lyrical existentialists are speaking of* the healthy life. *They are telling
us that to exist fully as human beings is to take on the full
responsibilty for being human. They are saying that to exist
with evergrowing psychological and physiological health*

and power means to assume an evergrowing responsibility and control of our lives.

Kierkegaard, Nietzsche and Camus are what I have come to describe as somatic philosophers, *and this is what separates them off from the traditional skein of intellectual philosophy. Using a psychophysiological analogy, we might say that traditional philosophy is left-hemispheric, whereas the somatic philosophy of these men is both right and left hemispheric. That is why their philosophy points to a whole view of human existence. And, just as obviously, this inclusion of right hemispheric brain functions accounts for the lyrical qualities of their writings: the artistic qualities of their philosophizing are a direct testimony to this broader, more inclusive vision of human existence.*

Thus, they are what I have suggested: the lyrical existentialists. And they have a lively and practical wisdom to offer us. It is a wisdom that is useable and liveable, and they invite us to use it and to live it. To the degree that each of us begins to use and live this somatic wisdom we shall have moved into that future state which all three of these philosophers envisage as the inevitable destiny of humankind if we are to survive and if we are to grow in power and health as a species: the state of human freedom, that fair realm where we, as humans, have finally affirmed ourselves in our deepest roots and have taken possession of ourselves. As the lyrical existentialists express it, this is the moment when we have "become ourselves."

It is with these two impressions in mind that I can recommend this reading to you. First of all, it is a good book— which is to say it is sound and artful in its presentation. But second and best of all, it is a healthy book. It is good for you.

Thomas Hanna
Spring, 1985

CONTENTS

There is many a man who has always been merry and yet stands so low that even aesthetics regards him as comic. The question is whether he has not been joyful in the wrong place. And where is the right place? It is . . . in danger, above seventy thousand fathoms of water, many, many miles from all human help, there to be joyful—that is great!

Søren Kierkegaard

If I be fond of the sea, and all that is sealike, and fondest of it when it angrily contradicteth me:

If the exploring delight be in me, which impelleth sails to the undiscovered, if the seafarer's delight be in my delight:

If ever my rejoicing hath called out: "The shore hath vanished—now hath fallen the last chain—

The boundless roareth around me, far away sparkle for me space and time—" well! cheer up, old heart!

Friedrich Nietzsche

I have always had the feeling of living on the high seas, threatened, in the heart of a royal happiness.

Albert Camus

THE
LYRICAL
EXISTENTIALISTS

Introduction

Søren Kierkegaard and Albert Camus were born a century apart: in 1813 and 1913. More than this, they were born a world apart. Kierkegaard first saw life on the island of Seeland, the remnant of that last upward thrust of western Europe, whose rolling plains moving ever northward finally disappear into the chilled waters of the Scandinavian seas, seas which send quiet mists over Seeland in the spring and autumn, and quiet snows during the long winter. Denmark is, in truth, a melancholy and peaceful land, a somber and sturdy land, a land which crowns Europe and gazes down upon it as from a distance, contemplating. This was Kierkegaard's world.

But Camus was born under the piercing, dry sun of Algeria, a land which can know neither chill nor melancholy, and which fears only mist and time. It is a southern land, a land resting under and apart from Europe, its people looking northward at Europe through an air which is dry and warm and washed clean by the ancient Mediterranean. This is Camus' world.

A third man, Friedrich Nietzsche, found birth in a world in between those of Kierkegaard and Camus. The time was in-between, for it was 1844. The place was also in-between, for it was Saxony, the old heart of Germany. And it was Nietzsche who partook of both these realms, linking together the misty world of the Dane and the burning world of the Algerian. Nietzsche was not to spend his whole life in Saxony but was to make a northern academic pilgrimage through Bonn and Leipzig, then southward to Basel, and later, in ever-increasing circles, he was to move restlessly through the sun-drenched cities of Nice, Genoa, Venice, Sils-Maria, and then, finally, Turin. Like Kierkegaard, Nietzsche was a child of the nineteenth century, yet he lived on into the century of Camus, dying in August, 1900. But the twentieth century could not claim Nietzsche for its own; only his body was washed up on its shores. His spirit was absent: it stayed behind, adrift somewhere in the nineteenth century, lost in its storms and cries.

It is more than coincidence that the worlds of these three men should be linked together. It is more than coincidence that three spirits of such different moments and places should impinge upon and complement one another and, so often, seem identical. Part of the explanation is surely that their lifetimes have encompassed an epoch which began with the clamorous and portentous advent of the nineteenth century and which endures into the present moment, an epoch which has seen the theories and fears of one century become the practices and dangers of another. We are not yet done with the nineteenth century, nor is it done with us: we still breathe its air. And it is not so much an inheritance as it is a continuing present which will not yet lapse into the past. This, then, is part of the explanation: these three men are contemporaries with one another and with us; we are all bound within the same epoch of history.

But there is another part of the explanation, and this lies not in the course of history but in the character of the men themselves. All three are sensitive, keenly observant men. Theirs is the temperament not of the scientist or of the rationalist, but rather of the poet. Their natural bent is neither that of the seeker nor that of the builder but primarily that of the man who feels, observes, and reacts. To the degree that these three thinkers are passive and sensitive before the world and its history, their reactions would be expected to be the same if the history in which they lived were the same. Such seems to be the case here, for we have to do with three "children of their times" who have sensitively mirrored an epoch which they share in common. Kierkegaard, Nietzsche, and Camus are observers and reporters of our period of history, and to the extent that this is a period of sickness and malaise, they are diagnosticians of our times. And if this analogy be not unjust, it is reasonable to say that if one wishes to understand our modern epoch in respect of its mistakes, its ills, and its possibilities, then one must come to know and understand the witnesses which these three thinkers have given to this period.

Yet there is more to this similarity than can be explained by a common historical moment and a common sensitive mirroring of this moment: it is the *way* in which these men have reflected their times. Here it is a question of those specific qualities in the world about them to which they are particularly sensitive. What are they primarily concerned with? The answer is brief and insufficient: values. The answer is insufficient because it suggests too much; it does not pinpoint that peculiar concern which all three men have brought to this problem. They are not primarily concerned with the material values that further the health, well-being, and productivity of society, nor are they primarily concerned with the social values which might accrue from a judicious arrangement of laws or production methods or ways of distribution. Neither of these concerns is primary even though both play an important part in the writings of each. What all three men were fundamentally interested in is the nature of value for the individual man, apart from his immediate engagement in the affairs of his fellow men. The question which undergirds and spurs all their questions could be phrased something like this: What can I or any individual do to achieve a completeness and satisfaction with my own existence which justifies me before the world and before my own being? Or, expressing it baldly, though perhaps not so clearly: How can I or any individual find holiness? The fundamental concern of all three men is with religious values, with the ways of individual existence which move toward finality, completeness, and wholeness. In this study of the Dane, the German, and the Frenchman, it will be made increasingly clear that these men are essentially religious philosophers. This is, of course, obvious in the case of Kierkegaard, but it is equally obvious, if one but reflects, in the case of Nietzsche: the very vehemence of his attack on Christianity is, in itself, testimony to his passionate concern for religious values. And with Camus it is the same: his religious concerns are as much shown by the particular ideas and institutions he has attacked as by the characteristic concern he has for a way of individual existence which he defends from attack. Kierkegaard the Christian, Nietzsche the anti-Christian, and Camus the non-Christian—all three are religious philosophers who would have every reason for being at loggerheads with one another, yet they break through their separate worlds and find a common ground which is peculiarly religious, peculiarly personal, and peculiarly related to the present era.

But even beyond this common religious concern which knits their worlds together, there is yet another ground for their meeting of minds, a ground which is at once an accidental personal characteristic and a necessary feature of their way of philosophizing. It is in this common trait that the present study finds its unity and its direction. All three men are lyrical existentialists. Their preoccupation with possible ways of individual existence, with ways of being, is central to their religious concern. The "inner," integral existence of a man is the problem which orients their thinking. Their thoughts turn constantly around the questions: What is the being of man? What is the being of the world? Under what conditions is the being of man emphasized and furthered? It is because of this fundamental concern with the nature of being that all three men can bear the title "existentialist." But the lyrical quality of their thought is an unusual and unexpected feature. It would seem here again that it is but coincidence that the works of all three men are flooded with lyricism, that it was a happy accident that each man *happened* to be a poet, *happened* to have a gift for lyrical expression. Yet this is not the case. And it will become increasingly clear in this study that the lyrical quality of these three separate philosophies is not an accident but a necessity; it is not a superfluous and pleasing complement to their way of philosophizing—it is unavoidable. If they felt compelled to sing rather than to speak, it is because what they had to say about the existence of man could not be directly told, could not simply be described and thrown out to the listener. They have sung because they were compelled to sing; they were poets made, not born.

We have before us, then, four suggested reasons— or, better still, four causes—for the similarity and, ofttimes, identity of three spirits whose particular worlds and moments were different. But before we look for this identity writ large in the general viewpoint of their works, it is important that we notice the impressive way in which it is writ small in curious parallels of their personal experiences, tastes, and special em-

phases of thought. Once we have probed these numerous similarities, our taste should be thoroughly
whetted for a general account of these three bodies of
thought and of the common voice which arises from
them.

It is interesting, for example, that all three of these
men felt that they had a mission in life, a special task
which they believed it was their destiny to fulfill.
Men who feel that they are marked out in such a way
are always a rarity, and the rarity is compounded by
the fact that these three men "happened" to think of
themselves in this way. Largely as a consequence of
this feeling, they related themselves to their times in a
prophetical manner. There are warnings and admon-
ishments in what they have to say, and these prophetical utterances are thrown out to an age which they
see to be in trouble. To speak of them as prophets is
to point up the fact that each had a polemical relationship with his moment of history. They are in no wise
dispassionate, ivory-tower thinkers at a dignified distance from problems of the moment; instead, they
were constantly absorbed in the crucial questions of
their day. And thus their attacks upon individuals and
institutions, as well as ideas, are as refreshing as they
are fierce. And these polemics were not footnotes of
formal treatises; they were essays, articles, and, at
times, common pamphlets, thrown out on the spur of
the moment and soon forgotten. Even so, there was
regret in none of these thinkers over the fact that
much of their labors was lost in the passage of time.
They did not feel that the greatness of their works
was in any way measured by their "imperishability."
This was, in part, due to their melancholy conviction
of the perishability of all works of men (Camus has
noted that within a few thousand years the works of
Goethe will be little more than archeological curiosi-

ties), and it also expresses their single-minded concern to be prophets to their age.

But this leads us to assert another common trait of the Lyrical Existentialists: they were "engaged" thinkers, who found their task and identity with transient contemporary issues. This is not a common trait among philosophers; hence, it is all the more surprising to discover it among three presumably disparate individuals. But the surprise broadens when we note some of the polemical blasts which they directed to their age. For example, they scorned parties and sects, indeed, they were almost instinctively contemptuous of any mass movement or popular conviction. And this contempt found its basis in a condemnation of the modern anonymous mass, in which the individual and his identity are drowned. Another thing is the antinationalistic bias which motivates much of their writing. None of them had more than a casual feeling of personal identity with their nations; the words "nation" and "state" were used by them with contempt, and even though they did have attachments to their native languages and landscapes, these men do not represent Denmark, or Germany, or France; they are Europeans. Their audience is not specific; it is universal. And this cosmopolitan quality of their works is a trait which, in the final chapter of this study, will be seen to have somewhat startling implications.

There is still more to be noticed about the prophetical engagement of the Lyrical Existentialists. An important conviction is their common denial of any progress in history; essentially, they are antihistorical thinkers who succeeded brilliantly, for the most part, in giving a dusting off to any historically oriented philosophy that came within their ken. This general attitude found specific application in viewing history since the opening of the nineteenth century as an age

of "dissolution," or "nihilism," or morbid "frenzy."
The meaningless and stultifying character of bourgeois life is roundly condemned by each man in his
turn, and all three emphasize the spiritlessness and
singular lack of integrity which are characteristic of
individuals in modern society. Or take another polemical issue, albeit a minor one: their bitter contempt for
journalism in general and the modern newspaper in
particular. These are some of the more striking of
their parallel convictions about the problems of their
times.

But there are other, more positive similarities, and
these are equally impressive. The Lyrical Existentialists have an extraordinarily intense interest in ancient
Greece, its myths, its culture, and its manner of philosophizing. It is significant that this interest drives
past Plato and centers either on the pre-Socratic thinkers or on Socrates as a man. The importance of this is
that they were seeking parallels for their way of thinking in a period of human history that was not strictly
Western but that predated the birth of the Western
philosophical tradition. This is another instance of
their cosmopolitanism, a trait which will eventually be
explained.

And should we not be somewhat surprised to notice
that all three men were, throughout their lives, ardent
lovers of the theater? Nietzsche theorized about the
theater, Kierkegaard analyzed its dramas, and Camus
took the final step of writing for the theater. Again,
there is nothing fortuitous in this common interest; it
is an expression of a more general viewpoint about the
nature of the most serious human problems and the
special ways in which they must be communicated:
not intellectually but immediately and existentially.
Related to this, obviously, is their general admiration
for the fine arts and their concern for aesthetic prob-

lems. Each of these men has had much to say about the nature of art, and their aesthetic theories are in accord. They saw art as an activity which is contrary to nature; in fact, a correction of it. And this, too, is a direct expression of their more general point of view. Each man possessed considerable poetic or dramatic talent and, from the beginning, made use of it as an integral part of his method of philosophizing.

An interesting fact in the personal histories of the Lyrical Existentialists is that all three, while still in their twenties, had various reasons for believing that they were near death. This confrontation with death made a profound mark upon the manner of their thinking but did not issue as a concern for immortality so much as it did in a deep desire to find and possess something in human life which endured, which was not subject to the ravages of temporality. Perhaps this has some part—though certainly not all—in the explanation of the most pervasive quality of their manner of philosophizing: they were "serious" thinkers. This is to say that the problems which drew their concern were not casual or dispassionate; these were serious personal problems, which could not be treated with disinterest or coolness. The issues in their philosophy are not "out there," separate and distinct from our lives; they are problems which arise out of the very task of existing as a human being. Hence, they do not say "this problem" but rather "our problem."

If this is not enough, we can finally note three other traits of their way of thinking. One of these is that the Lyrical Existentialists are all moral relativists, denying any objective foundation for the concepts of right and wrong. Another—and related—characteristic is the assertion that philosophy should not be considered as a revelation of truth but as something quite different: as the revelation of the moral nature of the thinker who produced the system of philosophy. And so their writings do not tarry for long with the outlines of a system; they quickly penetrate these expressions of a man's thought and speculate upon the kind of life which is reflected by this way of thinking. Lastly, it is a curious fact that each of the Lyrical Existentialists seems to address his remarks to a kind of moral aristocracy which is hidden among the anonymous masses of men. Their writings are not thrown out to "men in general" but are directed toward individuals. There is a peculiar personal confrontation which takes place between these thinkers and the individual who responds to their voices. A secret bond is formed, a hidden community grows, and this is the aristocracy which each of these men seeks to find and cultivate.

There are, perhaps, other parallels that could be indicated, but this is surely enough to impress us with the extraordinary identity which links Kierkegaard, Nietzsche, and Camus. As I have said, this identity is not accidental; it flows from the very nature of their way of thinking. Each of these surprising parallels has its explanation in the common voice of the three Lyrical Existentialists, and it is now time to listen to that voice.

Part One

SØREN KIERKEGAARD

THE MELANCHOLY
IMAGINATION

The leap is not an extreme danger as Kierkegaard would have it. On the contrary the peril is in the subtle instant which precedes the leap. To know how to maintain oneself on this vertiginous razor's edge, this is honesty, the rest is subterfuge.

ALBERT CAMUS—*Le Mythe de Sisyphe*

CHAPTER ONE

THE INITIAL STEP

It was 1834, and Søren Aabye Kierkegaard was in Copenhagen. Four years in the university were now trailing in the wake of his twenty-first birthday, and already his mind was playing over themes for future poetic works. He fancied he would become a poet, and with a searching intuition he came to be fascinated by those exceptional legendary individuals whose significance far exceeded that of ordinary dramatic heroes—figures such as Faust, Don Juan, The Wandering Jew. The legendary stature of these men fascinated him; the pattern of their lives gave a certain meaning to life itself and to the tragic or bold or pathetic existence which a man might carve out of life. But beneath the play of his imagination the young student was inadvertently searching for more than a literary subject; much more. He was searching out his own destiny. The legend which had first caught his eye and held him was that of The Master Thief, and this seems most fateful. The Master Thief was a person of the order of the English Robin Hood or the North German Till Eulenspiegel, a truly free and mischievous person, whose very *raison d'être* was to be in conflict with the established order, whose very existence depended on the danger and challenge which the life of the bandit and miscreant involved. The Master Thief was the cunning, independent spirit who outwitted the authorities, broke the laws of society, and yet loved and gave of himself to ordinary people; a man who was able to sacrifice for the good of others and yet remain free of the bonds which others would cast over him. The Master Thief was a being who was related to his world in tension and who, in essence, was alone; he breathed only the air of the quiet and desolate plains. There was good reason for such an individual to seem strangely exciting and compelling to Søren Kierkegaard for, indeed, he sensed the lines of his own life in this legend; it was his own image.

It is a rare and precious event in human affairs when there arises among us an individual who conceives of his life as a task, who feels that he was born for a purpose, that he was picked out, chosen for some deed. Such men are few and infrequent. It is perhaps not extraordinary when there are those who feel they have a calling or gift and proceed to develop their lives in this direction. This kind of vocation we can understand. But it is quite another thing when an individual appears in our midst believing he was brought into life to serve some purpose, that his life is not really of his own choosing but was set and planned by circumstances or intentions beyond his ken and beyond his power to alter them. Individuals such as this are of a different order and their lives are stamped with the peculiar brand of the religious. They are the prophets, the "chosen ones" of human history, and Søren Kierkegaard, with an early and quickly developed consciousness, came to realize that his life was stamped by the religious, that he was chosen for a purpose.

Once such a realization comes to a man his existence is suddenly transformed; in one stroke the future and the past become enlightened, and the span of one's years is bounded by meaning: there is a task to be done and beyond this is death, there is something to be completed and, after this, nothing. And for such an individual, time itself is transformed. Now every second is precious and pregnant; it has a meaning and begs to be used. Time, so transformed, now becomes limited, like just so many grains of sand. Every instant now has its allotted task and cannot be lost, lest death come and the life task be incomplete and the chosen life be unfulfilled, lest a life of meaning fall into complete meaninglessness for the want of a second. When time is so transformed the individual meets every moment with a feverish haste, and existence becomes a ceaseless activity and creation. This is the kind of individual that Søren Kierkegaard became and the kind of anxious creativity which poured forth from him. And this is where we must begin if we are to understand Kierkegaard and what he had to tell us. We must begin with the understanding of what time meant to him. Curious as this may seem, if we have understood this we shall enter into the complexities of his world with a clear vision and a sure foot for all the tricks and dialectics of his thought.

Allow me to express the question which may be in the Reader's mind at this moment: "Don't you have this turned around backward? Isn't it rather the case that Kierkegaard was feverishly concerned with the eternal, with the 'leap,' with the infinite, and an 'eternal happiness'? Isn't his concern with eternity the very stamp of his religiousness, the typical religious attitude?" I can reply to the Reader that he is correct, that this is true about Kierkegaard. But it is only half the truth. Indeed, he was infinitely concerned about eternity, but (and this is what is decisive) he was also infinitely concerned about time. Perhaps no thinker before him has been so seriously concerned with temporality. We quickly see how much value he put on time when he says, "Five days—how much is that? Indeed it is not so much as a clause in the paragraph, at the most it is a particle, a 'meanwhile' which is merely the beginning of a sentence. But five days might very well turn a man's hair gray." [1] These are not the words of one who discounts time for the sake of some higher reality, nor, moreover, do we find an impatient desire to escape time in these more poignant words:

> Oh, in loneliness I never have wished for death. I do not understand how men can suddenly become torpid enough to wish for death. For me on the contrary, the more it grows dark around me, the more I wish to live, in order to hold out by myself, to see if my enthusiasm was an empty word or . . . penny beer, which foams indeed— but by a foreign admixture.[2]

The absolute importance which Kierkegaard attributes to temporality becomes even more evident when he says that

> The religious individual has lost the relativity of the immediate consciousness, its distraction, its time-wasting activity—precisely, its wastage of time; the absolute consciousness of God consumes him as the burning heat of the summer sun when it will not . . . abate. But so he is sick; a refreshing sleep will strengthen him, and sleep is an innocent employment of time . . . but one who has merely gone about with a great plan in his head, for him the cry of the watchman is indeed a sad memento, and the approach of sleep more saddening than the coming of death; for the sleep

1. Søren Kierkegaard, *Stages on Life's Way,* trans. Walter Lowrie, Princeton, Princeton University Press, 1940, pp. 407-8.
2. *Ibid.,* p. 347.

of death is only a moment and a momentary
check, but sleep is a long delay.[3]

And so it seems that the individual who is absolutely concerned about eternity is equally concerned
about time; in fact, to the extent he is concerned about
the former he is to the same degree concerned about
the latter. This is a peculiar contradiction; quite "unphilosophical." And yet it is the thought which permeates the whole of Kierkegaard's writings. How is it
possible for the individual to be turned in contrary
directions? How can two such concerns exist simultaneously in one being, ignoring the law of contradiction itself? The answer, for Kierkegaard, is both obvious and simple: "The existing subject is eternal, but
qua existing temporal." [4] So then here is our contradiction: the existing individual is both eternal and temporal. And be assured that this is stated neither as a
pious hope nor as dogmatic conviction; Kierkegaard
states this as an obvious truth about human existence.
It is, for him, a truth so evident and necessary that
without it there is no way even of accounting for the
past, present, and future. Nor is there any way of
understanding human consciousness which is that "instant" cutting time into its divisions. Let us allow Kierkegaard one more citation in order to drive this point
home:

> The instant is that ambiguous moment in which
> time and eternity touch one another, thereby pos-
> iting *the temporal,* where time is constantly in-
> tersecting eternity and eternity constantly per-
> meating time. Only now does that division we

3. Søren Kierkegaard, *Concluding Unscientific Postscript,*
trans. David F. Swenson and Walter Lowrie, Princeton, Princeton University Press, 1941, p. 433.
4. *Ibid.,* p. 76.

talked about acquire significance: the present, the past, and the future.[5]

Here we have it then: the instant of human consciousness is constituted partly by something eternal and partly by something in time, and these two realms are brought into some kind of interplay and interaction within the existing individual, and without this interplay there would be neither consciousness nor time. The Reader should be cautioned at this point not to be put off by such words as "eternal" and "infinite"; they are, of course, old words filled with the profuse and contradictory inheritance of Platonism and Christian theology. If these terms are disturbing, then perhaps other words may be used to describe what Kierkegaard is indicating to be a given reality in human existence. In fact this is precisely what will happen when, later, we turn to consider the writings of Nietzsche and Camus. In Kierkegaard we discover the difficult and enormous effort to pin down with words a truth about human existence which for centuries had been slipping through the hands of both philosophers and theologians, and if his terminology sometimes seems imprecise it is only because what he had to say was quite novel and the words were not there to express what he wanted to communicate. In part, this is why he coined so many terms of his own, and, in part, this is why he sought another means of expression: the lyrical method of indirect communication. And so the caution to the Reader is a two-edged warning: If the Reader be a Christian he should not, at first hearing of the words "eternal," "infinite," etc., bound off at full bay into the woods of theology like hounds to the peal of the clarion, nor should the

5. Søren Kierkegaard, *The Concept of Dread*, trans. Walter Lowrie, Princeton, Princeton University Press, 1944, p. 80.

Reader, if he be a mossy-eared empiricist, positivist, or what have you, drop the whole idea of the chase at the sound of these same words and head back to the familiar boredom of the city. For either kind of Reader there is something extremely important and quite unexpected in the thought of Søren Kierkegaard from which he can profit.

The promise has been made that if we understood the meaning of time for Kierkegaard we would become both clear-visioned and sure-footed before the complexities of his philosophy. We have already taken the first step toward the fulfillment of this promise, and now we shall take the next three. The problem before us is to understand how it is that you or I— the existing individual—can be defined by and absolutely concerned with time and all that this entails while simultaneously being defined by and absolutely concerned with eternity. The task is to see what it means to be turned toward the realm in which time has its rule, and then turn about and examine this presumably contrary realm of the eternal. After this, perhaps, we can put these two realms together. So then the steps are three, i.e., (1) a consideration of the world of time and finitude, (2) a consideration of individual self-consciousness where eternity reveals itself, and (3) a discussion of the way in which these two realms combine to constitute the existing individual. In the course of these three steps we shall come across those more salient features of Kierkegaard's thought—the *spheres of existence*, the *leap*, psychology, and, of course, Regina—and, because of this more simple procedure, we can perhaps understand these well-known features in a clearer and more complete way than heretofore.[6]

6. A word to Kierkegaardian scholars. In the course of what follows, reliance will be placed chiefly on the pseudonymous

writings of Kierkegaard. This is done not without appreciation of the insistence of many scholars that Kierkegaard is to be read and interpreted only with strict reference to his sermons and other devotional literature. There are perhaps some who even go so far as to say that the "real" Kierkegaard is found only in these devotional pieces and that the pseudonymous writings are deceptive and unreliable accounts of Kierkegaard's "true" position. There is, I feel, a patent absurdity in this viewpoint, derived not simply from a misunderstanding of the pseudonymous works but as well from an amazing deprecation of the obvious importance which Kierkegaard attached to these numerous works. But the essential motivation in this viewpoint is the conviction by Christian scholars that inasmuch as Kierkegaard was from the outset of his writing career a Christian, we should at all points refer back to the Christian writings for proper orientation into what was actually going on in Kierkegaard's mind at any period of his pseudonymous works. This seems largely to be a defensive reaction to those who have seized upon the pseudonymous writings with total disregard for the accompanying devotional writings with which Kierkegaard intended to indicate his abiding Christian convictions. The rationale behind this is that Kierkegaard was a Christian, and, therefore, the Christian writings reveal the "real" Kierkegaard.

Now this seems to be a most reasonable position to take, but the problem which undermines it is this: even though Kierkegaard did indeed term himself a "Christian," just what kind of Christian is he, if at all? Simply to accept his being a "Christian," as if this were a rigidly defined category, ignores the fact that if Kierkegaard was a Christian he was one in a quite novel sense. It is a question for open debate as to whether the way he understood Christian faith is actually "Christian" and whether the main tradition and currents of Christianity can be reconciled to his conception of Christianity as "the existential communication that the eternal God became a man in time." His polemical assertion that Christendom, as he saw it, had absolutely nothing to do with Christianity should, at the very least, be a warning to theologians not to be too hasty in claiming him for the Christian heritage. For one to identify his theological convictions with those of Kierkegaard involves the doubly difficult assertion that (1) "I am a Christian in the way that Kierkegaard sees Christianity" and (2) "The way in which Kierkegaard sees Christianity is truly expressive of essential Christianity."

In the end, then, we have a question subject to scholarly, historical debate, and, of course, it is a question by its very nature insoluble; one simply takes a stand and hopes he is right. As in so many scholarly problems, an assertion of faith is finally required. But, in the meanwhile, if we are to discuss Kierkegaard at all we must admit that the question about where the "real" Kierkegaard lies in his literature is a completely open matter. And the scholarly debate will necessarily take place first, with a consideration of how the pseudonymous works describe the human situation (which is their purpose) and, second, to see how this basic description necessarily transforms the question as to "what it means to be a Christian." The work begins in the pseudonymous writings, for at least here we are in face of matters which are not scholarly but rather which involve the re-reading of "the original text of the individual, human existence-relationship, the old text, well known, handed down from the fathers. . . ." These matters are real to all of us and, to a degree, should be verifiable by all of us.

Viewed as a "Christian" thinker, Kierkegaard is a man who has written a rambling 999-page prolegomenon for a theological treatise of 1,000 pages; what he had to say on the final page was rather simple, but he could not quite say it until the entire nature of human existence had passed in review. In the following essay we are mostly concerned with the first 999 pages, and our concern is not with a scholarly exegesis but merely with understanding what this marvelous spirit had to tell us. That this is the proper procedure is the most evident of all things; it takes but little imagination to guess what Kierkegaard himself would say to all this: "The man who says that one can understand my writings only by painstaking scholarship is, be assured, precisely the one man who will never understand my writings."

CHAPTER TWO

TIME, REGINA, AND THE WORLD

LET US SAY IT once more: for a man who reportedly yearned for an "eternal happiness," Søren Kierkegaard was almost incredibly concerned about the finite limitations, conditions, and problems in the world that pressed about him. The first important fact we must constantly bear in mind about Kierkegaard the thinker is that he unconditionally accepted the finite, temporal world as serious. To use an expression which will gain great currency in the course of these pages, Kierkegaard accepted unquestionably the given reality of this world. For him, this finite world was *real;* it was not apparently real, somewhat real, or real to a degree: it was *wholly* real, a sovereign realm which possessed its own laws, its own conditions to which the existing individual was subject. Unless this is rigidly kept in mind we immediately fall into misunderstanding about Kierkegaard. Apart from the realm of the eternal, which will be discussed in our second step, there is the other direction toward which the individual faces, and this is the temporal world which is indisputably, inescapably real.

When one accepts the conditions of finitude and temporality as real, then the existential attitude appropriate to this acceptance is the awareness that what happens in this world is, for my existence, a *serious* matter. The difference between saying the world is real and treating it as serious is, for the existing individual, exactly the difference between the world being unreal or being real. An intellectual affirmation does not suffice to make the world real; only he who exists in the world, aware of the serious threat of its reality can know about the reality of finitude and temporality. It is just this kind of reality that Kierkegaard recognized, and it was just this kind of seriousness that he felt about what the world offered him. The crucial experiences which are the lot of every man's life were events which Kierkegaard could not slough off or play down; they had to be dealt with, understood, and, if possible, conquered. The events of love, marriage, anguish, disappointment, despair, laughter, and suffering—all of these are crucial, recurrent events in human experience and cannot be escaped or denied. Nor did Kierkegaard attempt to escape them. What philosopher or theologian before his time has shown such concern with these crucial human experiences as even to compare with the unprecedented manner in which he attempted to understand the infinite dialectics of the love relationship, even though (and this is a decisive word) he had foregone this relationship and put marriage behind him? Certainly Augustine does not bear this comparison, for the soul-searching confession of his pilgrimage to conversion is a chronicle of the illusory and unreal paths he explored before being granted the ultimate "reality" of the Christian faith. In regard to the recurrent experiences of human existence, Augustine, too, set off at full bay into the theological woods, leaving the thorny problem of finitude discarded and transcended.

But with Kierkegaard it was otherwise. He could never discount the importance of involvement with the world, and this precisely because of the undeniable reality which the face of the world presented to him. The striking example of this was Regina: Regina Olsen, the lovely daughter of the departmental secretary of the Danish treasury. She was fourteen and he was twenty-four when they first met, and he saw her through that distance of ten years with the eyes of sagacity, experience, and uneasy sadness which are the signs of maturity; and they are the eyes which could see in Regina all that was lovely, feminine, and fresh, all that was irretrievably lost in the dying of his own youth and which he could reclaim and possess only in the incarnation of youth which was Regina. Two years later he proposed marriage and was accepted. They became engaged. And thus began a curious story, a strange involvement that Kierkegaard was able to break away from but from which he was not, to the end of his life, ever to break away. Regina and all that she represented was never to be forgotten by Kierkegaard, and the loss of her was never to be completely atoned for or justified. There is, I think, no more fitting and poignant symbol for what the world meant to Kierkegaard than the image of Regina Olsen. She was lovely, complete, the promise of happiness, and yet there was something more which beckoned him away from her: an eternal happiness.

There is much that will ever remain inscrutable in the reasons for Kierkegaard's perfectly deliberate break with the young woman he loved. If the Reader has understood what has already been said about what it means for a young man to feel that he was born with a mission, then it should, in part, be understandable why such a person would refuse to involve another being in his life's purpose—not only for the sake of his purpose or for his own sake but also for the sake of the other being as well. In this respect Kierkegaard not only saved his own life but the life of Regina. After all, it is most likely that she would never have comprehended either his actions or his motives, and most certainly Kierkegaard was fully aware that a marriage could not be allowed on this basis.

But, again, I believe we misunderstand Kierkegaard (and his philosophy) if we simply say that he gave her up because his life's purpose promised something higher. No, this would be tantamount to saying that Kierkegaard quite deliberately gave up the world, and this he did not do. There were other and more determinant reasons for his action, and these lay in his own personal history. One was his melancholy, his constant tendency toward periods of morbid depression, a state of mind which at times had led him to contemplate suicide. Another was his own family history and the strange father whom he loved, a father afflicted with his own peculiar morbidity and sense of guilt which led him to feel that his children would be made to pay for the sins of the father. And the sin? Kierkegaard felt that in marriage he would need to reveal his entire life to Regina, and how could he bring himself to reveal to this girl that his mother had become his father's wife only after being seduced and made pregnant by his father? Another reason was surely his own physical debility, coupled with the prospect (firmly believed by his father) that he would die at an early age. There were, perhaps, other and more obscure reasons, but all these more painful facts in his personal history drew together in one awful vortex, completely drowning any hopes Kierkegaard could have had for a happy marriage.

And so Regina was forsaken. Almost as soon as the engagement was announced, he knew that it was impossible. His attempt to be a part of the "universal" aspects of human life could not succeed. He was unable to be a partner to the happiness of marriage. He was an "exception" to it. Regina was forsaken, but she was not forgotten; she remained a haunting presence, which sought its way into all his thoughts and found its place in his writings. In forsaking Regina, he had not forsaken the world, but rather stood off at a distance, attempting, with a certain sadness, to understand it and come to terms with it.

So it should be borne in mind that the strange, calculated abandonment of Regina was not a theological act but was motivated principally by the more obscure elements in a personal history over which the light of melancholy had, from the beginning, shone. Or, to express this in another manner, Kierkegaard means precisely what he says when he terms himself an "exception"; this is to say that there is no ultimate theological ground upon which he could recommend that all men forgo marriage; rather, it is the case that all men should marry and participate in a relationship which is universally offered to all men—that is, all men except those who for valid personal reasons must be exceptions to this relation. To be an exception was not a joyful and assured choice for this twenty-six-year-old Dane; it was a painful and difficult necessity which was recognized and assented to. There is poignancy in this happening, the submission to a necessity which, if we but reflect upon it, is an even more subtle example of the keen appreciation which Kierkegaard had of the love relationship and what is required for it to be a healthy relationship.[1]

We have said that Regina was a symbol for the world. This is not quite correct, because it is a somewhat traditional way of speaking. To be quite precise, the abstract term "world" is a symbol for Regina who was a concrete, existing reality. If the Reader understands the difference between these two viewpoints, then he appreciates the decisive quality which the existential attitude introduces into philosophical thinking. In this way we can more clearly see the signifi-

1. Kierkegaard, *Stages, op.cit.*, p. 173.

cance of a writing career which devoted a large part of its labor to an oblique discussion of Regina Olsen and a direct discussion of women, the love relationship, and the nature of marriage.[2] In all this, Kierkegaard was focusing his thought on a few of the primary existential realities which go together to make up the world in which all individuals exist. There is in Kierkegaard no systematic and exhaustive treatment of all conceivable existential realities, no attempt to give a complete "existential" run-down on everything which makes up the concept "world." This is not simply because of the impossibility of such a task (which is, of course, the case), but it is chiefly because it was these particular existential realities which Kierkegaard, as an individual, knew best; these were things which had happened to him and seriously engaged his thought, and thus they were the areas in which he could best fix his thought. This insistence on discussing only those problems of one's personal experience is exactly the same attitude we shall later discover in Albert Camus, who intransigently insists on discussing only those problems *within* the boundaries of "what I know" and never *beyond* these boundaries of personal certitude.

It should be quite clear now why Kierkegaard's exception to marriage has no implication that such a relationship of individuals has less importance or less value than other ways of existing. In fact, marriage is supremely important, so much so that he can say:

> Marriage I regard as the highest *telos* of the individual human existence, it is so much the highest that the man who goes without it cancels with one stroke the whole of earthly life and retains only eternity and spiritual interests—which at the

2. This involves, in whole or part, *Fear and Trembling, Repetition,* both volumes of *Either/Or,* and *Stages on Life's Way.*

first glance seems no slight thing but in the long
run is very exhausting and also in one way or another is the expression of an unhappy life.[3]

Few other passages in Kierkegaard indicate more
poignantly how it was a necessity and not a choice
which left him with "only eternity and spiritual interests," thereby leaving him an "unhappy life." Such
an unhappy life is a broken life which suffers from
the loss of something in the world. Life is not to be
lived in this manner, and Kierkegaard goes to great
pains to show this, and in this very act consciously
sets himself up as a negative example, an illustration
of what not to be.

Søren Kierkegaard was intensely concerned about
the world and those particular experiences of it which
had been offered him. And, with this thought firmly
in mind (it is, remember, our first step), we can view
the broader aspects of this central portion of his
thought. Kierkegaard has great fun throughout much
of his pseudonymous writings in satirizing the efforts
of "positive" thinkers—the philosophers who, beaver-
like and with a consitutional myopia, plug away at
building up a system of ideas which supposedly accounts for the world but somehow leaves out one important and illusive factor: the individual philosopher
himself who is the shifting, changing, nonstatic, and
becoming component of that world which the positive
thinker builds. He builds his systematic world, seals
it airtight when the last brick is in place, and then
stands back and admires it, oblivious to the fact that
with that last brick he sealed himself out of his world
and will forever remain outside. It is not, in the end,
his world; there is no way for him to exist in it. And
so it is, according to Kierkegaard's analogy, that the

3. Kierkegaard, *Stages, op. cit.*, p. 107.

positive thinker builds a castle but lives in a hut alongside it. The one thing wrong with positive thinkers is
that they never capture the real world, simply because
they have no idea of the serious reality of a real
world. A real world is one in which the thinker is
"caught"; he cannot deny or extricate himself from
the real world, for to do so would be to deny the conditions, pressures, and determinations which comprise
the real world of the existing individual. Such a philosopher must recognize the negative aspects of reality, the temporal and finite conditions which bind and
limit him both in thought and action. Not to recognize
these negative features of reality involves one in a
rather laughable situation, i.e.:

> If a dancer could leap very high, we would ad-
> mire him. But if he tried to give the impression
> that he could fly, let laughter single him out for
> suitable punishment; even though it might be true
> that he could leap as high as any dancer ever had
> done. Leaping is the accomplishment of a being
> essentially earthly, one who respects the earth's
> gravitational force, since the leaping is only mo-
> mentary. But flying carries a suggestion of being
> emancipated from telluric conditions, a privilege
> reserved for winged creatures, and perhaps also
> shared by the inhabitants of the moon—and there
> perhaps the System will first find its true read-
> ers.[4]

The intellectual denial of the negative factors of reality is exactly as successful as the physical denial of
the force of gravity: both involve a kind of idiocy.
And, leaving satire for a moment, if we allow Kierkegaard to express himself directly on this subject he
says that

4. Kierkegaard, *Postscript, op. cit.,* pp. 112-13.

Negative thinkers therefore always have one advantage, in that they have something positive, being aware of the negative element in existence;
the positive have nothing at all, since they are deceived. Precisely because the negative is present
in existence, and present everywhere (for existence is a constant process of becoming), it is necessary to become aware of its presence continu-
ously, as the only safeguard against it. In relying
upon a positive security the subject is merely
deceived.[5]

And, in going on to explain the basic significance of
this negativity, he brings us back once more to a
phrase already familiar, i.e.:

The negativity that pervades existence, or
rather, the negativity of the existing subject,
which should be essentially reflected in his thinking in an adequate form, has its ground in the
subject's synthesis: that he is an existing infinite
spirit.[6]

Here we are once again back to the notion that
every individual is a synthesis, an existing infinite
spirit. This is the curious and unprecedented turn of
events in the existential philosophy of Kierkegaard: it
is the insistence that the reality of the world which
philosophy seeks to capture finds its ultimate basis not
in the abstractly isolated realm of sensuousness and
rationality but in the synthesis of this in the existing
infinite consciousness of the individual. There is no
"outer" reality, but rather the outer world becomes
real only in relation to an "inner" reality, only in
synthesis with this inner reality. The Reader has al-

5. *Ibid.*, p. 75.
6. *Ibid.*

ready been told that no matter what his philosophical orientation he would find "something extremely important and quite unexpected" in the philosophy of Søren Kierkegaard. And as far as our first step is concerned, this is it. It is the flat insistence that neither the purely objective nor the purely subjective philosopher, neither the positivist nor the mystic, will ever grasp the world in its reality; that the former, by espousing only outer events, automatically excludes himself from such a world, and that the latter, by wholly denying the reality of such outer events, cuts himself off from the given reality of the world, a given reality which it is impossible to deny. In opposition to these two fragmentary approaches, Kierkegaard maintains that the outer world is absolutely real and serious and is so not because of any mysterious virtue of its own, but because it is existentially related to the synthesis of human consciousness. There is no reality for the world without existence, and the world finds this existence only in the individual who is an "existing infinite spirit." It is only in conjunction with the instant of human consciousness that the world becomes real; until this conjunction is made there is no reality either for the world or the individual, simply because neither has come into the existence which the existing finite spirit bears.

We know then that time is real, that personal human relationships and especially love and marriage are serious and paramount events. We know that the particular limitations which hinder our thought and action are serious and undeniable parts of our discovery of the world. We know, as well, that that absolute finite limitation, death, is equally a real part of that world in which we exist. It is actually the most absurd reality in our existence: the certainty that one's being will cease to be, that something in existence will

break the synthesis which constitutes existence. Kierkegaard knows that "Immortality is the most passionate interest of subjectivity,"[7] and this is a knowledge
and a yearning which deeply color the thought of all
three Lyrical Existentialists. First of all and last of all,
he knows he will not endure: this is the painful
consciousness of death which is ever present and ever
threatens "me."

> If death is always uncertain, if I am a mortal crea-
> ture, then it is impossible to understand this un-
> certainty in terms of a mere generality unless
> indeed I, too, happen to be merely a human being
> in general. But this is surely not the case, and it
> is only the absent-minded . . . who are merely
> human beings in general . . . ; and in the same
> degree that I become subjective, the uncertainty
> of death comes more and more to interpenetrate
> my subjectivity dialectically. It thus becomes
> more and more important for me to think it in
> connection with every factor and phase of my
> life; but since the uncertainty is there in every
> moment, it can be overcome only by overcoming
> it in every moment.[8]

Death, too, is one of those negative aspects of human
existence which must be faced, thought about, and
constantly struggled with. It is a reality which is not
future but is ceaselessly present and thus must be
overcome "in every moment." The bounds of finitude
press about the existing individual from all sides and
in all moments, and he shall not escape them; they
define his very existence.

The world and all its threat, challenge, and promise
engulfed the mind of Kierkegaard, and he accepted

7. Kierkegaard, *Postscript, op. cit.*, p. 155.
8. *Ibid.*, p. 149.

it, honored it, and struggled with it, even though it was his fate to have forgone part of the happiness which it offered him. Time, Regina, and the world: they all came together, coalesced, and signified reality; and he met them with a passionate interest and penetration that were peculiar to him. His mind roved wider and deeper even than this, and he explored with an unwonted keenness the subtler and more hidden events which come from the confrontation of the individual and his world, psychological tangles of infinite complexity which arise inevitably out of the "human existence-relationship." But these questions push us more into an examination of the individual consciousness. These states which are called despair, dread, and repression, and which may, finally, break through into freedom, are ways of existence peculiar to the synthesis that makes up the self. And what Kierkegaard would have us know is that without the absolute reality which the world offers there would be no way of accounting for the self, nor at the same time would there be any possibility of accounting for the world without the existence of the individual consciousness. The two go together; they are one, but one in a type of synthesis. And hence there is no other way for the self-conscious individual to know himself and deepen this self-consciousness except through the world. Here is a last word from Søren Kierkegaard which will bring us to take our second step into the realm of his thought:

> The individual has his teleology in himself, has inner teleology, is himself his teleology. His self is thus the goal towards which he strives. This self of his, however, is not an abstraction but is absolutely concrete. In the movement towards himself the individual cannot relate himself nega-

tively towards his environment, for if he were to do so his self is an abstraction and remains such. His self must be opened in due relation to his entire concretion; but to this concretion belong also the factors which are designed for taking an active part in the world. *So his movement, then, is from himself through the world to himself.*[9]

What does it mean to have an inner teleology and to strive toward one's self? To understand this we must consider the individual self-consciousness and the eternal which is revealed therein. Thus, we come to our second step in the understanding of Kierkegaard.

9. Søren Kierkegaard, *Either/Or*, Vol. II, trans. Walter Lowrie, Princeton, Princeton University Press, 1944, pp. 229-30 (italics my own).

CHAPTER THREE

THE PRODIGIOUS WEIGHT OF GOD

FRIEDRICH NIETZSCHE was one of the great speculative psychologists of modern times, and those who have studied him as such have found that his dominant concern as a psychologist was with healthy and unhealthy states of mind. Søren Kierkegaard was also a psychologist, and easily a peer to Nietzsche; he too was centrally preoccupied with healthy and unhealthy psychological states. Healthiness was the theme and justification of their explorations in this realm, and even though it is their brilliant studies in unhealthy, pathological states for which they are most famous, it was the concept of the healthy individual which guided them in all such researches. And the amazing thing is that although neither profited from the other's speculation, nor did they actually profit from the research of others, still they shared the same concept of what it means to be healthy. This is a curious pass, another of those "coincidences" among the Lyrical Existentialists which are not at all coincidental. This common conception of the nature of health derives simply from their common understanding of the nature of man and his world. The working concept which both of them had of health was that it was a condition in which all constituent aspects of an individual's existence are allowed to have full play in the conscious life.

The psychological value of this working concept is, I think, obvious, although some of the ultimate ramifications of this concept may be obscure. The obvious implications of such a concept are that the given drives, impulses, emotions, and frustrations experienced by the human psyche are not to be thwarted, ignored, or repressed but rather are to be consciously faced, and expressed, and accepted. This viewpoint is one which has ultimate confidence in the individual and in his constitutional ability to remain healthy. It is a viewpoint which conceives of the healthy individual as the bearer of a constant tension, a tension which he is constitutionally able to endure and satisfactorily cope with. Of course, this is, at bottom, a conviction or faith about the nature of the given individual which is not cautiously ventured as a clinical hypothesis: it is an absolute conviction about the human individual which carries out into ultimate assertions about human existence itself. This conviction that the existing individual, as constituted, attains the optimum condition of existence only when all aspects of his existence are held in tension within consciousness—such a conviction involves an understanding that there is some effective force operative in this conscious tension which stabilizes, guides, and guarantees a continuing satisfaction within this state. There is the implication within this psychological concept that a man is truly and fully a man only in just such a state of conscious tension, and that this kind of tension is a state of health. Putting it in the most general terms, the Lyrical Existentialists describe this tension as that between the individual and his world—the world of finitude that we have just now considered. And all three thinkers have an acute awareness of the fact that the body is part of this world, a part which, to the individual, is the most immediate and intimate aspect of the world which gives itself to his conscious life. We know already about the absolute reality which Kierkegaard granted to the world in all its aspects; it comes to us now to consider how, in relation to this world, the individual may discover something about himself which is separate from the reality of his given world, something which puts him in tension with this outer experience that environs him.

The discovery of this tension within the individual's consciousness is an event which marked Kierkegaard's thought from its very inception. In truth, this is the central theme of the many-faceted first work, *Either/Or*, and—as I hope will become evident—is the undergirding theme of the entirety of Kierkegaard's thought. The discovery of this divided consciousness and its tension is not made by any rational philosophic means nor is it, properly speaking, a discovery which can be made by psychological observation; rather, this is a discovery which an individual can make and verify only within his own personal experience and then, afterward, can apply to the experiences of other individuals as being the "unseen" event which takes place behind what we know of their experiences. What I am saying is that this is an existential discovery, one which can never be discovered by objectively reading the patterns of the world. The event does not take place in the world which is outside us; it takes place only within individual consciousness and, hence, by the very nature of things, can be known only within each of us in our solitude. We may infer similar experiences in others only by analogy from our own primary existence.

"My soul is so heavy that thought can no more sustain it, no wingbeat lift it up into the ether. . . . Over my inmost being there broods a depression, an anxiety, that presages an earthquake." [1] These are the words, sample words, of an individual in psy-

1. Søren Kierkegaard, *Either/Or*, Vol. I, trans. David F. and Lillian M. Swenson, Princeton, Princeton University Press, 1944, p. 23.

chological trouble: something in the world has failed him, disappointed him, abandoned him. Something is not right. Between his brooding consciousness and the bright world there has arisen a difficulty which "presages an earthquake." It is in the section of *Either/Or*, Vol. I, called "Shadowgraphs" [2] that Kierkegaard considers the problem of what it means for something to go wrong in an individual's relation to his world. The "shadowgraphs" concern certain types of persons who have given something in the world their full confidence, who have found something in the world in which they can wholly believe, find hope and happiness. They are the classical literary figures of Marie Beaumarchais, Donna Elvira, and Margaret; all of them have found something in the world to which they gave themselves in complete confidence and passion, and all of them were betrayed and came to grief. The spectacle of these women being deceived by their extraordinary lovers is the concrete exemplification of how the individual can be deceived by the world. In all three cases the reaction to the deception is pathological; each of the betrayed women is hopelessly caught in a state of mind which Kierkegaard calls "reflective grief," a sorrow which is inward, hidden, and self-perpetuating. Her grief is that of one caught in the paradox of loving someone who is revealed as a deceiver; the love is directed toward an individual who *is* the object of this love but who has also shown himself also *not to be* the object of love for which she has taken him. How can she believe that the object of her love is deceptive? This is a paradox. How can she understand what has happened? Is he *really* a deceiver or only seemingly so? Shall she hate him and feed her pride? But how could this help?

2. *Ibid.*, pp. 137-76.

For if he is truly contemptible, then her hate would not bother him at all. What can she do? She enters with this paradox more and more into a reflective grief, sealing herself off from the outside world in an inner world of restless grieving. No verdict or solution will emerge from this condition.

This "shadowgraph" is a dark, inner picture of the subjective life which has been projected outward as if it were an objective event. The picture is that of a sickness which arises from the inability of an individual to reconcile his own confidence and love for the world with the discovery that the world does not respond to or accord with this confidence. There is a conflict here which cannot be bridged over or annulled, a difference between what one has expected of the world and what the world has turned out to be. And the insolubility of the conflict rests in the continual belief of the individual that the world must respond and conform wholly to one's desires, that the world *be* a world in which one can love and confide and hope. The inability to recognize the world for what it *is* is the source of the sickness. It is the refusal to recognize that the world cannot correspond with the absolute and infinite nature of our demands upon it, because the world is finite. The unhealthy psychological state which Kierkegaard depicts for us is the refusal to accept the finite and temporal limitations of the world, the refusal to accept its reality. That the object in question here is a loved one is, after all, an incidental matter; this is but a concrete example. The same grief can arise with any kind of goal, ambition, or desire which one pursues in the world. Whatever it may be, frustration can be its result, and, in the case of intensely personal goals, this frustration may be radical; and if one still insists that the world respond to this desire, then unhealthy inner grief begins its growth. As long as this insistence lasts, the sickness will last, and Kierkegaard, one of the most penetrating religious philosophers of modern times, has given us the surprisingly irreligious answer that the only way that such an individual can find the health of the religious life is by realizing that he is finite. Thus do we see that, in making his first step in the direction of the eternal, Kierkegaard pays his greatest respect to the reality of the world. Only in realizing the finitude of one's existence in this world does one discover the eternal which is within. Despair of the world and thereby find yourself!

Such psychological crises—which may appear in innumerable forms in the lives of individuals—reveal two truths about the world. First, that the world is real and serious, that it has a character of its own which cannot be ignored, and, secondly, that the most general character of this real world vis-à-vis the self-conscious individual is that it does not correspond to the needs and demands of the individual. There is a given disjunction between the individual and his finite world, and this disjunction is discovered in moments of concrete personal crisis. Both the crises and the truth which they imply are inevitable within human experience, but nothing is inevitable about what follows. Kierkegaard urges us to despair of the world and no longer trust our hopes to something which is foreign to our control, but the person so deceived by the world might quite well persist obstinately in the hope that somehow the world of finitude will bear out his trust in it. This would be a case of blind faith in the world which, no matter how often deceived, defeated, and wounded, refuses to believe that the world is not an ally of the individual. And this is indeed a case of blindness; it is the inability or refusal to recognize and profit from the truth which is implied in a frequent human experience.

We see, then, that Kierkegaard is concerned with such psychological crises from neither a speculative nor a dogmatic viewpoint but simply because such crises imply something quite basic about the nature of human existence. The foundation stone of Kierkegaard's understanding of human nature is this discovery of disaccord between the self-conscious individual and the world which is the object of this consciousness, and it is essential to recognize that Kierkegaard appeals to the universal ground of human experience for proof of this assertion. Later, in speaking of Albert Camus, we shall recall this entire discussion and discover that Camus, in making the same point about the individual and his world, goes to experience for his proof and requires no other proof than this.

This crucial experience to which Kierkegaard points is something quite elemental in human affairs; in truth, it is part of a man's experience from childhood on. A child discovers that his desires are not answered: "You can't have everything you want!" There is some educative value in this, and the child may profit from it. But there still remains hope, and in hope one may look forward to the time when one *can* have something he wants. Hope tempers this education and sustains one's confidence in the world. Such confidence may and does endure into the adult life, there being the day-to-day belief that if one entrusts his personal hopes to events in the world everything will probably "turn out all right." The "probably" indicates a cautious attitude, a cautious trust in the world. The education is not yet and may never be complete. The original fetal confidence in the environing world hangs on as a remnant. So that we might chance upon a man who, for eight hours a day, is a scientist; by professional training and instinct he is entirely awake to the finite conditions and restrictions of the physical or psychological world which he explores. But, after his eight hours are finished, he turns his mind away from his studies and goes to his home, his family, his entertainment, his meditations; he puts his hopes, his trusts, his most earnest desires in these extracurricular areas, and, with an ever-growing remorse and disappointment, realizes and chafes before the fact of a love which does not grow warmer, of friendships which molt into routine, of pleasures which cease to give pleasure, of a day-to-day existence which has metamorphosed into a twilit sadness without justification, without promise, without meaning. And then, one fine morning, he takes his life; he has refused to exist in a world which will not bear the meaningfulness which he demands that it bear. With the sharp crack of a revolver, this hypothetical life comes to an end, and, in summary review of this life, we must say that the man was rather blind; he did not apply to the whole of his existence that consciousness of finitude which he applied to his professional studies. The problem was not that he was a scientist; rather he was not enough a scientist. He was naïve about that which he could least afford to be naïve about: his personal existence.

There are infinite ways in which this kind of life might be imagined, but, whatever direction it may take, such a life is characterized by Kierkegaard as being "aesthetic." The individual who puts his confidence in the workings of the world and allows its arbitrary events to be the arbiter of his hopes—such an individual is, says Kierkegaard, caught in an aesthetic existence, i.e., his consciousness is turned outward in a state of perceiving, of hanging onto and drinking in the train of inner emotions and outer events which make up his perceptive (i.e., aesthetic) world. To use an expression of Kierkegaard's which is quite exact, the aesthetic life is the life of the "spectator"; it is an individual existence which is turned outward—and only outward—absorbing, viewing, and reflecting the changing kaleidoscope of his sensible world. At a later date, when Nietzsche scorned the typical German as absorbed in beer and Wagner he, also, was pointing to the aesthetic type of life. This was why he could write that "the Germans are not even shallow, in truth they have not even broken through the surface of things!" And, at a still later date, when Camus says of our own day and times that modern man is chiefly characterized by being a fornicator and a reader of newspapers, he is again simply speaking of the aesthetic life.

But the aesthetic life is an extremely fragile existence—fragile because its fate lies beyond, outside the individual. And it is exactly this which dominates the aesthetic life: fate, or call it fortune, or call it luck. The individual himself does not control his existence, for he merely preys upon the sensuous world to sustain him; nor, in the ceaseless play of outer events, does the individual find a purpose; for him the moment is what matters, and any purpose transcends any of his given moments. The aesthetic existence, then, is completely dependent upon external circumstance, and thus it is fragile and in danger. In short, harking back to our first words, the aesthetic life is unhealthy. As long as it does not bring to consciousness the fact of the world's noncorrespondence with its desires, it is unhealthy; all the constituent aspects of the individual's existence have not been brought into the play of consciousness. The aesthetic existence is simply false to the constituted nature of human existence and cannot survive with impunity. Kierkegaard's statement about this is clear enough:

The *immediate* man (in so far as immediacy is to be found without any reflection) is merely soulishly determined, his self or he himself is a something included along with "the other" in the compass of the temporal and the worldly, and it has only an illusory appearance of possessing in it something eternal. Thus the self coheres immediately with "the other," wishing, desiring, enjoying, etc., but passively; even in desiring, the self is in the dative case, like the child when it says "me" for I. Its dialectic is: the agreeable and the disagreeable; its concepts are: good fortune, misfortune, fate.

Now then there *happens*, befalls (falls upon) this immediate self something which brings it to despair; in no other way can this come about; since the self has no reflection in itself, that which brings it to despair must come from without, and the despair is merely passive. That wherein immediacy has its being, or (supposing that after all it has a little bit of reflection in itself) that part thereof to which it especially clings, a man is deprived of by "a stroke of fate," in short, he becomes, as he calls it, unfortunate, that is, the immediacy in him receives such a shock that it cannot recover itself—he despairs.[3]

It is when this grasp upon immediacy has received a shock that an individual discovers the possibility of asserting himself against this immediacy, of originating an action which has its source within his own conscious world. This is an action which has arisen as a basic reaction to his immediate experience; it is a

3. Søren Kierkegaard, *The Sickness Unto Death,* trans. Walter Lowrie, Princeton, Princeton University Press, 1941, pp. 80-1.

consciousness which has sprung into being as a self-consciousness, a double reflection which suddenly puts a distance between the individual and his world. This primal action Kierkegaard calls "despair," and this despair is a positive action which asserts an autonomous self against the world *of* the self. From this point onward the world is no longer the same, for existence is no longer the same: a reality other than that of the world has come into competition.

What Kierkegaard has called "spheres of existence" are simply descriptions of the ways in which the conscious individual exists in relation to the world of his immediate experience. The aesthetic way of existing finds its fullest, purest expression in eroticism, but this personal mode of existence is not solely limited to this kind of relation to the world. There is, as well, a possible intellectual side to the aesthetic life, which involves this same unblinking, wide-eyed immediate relation to the world and whose blind side consists in the inability to see the threat of finitude in this world. The intellectual expressions of this positive direct relationship to the world are what Kierkegaard has scored almost unceasingly by intricate metaphysical argument, by bombast, by ridicule, by scorn, and by satire. It was the aesthetic intellectual whom he saw in the forefront of the wave of systematic thought which Hegelianism had engendered throughout Europe. And nothing was more apparent to Kierkegaard than that these colossal intellects, although able to comprehend all human history within their system, could not understand (indeed did not care to) that modestly simple problem: what does it mean for me, an individual, to exist? As long as such a philosopher was unable to account for his own particular life within the web of his system, then he was, as a philosopher, guilty of being infinitely con-

cerned about something which didn't concern anyone. Within the system's maze of abstract forms
Kierkegaard wondered where there was a place for
the concrete existence which alone could justify and
give the system meaning. The positive thinker would
never touch upon real existence until he recognized
those negative finite realities which constitute the
stumbling block for all well-greased systems. One
may have the logical, static form of the system or one
may have the existential, but one may not have both.

Perhaps, then, we can appreciate what Kierkegaard
intends when he says that the conscious state undergirding eroticism or positive thinking is a state of
mind in despair. This is to say that the aesthetic
consciousness is an incomplete, limping, half-blind
consciousness that is ill-constituted and is apt to
crumble without warning. In short, the aesthetic state
of mind is unhealthy simply because it excludes from
consciousness the wider realm of individual existence.
It is a false consciousness, false to what *is* the constitution of individuality. Thus do its active expressions
end in boredom, unhappiness, anxiety; and its philosophical expressions end in false assumptions about
reality. Both the thought and the actions of the
aesthetic consciousness are unhealthy.

The picture which Kierkegaard paints us is this:
the natural and childlike aesthetic consciousness discovers its unhealth in a crisis in its relation to the
world; recognition of what has been revealed in this
crisis invites the individual to despair of the world as
being the sole constituent of his existence; this act
of despair is the prime act of the conscious self in
asserting its autonomy in face of the world and is,
simultaneously, the rediscovery of health in new
terms, i.e., in terms of a consciousness of difference
and tension with one's world. Now what is already

obvious in this process is the fact that if the aesthetic crisis points to another state of mind and is "invited" to this wider consciousness, then there has been, from the beginning, a teleology implicit within the structure of human consciousness. Hence, the understanding which Kierkegaard has of human consciousness is that it is not given as a simple structure, all of whose constituent factors and possibilities are on the same level, and whose variations and transformations are only a matter of degree and only a matter of varied constellations of these given factors. Rather, Kierkegaard contends that human consciousness is a complex structure whose constituent factors and possibilities are not given as immediately active on the same level, but that consciousness carries within it a teleology which is the seed of its destruction and its subsequent reconstitution in a decisively distinct manner. Thus, the point which I wish to make clear is that this teleological factor which Kierkegaard sees in human consciousness is not, as some Kierkegaardians foggily contend, something present only in the religious life, but rather it is present as a given quality in human consciousness from its very inception. This is to say that there is a directive, teleological factor in the very constitution of human existence or else there is no such thing. For Kierkegaard, it is a primitive, inescapable factor of human experience.

So then, a teleological directive is revealed in the individual consciousness, and, recalling something said earlier, it was noted that Kierkegaard's conception of health as the tense conscious acceptance of all aspects of one's existence implied the presence of some force which guaranteed and stabilized this kind of consciousness. This stabilizing force is seen by Kierkegaard as being in the individual who "is himself his teleology. His self is thus the goal toward which he strives." Thus, if I read Kierkegaard correctly in this most essential point, he is saying that no matter how great the tensions within consciousness, health is guaranteed to the open-minded acceptance of these conflicting pressures by an increasing capacity to accommodate these pressures. This is to say that the teleology of the individual involves an unbounded possibility for containing a growing consciousness of the individual's conflict with some aspects of his environment. Or, to express this notion in its dual aspect, my inner teleology not only means a guarantee that I *can* retain sanity under increasing conscious tension, but it also means that I am "invited" toward intensifying this conflict so that I *can* expand this inner capacity for conscious tension. This may at first seem an unnecessary attempt to psychologize this central aspect of Kierkegaard's thought, but it is forgivable, I believe, if we understand that it is only by such means that this most crucial Kierkegaardian theory is to be brought out of the realm of fancy and into the area of discussion and criticism.

Everything said about Kierkegaard thus far concerns his philosophical ideas. As was said at the beginning, we are not directing our thought to the question "What does it mean to *be* a Christian?" but rather to the primary question "What does it mean to *become* a Christian?"—or, as Kierkegaard himself has rephrased it, "What does it mean to become an individual? What does it mean to exist truly as a man?" This is being strictly true to Kierkegaard's own intentions, and, inasmuch as this second question involves philosophy, we should take Kierkegaard's philosophy seriously, attempting to make sense of it, or else we should not take it at all. This is not an unnecessary polemical note but rather a necessary remark for anyone who feels that it is absolutely crucial that we find some cogent and meaningful manner in which to discuss religious ideas with the rest of the thinking world. Kierkegaard makes claim to an important place among the religious spokesmen of the modern world, and, hence, he must be taken seriously and critically even by those who fear that absolute critical honesty may destroy what seems to be the last philosophical support for religious values in face of a religious twilight which threatens to leave us a nighttime world of total immanence and objectivity.

So then, the aesthetic existence is unhealthy; its death is always imminent; it awaits circumstance, and —this present—it dies if the individual forsakes it in his despair of immediacy. Kierkegaard sees this act as the central moment in the growth of an individual, the birth of a new world of possibilities. The backward push of despair is the shove away from the shores of security and into the uncertain and obscure waters whose farthest reaches are beyond human help and over an abyss of "seventy thousand fathoms." With the death of the aesthetic something else is born within the individual; it is the push into what Kierkegaard terms "the ethical" where freedom and the eternal are for the first time tasted. One has now entered within a new "sphere of existence."

It is in regard to the spheres or "stages" of existence that one must be most thoughtful and careful in reading Kierkegaard. He tells us that there are three and, later in his writings, distinguishes yet a fourth sphere: the aesthetic, the ethical, immanent religiousness, and paradoxical religiousness. How are we, in all honesty to ourselves, to make sense of these distinctions? There is much confusion in regard to Kierkegaard's spheres, and it is certain that a major cause of this confusion is the attempt to see these distinctions baldly and literally as clear-cut categories with no reflective effort made to understand the basic continuity and drive which link these spheres together. For Kierkegaard, the two basic possibilities of human existence are to exist in immediacy or to exist in self-conscious freedom in estrangement from immediacy. It is either one or the other. And in the same basic fashion we must understand that the spheres express these two possibilities in terms of the aesthetic on one hand and the ethicoreligious on the other. It is, by definition, the very nature of the "existing infinite" individual which limits these possibilities to two. One may exist qua temporal or one may exist qualified by the eternal. The former has many varieties and forms, whether erotic, intellectual, or speculative; the latter has not varieties so much as differences of degree according to which one's self-conscious estrangement from immediacy is accentuated, qualified, and made more intense. The difference between the "ethical," "immanent religiousness," and "paradoxical religiousness" is not categorical but one of degree. For Kierkegaard, the only existential categories are the aesthetic and the ethicoreligious.

In the light of this it should be apparent why—as was noted a moment ago—Kierkegaard considers despair of immediacy as "the central moment in the growth of an individual." He makes this amply clear when, in *The Point of View*,[4] he contends that all his pseudonymous works point either "away from the poetical" or "away from speculation." But what do they point *to?* The answer: ". . . the great thing is not to be this or that but to be oneself, and this every one can be if he wills it."[5] Let us now explore the ethical, that frontier of the ethicoreligious, to see what

4. Søren Kierkegaard, *The Point of View*, trans. Walter Lowrie, New York, Oxford University Press, 1939, pp. 74-5.
5. Kierkegaard, *Either/Or*, Vol. II, *op. cit.*, p. 150.

it means to "be oneself."

The word "despair" has been used enough times already for the Reader to have become impatient for some definition. Let us turn the word about and ask, What is the opposite of despair? It is hope. But hope in what? Hope in finding satisfaction and happiness solely in terms of those limited temporal conditions which comprise one's immediacy. It is this hope, this faith in immediacy which despair shakes itself free of. Kierkegaard says much about despair but little about hope, yet these are the contrary faces of the same coin, and the Lyrical Existentialists are of one accord in their insistence that hope is the individual's mortal enemy. For it is hope which sustains one's relationship and confidence in the immediate world. It is hope which arises from tragedy with the deceitful invocation to start anew, that "things will be different next time," that this particular tragedy is not final, not definitive, but was only bad luck, an accident, a case of untimely, star-crossed occurrences. It is hope which blinds a man to the reality and lesson of his tragedies; it is that which a man seizes and clings to rather than face the bleak and frightening alternative of inner transformation. It is hope, this one word, which expresses the essence of one's faith in immediacy, for without hope the individual would not rearise, ever optimistic, from the disappointments, the deceptions, the confusions, and tragedies of his personal history. For all three Lyrical Existentialists, hope is a lie; it is a lie to oneself about reality, which keeps the individual dependent upon his finite environment, ever blinded to the possibility of independence, of self-discovery, of freedom.

> . . . it is my conviction, my victory over the world, that every man who has not tasted the bit-

terness of despair has missed the significance of life, however beautiful and joyous his life might be. By despairing you do not delude the world in which you live, you are not lost to it because you have overcome it. . . .[6]

Despair is an act, a negative act in which all hope in one's world is abandoned. What is frightening about despair is its absoluteness: it is complete abandonment, a cutting-off, an irrevocable push away from the shore. And in this strange circumcision of despair one has lost everything: it is an unprecedented act of courage and honesty. In honesty one has chosen to forsake one's world: he no longer belongs to it, it no longer belongs to him. But, then, where has this courageous honesty led him? Previously he had clung to something, now he clings to . . . nothing. And this is precisely the miracle which Kierkegaard sees in despair: when in despair one has nothing to cling to, one is alone, possessing nothing but oneself. In this moment of total loss and total discovery the individual makes his first discovery of an existence which is absolute (not relative), free (not contingent), eternal (not temporally confined), and infinite (not limited in possibility). In despair and recovery of oneself the transformation is made from one way of existing to another. One *is* different. One has taken a step which holds the world at bay; one now has the instrument of freedom which puts the world at a distance. And what must be remembered is that this miraculous discovery, if it be a "conversion," is a conversion without benefit of external help either of men or of gods. It is, for Kierkegaard, a possibility for any individual, rooted in his nature of being an "existing infinite individual." It is the possibility of being oneself and "this every

6. *Ibid.*, p. 175.

one can be if he wills it."

Despair, then, as the refusal to put hope in immediacy, is an act, an internal act of enormous import and yet one which is quiet and unseen. One watches a man, sees no change, yet he is no longer the same individual: he *was* one individual, he now *is* another. Of course there is no observable change; it is because the change has nothing to do with the temporal; it has everything to do with the eternal which a man has discovered with a new consciousness of selfhood. But we must deepen this discussion even more, for the intention of the present pages is to probe as sharply as possible into the Kierkegaardian view of human nature in terms of which we can make sense of these transformations from one sphere to another. If the Reader has some understanding of the act of despair ("some" understanding is the most that one can expect, given the hidden nature of despair), then we can sketch in the fuller picture of this event in terms of a favorite word of Kierkegaard's: repetition. Among the many students of Kierkegaard I think there has been no serious concern to understand the crucial significance of "repetition" in relation to the whole of his thought. And this is largely the fault of Kierkegaard himself who, when he first began using the term, was not, I think, certain about the ultimate import of the term. Certainly, in the book *Repetition*[7] we can learn very little: the title holds a fascinating promise, but the book itself proves to be one of the least important ever written by Kierkegaard. But the failure of the book should not lead us to assume the unimportance of the term, inasmuch as either the term or its meaning finds application throughout Kierkegaard's writings. The Reader should find that the un-

7. Søren Kierkegaard, *Repetition,* trans. Walter Lowrie, Princeton, Princeton University Press, 1941.

derstanding of this term will shed much light on Kierkegaardian philosophy as well as on the Lyrical Existentialists as a whole. Moreover, once we have seen the significance of repetition, not only shall we have a firm grasp of the meaning of despair but, as well, we shall have a specific conception of the dialectical nature of the ethicoreligious sphere.

What is repetition? It is the process of losing something and then regaining it in a different manner. And what initiates this process? The voluntary act of losing something, of giving it up. Thus, Kierkegaard sees repetition as an inward action which must be "willed."

> It requires youth to hope, and youth to recollect, but it requires courage to will repetition. He who would only hope is cowardly, he who would only recollect is a voluptuary, but he who wills repetition is a man, and the more expressly he knows how to make his purpose clear, the deeper he is as a man.[8]

Repetition gives us an "aesthetic" example of repetition in relation to a young man's troubles with his fiancée, but a more striking example of this principle is found in *Fear and Trembling*,[9] published simultaneously with *Repetition* in 1843. Here we find the problem of Abraham, whose faith is so complete that he has forsaken his love for the beloved son, Isaac, in light of the higher divine command to make a sacrifice to the Lord. Isaac himself will be that sacrifice, and Abraham has suspended his human, ethical love of Isaac in favor of that higher "divine madness" of faith, yet, paradoxically, Abraham believed that he would

8. *Ibid.*, p. 5.
9. Søren Kierkegaard, *Fear and Trembling*, trans. Walter Lowrie, Princeton, Princeton University Press, 1941.

somehow regain Isaac. And so it was: the Lord provided the ram. Abraham forsook his son because of his faith and then regained his son because of his faith. This is a paradox, an absurdity. Precisely so: Abraham believed "by virtue of the absurd." ". . . to be able to lose one's reason, and therefore the whole of finiteness of which reason is the broker, and then by virtue of the absurd to gain precisely the same finiteness—that appalls my soul. . . ." What is this? Why, it is repetition. Abraham has lost something and regained it in a different manner. We have noted that repetition is initiated by a "voluntary act of losing something." In the case of Abraham, Kierkegaard calls this act "infinite resignation." Not surprisingly, the same process pops up again in *Stages on Life's Way* in the section "Guilty?/Not Guilty?" which follows the tortured confessions of "Quidam's Diary." Here we find the act of "infinite reflection" by virtue of which Quidam holds his love for the girl and yet rises above it. This is a "double-movement," a dialectical act of freedom. In reference to Quidam it is said that

> Freedom indeed does not mean that he is to give up his passion, but freedom means that he uses the passion of infinity whereby he might give it up in order to hold it fast. . . .
>
> So in the infinite reflection freedom is won—a freedom which may be affirmative of love or negative.[1]

And it is Judge William who, in *Either/Or*, Vol. II, sets himself the task of showing that when, in marriage (the ethical), one forsakes the purely sensuous delight of immediate love (the aesthetic), one regains this immediate love in a new manner, transfigured and

---

1. Kierkegaard, *Stages, op. cit.*, p. 376.

ennobled.[2] Or again, the same Judge William elaborates the principle involved in this by analogizing personality to a circle: the aesthetic personality finds itself off center, buffeted about on the periphery of the circle, whereas the ethical personality finds itself in the center of the circle, dominating all that surrounds it but not controlled by it. The move from the periphery to the center does not mean to lose the periphery but rather to possess it as it should be possessed. This, again, is the act of repetition, but Judge William now tells us that the process is initiated by *despair*. So then, "infinite resignation," "infinite reflection," and "despair" are all varied expressions for the initial act producing repetition whereby what is lost is unexpectedly redeemed.

> By despair nothing is destroyed, all of the aesthetical remains within a man, only it is reduced to a ministering role and thereby precisely is preserved. Yes, it is true that one does not live in it as before, but from this it by no means follows that it is gone.[3]

Viewed in this perspective, despair takes on a larger meaning in terms of the context of repetition. The reader of Kierkegaard has not understood enough if he vaguely concludes that despair somehow introduces one into the ethicoreligious. This would be a treacherous understanding, because it makes Kierkegaard appear a mystic. Despair, taken by itself, is simply a negative decision in respect to immediacy; but this shove away from the shores of the aesthetic is only the initial act in a process which Kierkegaard sees as indigenous to human consciousness. Obvi-

2. Kierkegaard, *Either/Or*, Vol. II, *op. cit.*, pp. 25-7.
3. *Ibid.*, p. 192. For another interesting remark *re* repetition, *vide* Kierkegaard, *The Concept of Dread, op. cit.*, pp. 132-3.

ously, no one can turn away from his immediate environment; no existing human being can point heavenward toward a starry infinity and rocket upward, shaking the dust of immediacy from his shoes. No, for the "existing infinite individual" only one course is possible: that of the despairing choice, inaugurating an inner transformation which recreates one's relation to his immediate world. Repetition is a double movement, a dialectical event expressive of the very being of the individual, a being which is itself dialectical: both finite and yet infinite. One cannot realize infinity without regard to one's finite existence; it does not disappear, it becomes qualified. If the existing individual is a synthesis, then he will remain a synthesis no matter what transformation he may undergo. Each aspect of his existence will qualify the other. Even over seventy-thousand fathoms of water he will still have the shores of finitude in sight; they loom before him, never vanishing, and the flood tides of existence ever draw him back, lulling him toward the shores unless he fights against them in a never-ending struggle. Despair puts a man in conflict with his environment, and as long as a man remains in this ethicoreligious conflict he shall never escape despair, for this is the "sickness unto death," the awesome realization of the inescapability of struggle, of tension, of becoming, of the infinite task of becoming an individual. The despair which creates the ethicoreligious personality does not cease with one repetition, but repetition itself will be repeated into infinity. The negative push of despair constantly recreates one's conscious relation to the aesthetic realm. So it is, I believe, that in understanding the terms "despair" and "repetition" we have come to grips with some of the central concepts which Kierkegaard uses to describe the possibilities of human existence; and without this basic understanding there is little possibility of seeing the basic human situation which gives content and continuity to the term "spheres of existence." In a beautiful paragraph Kierkegaard has written a fitting summary to this discussion of despair.

> So, then I bid you despair, and never more will your frivolity cause you to wander like an unquiet spirit, like a ghost, amid the ruins of a world which to you is lost. Despair, and never more will your spirit sigh in melancholy, for again the world will become beautiful to you and joyful, although you see it with different eyes than before, and your liberated spirit will soar up into the world of freedom.[4]

Does this aid in understanding the transition from the aesthetic to the ethical sphere? I think so. More than this, it should enable us to understand the curious meaning which Kierkegaard attaches to the term "ethical." Kierkegaard does not stand alone in his unique use of the word ethical; it is a problem common to all three Lyrical Existentialists and has become a thorn in the side of many of their interpreters. Certainly, morality is a central concern of both Nietzsche and Camus, and especially in the case of Camus this concern is quite specific and contemporary. It is clear enough that Camus is a moral philosopher; yet the troublesome problem is that it is impossible to pin him down to any given position or principle of morality. It is for this reason that he is held in suspicion or contempt by any and all who have chosen definite policies, parties, or politics. He somehow remains aloof from objective commitments, being neither to the right nor the left, nor rigid nor libertinarian but rather all of these and yet none of them.

4. *Ibid.*, p. 184.

Why is this? The answer is the same for all the Lyrical Existentialists and is characteristic of their ethical thought as a whole. The answer is that, for them, ethical conduct does not find its source in any objective situation or principle but rather in the *manner* in which the individual determines himself in relation to a specific situation. Or, localizing this to Kierkegaard's thought, we would say that the ethical is revealed in the subjective state of mind with which the individual relates himself to his immediacy. The Reader can see that in speaking of despair and repetition we have already been sketching the outlines of the ethical, which is descriptive not of external conduct but of a state of being and an inner activity. Let Kierkegaard himself elucidate this point.

> If you understand me aright, I should like to say that in making a choice it is not so much a question of choosing the right as of the energy, the earnestness, the pathos with which one chooses. Thereby the personality announces its inner infinity, and thereby, in turn, the personality is consolidated.[5]

This is a helpful citation, for it stresses the inner activity essential to the birth of the ethical consciousness. Choice is the central term here, and energy, earnestness, and pathos are the purposeful activities which buttress this choosing. The difficulty for most readers in this area is not that Kierkegaard's term "ethical" is ambiguous but rather that it has a double meaning: on the one hand it refers to a conscious state of being and on the other it refers to what is best called "right conduct." This is to say that Kierkegaard's use of the word "ethical" has a subjective and an objective reference.

5. *Ibid.*, p. 141.

And here we are at the root of the problem, for it is his intention to tell us that the foundation and source of all right conduct is in a particular state of mind, and that without this given state of mind all conduct is either anarchic or moral puppetry. Lacking a subjective source, moral conduct is determined by the "more or less" and the relativity of the finite world; finitude can give us nothing which is absolute and categorical. But for one who has despaired of finitude and stands related to it in isolated independence, absolute choice is possible, indeed, is necessary. In terms of finitude there is but a negligible difference between honesty and slyness, such a slight, forgivable difference; but in terms of infinitude there is an absolute difference. In terms of finitude the butcher can hardly be bothered if his scales just happen to overweigh by one ounce, but to the ethical consciousness this ounce weighs a ton. We are dealing in this instance with basic categories and basic distinctions. In the world of finitude there is no choice but only calculation, an adjudication of relative factors: only this and nothing more can be demanded of objective-mindedness. But if, in infinite resignation, finite determinants have been despaired of, then there is but one unique and simple determinant of conduct: oneself. And this is exactly what it means to be in possession of oneself: all relative determinations have been forsaken and one stands alone, isolated, the only remaining determinant.

This is why Kierkegaard speaks of the ethical as based on freedom—for one *is* free. And this is why there is an either/or, an absolute—for one is absolutely and irrevocably responsible for his choice; there are no conditions, no extenuating circumstances, there is that single one, the individual, who stands alone, free, and absolutely responsible. Kierkegaard, as the father of Lyrical Existentialism, is the first one to admit that there is no objective standard for deciding right from wrong. He is exceedingly modern in his conviction of the relativity of objective moral standards. But his correction to this is the insistence that right choice and conduct do find an ultimate standard in the manner in which the individual makes this choice; that is, to the degree that the individual assumes freely and uniquely the absolute responsibility for his choice—to this degree is his choice "right." There is a fascinating more-than-modern consequence of this for all Marxists and scientific empiricists to ponder: it is only the good man who is good. Kierkegaard has withdrawn morality from the objective world to a degree not ventured by doctrinaire modern thinkers. The right choice is not dependent upon the right moment, or the right circumstance, or the right configuration of social/economic/psychological factors; the right choice is, ultimately, dependent upon the right choice, that is, it is self-vindicating. It is in this way that Kierkegaard has reconciled the double meaning of "ethical"; right conduct has found its source and its justification within a state of being. So then, there are quite obvious reasons for terming this an *existential ethics:* what one *does* ultimately depends upon what one *is*. And this is why it is only the good man who is good.

During this second step toward understanding Kierkegaard our problem has been to complement his views on time and finitude by developing his conception of the individual self-consciousness where eternity reveals itself. In this rather extended discussion the Reader has been asked to think about Kierkegaard's conceptions of health, of the aesthetical, of despair, and of repetition and the ethical. All this has been instrumental to our purpose, and the Reader should be aware that these at-first-glance disparate ideas come together to form a complex conception of the movement from the aesthetic to the ethicoreligious sphere of existence. It is now possible to round out our discussion by speaking more directly to the problem of the nature of self-consciousness.

There is no clearer analogy of Kierkegaard's conception of self-consciousness than that of the mirror. The man who exists aesthetically is like a mirror turned toward the world; he *is* that mirror and the mirror is nothing more than a reflection of the world. When Kierkegaard says that the aesthetical in man is "that whereby he is immediately what he is," [6] this is the principle of the mirror which has no other identity than that which it reflects at a given moment. But in despair the individual has put a distance between himself and the immediate, and hence the analogy is changed. The ethical existence is a double reflection: another mirror has appeared which reflects the first reflection. Now we have double reflection; we have consciousness of self, reflection of the fact of reflection. In this second situation it is no longer the case that one "is immediately what he is," but it is true to say that one *is not* immediately what he is. There can be no more exact description of self-consciousness than this. In double reflection, a gap, an infinite distance, has arisen between the knower and his world; he stands now at a distance, conscious of what he immediately is, and by virtue of this very fact that he, as an individual, is *conscious of* being something else, he knows that he *is not* what he immediately is. For those interested in the branch of philosophy known as ontology, it is worth while noting that this elementary yet dialectical observation is the central insight upon which Jean-Paul Sartre erects his extraordinary essay, *L'Etre et le néant*. He is refining

6. *Ibid.*, p. 150.

Kierkegaard's own ideas when, in a famous definition, he says that self-consciousness "is a being which carries within its being the consciousness of the nothingness of its being." [7]

If one has understood this analogical description of the individual self-consciousness, then it takes but little reflection to realize that in Kierkegaard's use of the words "freedom," "infinite," "absolute," and "eternal," all find their meaning in terms of this understanding of self-consciousness. And this is why, in the beginning of this treatment of Kierkegaard, the warning was made to the theologically inclined not to bound off at full bay at sounds of the words "infinite," "eternal," *et al;* and why, also, our more doctrinaire "scientific" philosophers should not draw their swords at the mention of the same words. Kierkegaard used traditional words which he thought could best indicate his meaning, but there is no doubt about the fact that throughout his writings he constantly struggles to prevent the reader from giving traditional interpretations to these terms. For Kierkegaard, "freedom" is born in and refers to individual self-consciousness; one is free in the *consciousness* of not being solely defined by finite determinations. For the same reason the individual is "infinite" in not being the finite being one "immediately is"; in this discovery the individual is conscious not of his being (which is the immediate component of his individuality) but of his *becoming,* a becoming which is infinite. The individual, moreover, is "absolute" in his consciousness of the solitary and total responsibility for what he becomes by virtue of his choosing. And, finally, the individual is

7. Jean-Paul Sartre, *L'Etre et le néant,* Paris, Gallimard, 1943, p. 85. (You will notice that Sartre here speaks of *conscience* rather than *conscience de soi.* For Sartre, the two expressions are equivalent, it being his understanding that all consciousness is self-consciousness.)

eternal in his consciousness of the incommensurability between himself and the temporal; in respect to the infinite task of becoming, a thousand years is equivalent to a day, and in respect to its pregnant possibilities, a single day is equivalent to a thousand years. It is this disproportion which is the mark of the eternal within the self-conscious individual.

It is the attainment of self-consciousness which Kierkegaard sees as the crucial moment in the growth of an individual. It is at this juncture that a man discovers freedom and responsibility and the awesome task of becoming; this is the mark of his entry into the ethical: "the ethical is that whereby he becomes what he becomes." [8] The world no longer has a compelling positive value for such a man; it has now become neutral. He is not concerned with the results of his choices but only with their purpose and with the purity of their single-mindedness.[9] But other than the freedom, the infinite, the absolute, and the eternal which are revealed in self-discovery, there is a basic discovery which towers over and behind these particulars: "For by the fact that he turns towards himself he turns *eo ipso* towards God, and it is a well-established ceremonial convention that if the finite spirit would see God it must begin by being guilty." [1] With these words the full intent and scope of Kierkegaard's philosophy burst upon us suddenly and powerfully. And it is for this reason that we must hold our thoughts in rein, lest they leap at traditional meanings. It is, indeed, for this reason that this entire discussion has been built up so carefully, lest the Reader should understand too little or too much in what is said.

8. Kierkegaard, *Either/Or*, Vol. II, *op. cit.*, p. 150.
9. Kierkegaard, *Postscript*, *op. cit.*, pp. 263-4 n.
1. Kierkegaard, *Concept of Dread*, *op. cit.*, p. 96.

The miracle of despair and self-discovery was, we have seen, a "conversion" without external aid of gods or men. And those discoveries of freedom, the absolute, etc. are not external and foreign experiences but are realities which find their very nature in the existence of the infinite existing individual. In the same way, when Kierkegaard speaks of God (or "God concept," or the "Infinite") he is referring to a reality which is inescapably a part of and indigenous to human existence. It would be unspeakable blasphemy, for him, to speak of God in any other fashion; and Kierkegaard has struggled to make this unmistakably clear: "As for God, he is never a third party when he is *present in the religious consciousness;* this is precisely the secret of the religious consciousness";[2] "For God is not an externality as a wife is, whom I can ask whether she is now satisfied with me; . . . because God is not an externality . . . *but the infinite itself* which has no need to scold, but whose vengeance is terrible . . .";[3] ". . . no, the eternal is not really a thing, but is *the way in which it is acquired*." [4] "He does not have to find the place where the object of his search is, for it is right beside him, he does not have to find the place where God is, he does not have to strive towards it, for God is right beside him, very near, near on every hand, omnipresently near, but the seeker has to be changed so that *he himself becomes the place where God truly is*." [5] God is present in the religious consciousness as a way of existing; he is the infinite task, the absolute goal which ever lures toward the depths of greater freedom, greater subjec-

2. Kierkegaard, *Postscript, op. cit.,* pp. 61-2 (italics my own).
3. *Ibid.,* p. 145 (italics my own).
4. Søren Kierkegaard, *Attack Upon Christendom,* trans. Walter Lowrie, Princeton, Princeton University Press, 1944, p. 100 (italics my own).
5. Kierkegaard, *Stages, op. cit.,* p. 461 (italics my own).

tivity, greater distance from the immediate world. The infinite is real; it is given in human experience. Thus is God real. Whether we say that the infinite is God or God is infinite—this is unimportant, I think, to Kierkegaard. What is important is to understand that this force is an effective reality woven into the being of every individual. To bring together Kierkegaard's notion of God with the conception we now have of the "infinite existing individual" we need but make two citations from *The Sickness Unto Death*. The first is this:

> Man is a synthesis of the infinite and the finite, of the temporal and the eternal, of freedom and necessity, in short it is a synthesis. A synthesis is a relation between two factors. So regarded, man is not yet a self.[6]

This sets the problem for us: Kierkegaard has linked together our discussion of temporality with our discussion of the eternal revealed in self-consciousness. This is a synthesis, but it is not complete; it does not exhaust all the constituent factors of human existence: even after we have taken account of the two conflicting realms of individuality, man "is not yet a self." What does this signify? It signifies that basic tenet already discussed: that we cannot say that the self-conscious individual *is* but rather that he *becomes*. When despair created a rift between the individual and his environment, it created a consciousness of this rift. For the simple, direct reflecting life of the aesthetic, there could be no consciousness of self simply because the individual was what he immediately was in a single, integral manner; there was a direct relation and reflection between knower and world, an identity of the two. But once a rift has been cre-

6. Kierkegaard, *The Sickness Unto Death, op. cit.*, p. 17.

ated between the individual and his world, what is it that holds this dialectic together, mediating between the finite and infinite, which simultaneously meet and compete within existence? What is it within this split which maintains and guarantees individuality and identity? It is the *self* which does this, says Kierkegaard; the self is that consciousness which rides above this conflict, mediating and sharing the tension between these two segments of existence. This is why there can be no self unless, in despair, one creates the schism which *requires* the conscious, mediating self. Self-consciousness rides on the shoulders of the finite and the infinite as a function of this schism, as its servant. It is the tense relation between the two. Elsewhere Kierkegaard has expressed this complex relation as being that between body (the finite) and soul (the infinite), whose synthesis is posited by spirit (the eternal).[7] When Kierkegaard speaks of the self, he is not pointing to some concrete thing or entity with a discrete psychological function; this is not the nonsense of a concrete will, or soul, or self which present-day psychologists have grown weary debunking. Indeed, Kierkegaard says that there *is* no self; rather, the self *becomes* as the changing, inconstant, tense relation between the immediate world about us and the mirror of consciousness which receives and reflects this world. And as a *becoming*, it is an unstable relationship which cannot posit itself (else it would "be" itself) but seeks to find a foundation outside itself in which it can posit itself and find rest.

But how can a relation find its foundation? The answer: only by increasing and intensifying itself; that is, only by becoming more and more a reflection of the conflict and tension which is the dialectical reality

7. *Vide* Kierkegaard, *The Concept of Dread, op. cit.*, pp. 79-81; and Kierkegaard, *Postscript, op. cit.*, p. 307.

of the infinite existing individual. This is why it was stressed earlier that despair is not an end in itself; the despair by which one loses and regains one's self and one's world in a different manner—this despair must be again and again repeated as a constant underlining and deepening of the reality of one's dialectical existence. This is not a thought problem, it is an existence problem, a task of living the truth of this dialectic to its ultimate point, to the point where it will no longer be necessary to despair, to the point where the self has found its foundation, to the point where one is completely and finally a whole individual.

> This then is the formula which describes the condition of the self when despair is completely eradicated: by relating itself to its own self and by willing to be itself the self is grounded transparently in the Power which posited it.[8]

This is the formula for completeness, this is the infinite goal toward which self-consciousness is driven. This is that guarantee of health of which we spoke which allows the human consciousness to bear an ever-increasing burden of tension, nay, which invites and compels the individual to bear this tension, which is the existential reflection of the reality of his dialectical existence.

The ethical sphere is but the initial stage of this tension, it is that state of mind whereby a man turns toward his world, which has now become "neutral"; he is no longer concerned for his place in the world or for the results of his actions. He is concerned only with choosing in complete freedom and responsibility; his ethical task is to choose rightly in accordance with the universal demands which the world places upon

8. Kierkegaard, *The Sickness Unto Death, op. cit.,* p. 19.

all men, but to do this not because of the moral pressures of the world but because of his inner responsibility, that is, the ethical man chooses not from necessity but from freedom. But the ethical sphere of existence is only a transitional sphere of the ethicoreligious existence. It is but the initial push away from immediacy, which has not yet realized the full import of its inward task.

Kierkegaard says that the ethical existence reaches its limit and founders on the impossibility of fulfilling the infinite requirements of morality: it is the very fact of being a finite part of this finite world that rules out the complete fulfillment of a perfect, complete, and successful moral life. It is the recognition of this inability, this impossibility, which marks the fading of the ethical sphere, for despair of the ethical drives one to *repentance,* and in the despairing act of repentance one loses the world as a "neutral" field of action, rediscovering it as a hostile realm which never will and never could conform to the demands of the infinite. In this moment the individual has begun to exist religiously. The task of becoming has begun in earnest. With a negative shove he has begun to "die away from immediacy"; the world which once aesthetically had a positive value to him is now seen in its true colors as a negative value. He relates himself now to the world in opposition; the tension now becomes clear and sharp; he suffers under it. He suffers in order to maintain the tension, and the tension maintains him in suffering. But, existing like this, how far must he go, how long must this endure, how much must he increase this tense suffering until it reaches its terms? For the self to find its ground and its rest, this is the goal toward which he becomes, it is the "eternal happiness" which alone can quench the fires of this suffering. And here is the answer:

> . . . since an eternal happiness is a *telos* for exist-
> ing individuals, these two (the absolute end and
> the existing individual) cannot be conceived as
> realizing a union in existence in terms of rest.
> This means that an eternal happiness cannot be
> possessed in time, as the youth and the maiden
> may possess one another, both being existing in-
> dividuals. . . . But since an eternal happiness is
> just a little higher up in the scale than a maid, it
> is quite in order that the period of endeavor
> should be a little longer . . . that the whole of
> time and of existence should be the period of
> striving.[9]

The infinite task of becoming is just that: infinite,
endless. The power in which the self may be
grounded, the eternal happiness which beckons, this
is God who is "the infinite itself . . . whose vengeance is terrible." So then, even as the ultimate stage
of the ethical was repentance before the requirements
of the world, the ultimate and decisive stage of the
religious is guilt before the requirements of the infinite. It is here that man is caught over seventy-
thousand fathoms of water, completely alone, cut off
from the security of the world and the security of rest
in the infinite. Here in this limitless sea of becoming
man can never go back and yet can never really go
forward; he is caught under "the prodigious weight
of God, which by humiliation presses down as deeply
as it uplifts. . . ."[1]

And here we leave the religious individual, caught
in a wondrous and awful awareness of what it means
to exist, conscious of what he is both in his finitude
and infinitude and existing in this consciousness, hu-

9. Kierkegaard, *Postscript, op. cit.,* pp. 355-6.
1. Kierkegaard, *The Sickness Unto Death, op. cit.,* p. 197.

miliated and alone before the task of an infinite becoming. He has discovered a joy and a misery, a happiness and a suffering, a laughter and a despair. He has discovered what it means to exist as a man.

CHAPTER FOUR

LAUGHTER AND PATHOS

HERE ARE two imaginary situations concerning two imaginary gentlemen: Beauregard O'Flaherty and Isaac O'Flaherty. They are brothers. With single-minded purpose, Beauregard, upon completing his high-school studies, threw himself into the world of business, determined upon success. And, indeed, success he found. Day and night, body and soul he gave to his business, his very being was poured into it until finally these unstinting sacrifices were rewarded with success: he was proprietor of the largest warehouse in the county. Fame and acclaim followed: he became president of the local Lions Club, was initiated financially into the mystic community of the Shriners, was even made an elder in his church. Beauregard and his warehouse had done well. However, one evening just as Beauregard was savoring his after-dinner brandy (Courvoisier), the telephone rang and someone told him that his warehouse was on fire. By the time he arrived on the scene there was a lovely display of flame roaring from the center of the warehouse where the roof had just caved in. Hundreds of the townsfolk stood about heartily enjoying the pyrotechnics and deeply thankful for this providential interruption of the eight-o'clock television program. They watched Beauregard as he arrived, the wheels of his big automobile skidding dramatically as he came to a stop. They watched Beauregard also as he stood gazing at the total loss of his warehouse, the work of a lifetime, *his* lifetime, reduced to ashes overnight.

He wept, wrung his hands, and lay sobbing on the
ground as the last two walls collapsed. And the townsfolk, feeling embarrassed, walked away, leaving Beauregard alone and forlorn. The next morning Beauregard
was found dead in the master bedroom of his home.
The suicide note said something about "tragedy" and
"nothing left to live for." Four days later he was given
an impressive Masonic burial. The whole town seemed
to be there, and they meditated sadly on the bitterness
of this tragedy.

And then there was Isaac. He, too, after fitfully
struggling his way through high school, entered upon
a business career—this, too, fitfully. Between fits of
idle hours in a rowboat and meditation over a book
or a well-prepared veal cutlet, Isaac built his business. As the fates of business will sometimes have it,
he was lucky. Almost with no effort Isaac found himself successful; everything seemed to mushroom
and run by itself, and before many years had passed
he found himself the wealthiest resident of the county
to which he had moved after his high-school years.
He had built up the biggest warehouse in the county,
was respected, envied, and admired by one and all,
was a feared poker player of the local Elks Club, a
benevolent director of the Red Cross, and an un-
predictable deacon of the First Baptist Church. He
had done well, and success attended him at every
hand. However, one evening just as Isaac was savoring his third brandy (Courvoisier), the telephone rang
and someone told him that his warehouse was on fire.
By the time he arrived on the scene, the flames were
dancing brilliantly above the giant warehouse; the
roof had already collapsed, and Isaac watched bleakly
as the first of the walls caved in gracefully with an
earsplitting noise. Hundreds of his fellow citizens
were on hand, thoroughly absorbed in the spectacle

of light and noise and quite thankful that there was something to replace the nine-o'clock wrestling matches on the television. They watched Isaac as he stood gazing at the total loss of his warehouse, the work of a lifetime, *his* lifetime, reduced to ashes overnight. They were not unsurprised when they saw tears form in Isaac's eyes, but they were completely caught off balance when they heard a chuckling sound and realized that Isaac was laughing. They had never heard such laughter: Isaac shook, roared, and slapped his sides. They could hear him saying something about ". . . well, that fixes *my* wagon!" and ". . . hell of an expensive show I'm putting on for you people." And the citizens, feeling shocked and embarrassed before this strange reaction, left Isaac alone, still chortling and slapping his sides in the orange-and-yellow light. In a few moments Isaac, too, left, going home to finish his bottle of brandy. During the long night, as he sat there tippling, Isaac's face was alternately taken with expressions of profound seriousness and inarticulate hilarity. The next morning Isaac sold his house at a loss and wrote a whimsical letter to the mayor demanding payment for the extravaganza he had presented to the town last evening.

Comment: Although objectively we have two situations which are roughly identical, the reactions to this situation are contradictory: in the case of Beauregard the reaction is tragic; in that of Isaac it is comic. Explanation: although objective situations may be identical, reactions to them need not be identical. This is because the existing individual is both eternal and temporal; the objective situation in the temporal world does not necessarily determine one's reactions inasmuch as another facet of human existence may be brought into play: the eternal consciousness of the individual. The value of these two little tales is both simple and obvious: they illustrate that what is tragic for the aesthetic personality may very well be comic for the religious personality. Beauregard, existing aesthetically, found self-identity in immediacy; all that he had was outside him: he *was* his warehouse. So then, when the warehouse was destroyed, Beauregard was destroyed; there was "nothing left." But Isaac, existing religiously, found his self-identity in freedom, in opposition to immediacy; the warehouse was not Isaac, in fact, Isaac buttressed his self-identity precisely by the consciousness that the warehouse had nothing to do with him. It was a threat, a temptation, a negative value. And as a religious being, Isaac saw the comic contradiction of a man (himself) who, in the eyes of the world, had been utterly destroyed, having lost everything, and yet at the same time had lost nothing but rather had gained something, had discovered how free he was from immediacy, how much distance he could still create between himself and the world. That a warehouse should be compared to an eternal happiness, this is what was comic, and this is why Isaac laughed.

The comic and the tragic: few thinkers have been so concerned about these two human extremes as was Kierkegaard—not simply because he spoke about them a great deal (which, of course, he did), but also because he continually *used* them in his writings. Comedy and tragedy were inescapable experiences for Kierkegaard; they were crucial situations which shot through and emphasized the peculiar reality of human existence. What a superb use of the comic Kierkegaard displays in his satirization of Hegelianism, of aesthetic types, of "systematic" professors who explain all of time and existence yet forget their names. But the woof of the comic is threaded into the warp of tragedy, which also finds its place from the beginning to the end of Kierkegaard's writings: in both the pseudonymous and signed essays as well as the intense discourses which accompanied his more intellectual productions. What could be more poignant than the short story "A Possibility," [1] the quiet tale of the haunted man of Christianshavn which is "far, very far away from Copenhagen." Or the infinite sadness of the cemetery scene[2] where an old man and his grandson stand over the grave of the boy's father, quietly speaking of life and death. These are not isolated examples but rather samples from a vast literature whose significance depends upon these moments of human crisis.

Kierkegaard is not just a philosopher, nor only an existentialist: he is a lyrical existentialist. It is not enough to choose one's words carefully, building up a rational description of human existence: this is insufficient, it is an abstract picture without reality, it has only a possible application to the reality it pretends to reflect. It is the mark of the Lyrical Existentialist that words are insufficient to the task; it is not that they are too general or too uncontrolled, but rather that they are too precise, too direct and static to describe the shifting, luring, threatening reality which is the reality of each of us as existing individuals. For Kierkegaard, lyrical means were needed to describe existence; words were not always to be used directly but sometimes needed to be inverted, twisted, and turned, catching strange lights and new meanings, suggesting rather than indicating, provoking rather than unveiling. This is the basis of Kierkegaard's notion of "indirect communication." Not only is existence an art, but communication is an art, a "double reflection": one must communicate the fullness of

1. Kierkegaard, *Stages, op. cit.,* pp. 258-68.
2. Kierkegaard, *Postscript, op. cit.,* pp. 210 ff.

one's inner knowledge by artistically invoking that same inner experience within the listener. This was a Kierkegaardian doctrine, but, more basic than this, indirect communication was a Kierkegaardian necessity: *what* he had to say was inextricably bound to *how* he would say it, to speak of existence meant that one would speak lyrically. And lyricism irresistibly gravitates toward the extremes of subjective experience, toward moments of laughter and pathos. Thus is Kierkegaard the great practitioner as well as theorist of the comic and tragic.

Artistic expression is a crucial concern for the Lyrical Existentialists, and it follows that the theory and practice of this should be a fundamental key to understanding them. In this respect, Albert Camus offers a direct and enlightening parallel to Kierkegaard. It is interesting to observe that in his historical and social writings as well as his purely literary pieces, Camus' leading philosophical ideas are often quite general and vague, but when he turns his attention to art and speaks to the subject of aesthetics, his philosophy of revolt becomes quite precise and explicit. The explanation for this is not far to seek: aesthetics is crucial to Camus' task as a writer, so that when he begins to speak of the sources of creativity and creative expression, he finds himself faced with the task of justifying a certain conception of human existence. Before long we shall see the basic similarity of the Camusian and Kierkegaardian conceptions of human existence, but for the moment we must be content to point out this parallel concern for aesthetics. There is no need to belabor this parallel, for it is obvious: both men have clear-cut views on aesthetics and in both cases this aesthetic theory is immediately reflective of their central insights into human existence. When Kierkegaard speaks of comedy and tragedy, he is dealing with aesthetics, and he is simultaneously revealing to us what it means "to exist as a man."

So then, what is comedy and what is tragedy? In answering this, I think that we shall be in possession of the clearest description which Kierkegaard can offer us of the nature of human existence. In addition to this it becomes immediately apparent that a discussion of comedy and tragedy is the necessary complement to what we have already learned about the two existential categories, the aesthetic and the ethico-religious.

As Kierkegaard says, "The matter is quite simple."

> The comical is present in every stage of life (only that the relative positions are different), for wherever there is life, there is contradiction, and wherever there is contradiction, the comical is present. The tragic and the comic are the same, in so far as both are based on contradiction; but *the tragic is the suffering contradiction, the comical, the painless contradiction.*[3]

Here we have an exceedingly clear definition; two factors are in play: (1) a situation which involves a contradiction and (2) two possible ways of apprehending this contradictory situation. If the Reader will recall the case of the O'Flaherty brothers he will perceive that this defines their two situations. Their problem was, in both instances, the same, yet their apprehensions of this problem were contradictory, one tragic, the other comic. So then, this much is clear: we have to do with a contradiction and with two conscious ways of reacting to it.

The next question to ask is "What is behind these

3. Kierkegaard, *Postscript, op. cit.*, p. 459.

different ways of reacting?" The answer, again, is quite simple.

> The difference between the tragic and the comic lies in the relationship between the contradiction and the controlling idea. The comic apprehension evokes the contradiction or makes if manifest by having in mind the way out, which is why the contradiction is painless. The tragic apprehension sees the contradiction and despairs of a way out.[4]

The comic has "a way out"; the tragic does not. The O'Flahertys again bear out this point: faced with the contradictory situation of total identification and reliance upon a warehouse which no longer exists, one man is crushed by this and carries out *de facto* the self-destruction which had already taken place; but the second man sees humor in this contradiction because he knows it is false; his way out is his desire for freedom and independence through which he attains self-conscious identity in opposition to any finite situation. In this second instance it is the push away from immediacy which provides the way out.

In distinguishing the comic from the tragic Kierkegaard likes to use the geographically moral terms, *higher* and *lower*. The individual finds his way out of such contradictions in terms of a higher sphere of existence. And it is by clarifying these distinctions between higher and lower that we can round out this conception of tragedy and comedy. Here, for the sake of the Reader, we must paraphrase a lengthy but very revealing paragraph from Kierkegaard's *Postscript*.[5]

Even though we have seen the relative distinction between the tragic and the comic (as witness, the brothers O'Flaherty), this is valid only in terms of

4. *Ibid.*, pp. 462-3.
5. *Ibid.*, pp. 82-3.

immediacy (which is to say, in this case, from the objective, third-person viewpoint taken by Reader and Author in discussing this problem). But for the subjective existing thinker who has died away from immediacy and now has a doubly-reflected consciousness—for such a person this distinction vanishes, and he sees the identity of the tragic and comic: both are reduced to the consciousness of a discrepancy, a contradiction between the infinite and the finite within the existing individual. So it is a question of one's point of view: if one views a finite situation in the light of the infinite goal, this discrepancy is comic; if one views the infinite goal in the light of one's finite situation, this discrepancy is pathetic. These same two points of view are applicable to the way in which we view the subjective existing thinker who is "as bifrontal as existence itself." Viewed as a finite individual reaching for the infinite, he is pathetic in light of the discrepancy between what he is and what he seeks to become; but viewed as an infinite individual caught in the toils of finitude, he is comic.[6] Thus, depending upon the point of view, the ethicoreligious individual is in possession of and caught in both the comic and the tragic. The greater the degree of his pathetic relation to the infinite, the greater is his comic apprehension of the finite. As we would have expected from our previous discussion, the consciousness of the ethicoreligious individual is dialectic; it is

6. This view of the religious individual as both comic and pathetic is emphatically contradicted by Kierkegaard in a number of places (e.g., *ibid.*, pp. 431-2) with the claim that the comical is excluded from the religious consciousness. But this claim implies that the religious individual has made a break with finitude and no longer has to reckon with it, which, for Kierkegaard, is tantamount to saying that the religious individual no longer "exists." Whether Kierkegaard is confused on this matter or only obscure is a serious matter which comes up again in our discussion of paradoxical religiousness (cf. *ibid.*, p. 473).

dialectically comic and pathetic because the existing individual is a synthesis of the finite and infinite. Almost at every turn, the rich arabesque of Kierkegaard's thought refers back to this fundamental description of the individual as a synthesis.

This is the final step in understanding the thought of Søren Kierkegaard, and it was our task during this last phase of the essay to show how the competing realms of the temporal and the eternal combine to constitute the existing individual. The comic and the tragic have been chosen to elucidate this last task, because the understanding of their essential unity is nothing more or less than an understanding of the essential unity of the dialectic which constitutes human existence. The tragicomic consciousness is revelatory of what it means to exist in this world and yet not be completely a part of it; of what it means to exist freely and solitarily in terms of the infinite within oneself and yet not be completely a part of this infinite. This is a divided consciousness, a double consciousness, a suffering and happy consciousness, a consciousness of laughter and despair. Although quite simple at the beginning, Kierkegaard's conception of the comic and tragic is quite complex at the end. It is quite complex because, once this conception is meshed with the spheres of existence and with the notions of despair and repetition, we discover that there are lower and higher grades of the tragicomic consciousness. For him who exists aesthetically, the comic and tragic are contradictions which exist outside in immediacy. But in the despair of immediacy irony is born, and the ethical consciousness has within itself that comical appreciation of how, in the light of infinite demands of perfection, relative differences of "bad," "good," and "better" are insignificant, meaningless. And when the ethical existence despairs of its task and repents of its concern for immediacy, the religious consciousness is born which sees all finite determinations in the light of the comic while simultaneously it is tragically related to the goal of infinitude toward which it struggles. With the attainment of the religious consciousness an individual has brought the dialectical elements of his time and his eternity together; he has reached the "seventy-thousand fathoms" and now knows the joy of his accomplishment as well as the suffering of his ultimate task. The self-conscious individual himself is the bearer and guarantor of this tension, no one can help him, he is alone and beleaguered; the more he suffers this contradiction, the deeper will be his joy and the greater will be his suffering; and by the same token, his capacity for joy and suffering will be increased. There is no end to this, and the realization of the never-ending, never-to-be-achieved nature of this venture is the greatest suffering to be endured. "Now existence has racked him as hard as it can rack a man; to live under or hold out under this pressure is what may be called emphatically to exist as a man." [7]

In the course of these plodding steps through the tangles of Kierkegaard's philosophy two things have been readily apparent: we have here a description of the nature of human existence—that is, what constitutes this existence—but, in addition to this, we have a prescription for the way in which a man *should* exist. If this discussion of Kierkegaard has not completely failed in its task, then the Reader has seen that Kierkegaard's conception of what a man *should* be is rooted in and derived from his description of what man *is*. This is of absolute importance to the understanding of Kierkegaard, for his value

7. Søren Kierkegaard, *Training in Christianity*, trans. Walter Lowrie, Princeton, Princeton University Press, 1944, p. 189.

judgments find their origin not in rationality or ideal-
ism or theological dogma but in the "is" of human existence; this is the thoroughly humanistic aspect of
Kierkegaardian thought. When he says that from a
consideration of what the individual *is* he can conclude what the individual *should be,* he is making the
injunction that the individual *become* himself. This
is identical with Nietzsche's injunction, "Become
who you are!" and serves to point up the cardinal fact
that the Lyrical Existentialists, in their final choice of
values, are religious philosophers rather than moral
philosophers. If Kierkegaard were a moral philosopher, his highest injunction would be that man
should *do* something; as a religious philosopher his
exhortation is that a man should *be* something, should
exist in a certain manner. It is this that marks the
concerns of these thinkers as more basic than that of
moral philosophers; each man would maintain that
what an individual *does* is ultimately reducible to
what he *is.* This insistence on what a man should be is,
as I see it, essentially religious, but, lest this word be a
shibboleth for both the theologically inclined and
disinclined, I have contented myself with being
quite precise in describing these men as Lyrical Existentialists.

Our concern, then, with these spokesmen for Lyrical Existentialism is to root out their ultimate conception of what a man should be. This is, after all, the
final point toward which their evangelical concerns
have taken them. In the case of Kierkegaard, this
final point has been described as "thoroughly humanistic" and consists of the admonition to despair of
the immediate world and continue despairing of
any hope in immediacy so that the infinite possibility
of absolute freedom and selfhood may become an increasing reality. In this process the individual has

preened himself into an intense affirmation and re-affirmation of what he is; to become himself, he wills to increase the dialectical tension within the synthesis which constitutes him. To exist as a man means will-ingly to be conscious of one's dialectical nature and willingly to reaffirm it, ever conscious of one's finite trappings and of one's infinite task. This is the high point, the existential admonition, of Søren Kierke-gaard. To say that this is thoroughly humanistic means that it can be explained and discussed in terms of human existence itself. If Kierkegaard has (and he has) frequently phrased this in Christian terminology, and if his interpreters have (and they have) seen this admonition as Christian, this need not deter us. If Kierkegaard's existential admonition is humanistic (and it is), then we can translate it back into human-istic terms; the Christian translation of these terms is not basic but secondary, and it is just as possible —if not more so—to phrase this aspect of Kierke-gaard's thought in terms of Hindu theology as in those of the Christian.

So then, this brings us in direct confrontation with the most serious problem in interpreting Kierkegaard. Our entire discussion up to this point seems to be centered upon what Kierkegaard has called *Religious-ness A*, the immanent religiousness which is possible for any man qua man without reference to Chris-tianity. Kierkegaard would completely concur with us up to this point in our characterization of the tragi-comic consciousness as completely humanistic; he would be willing to withdraw the Christian terminol-ogy with which he has, at times, inadvertently de-scribed Religiousness A. Thus, we have been on firm ground this far. But having made the assertion that the tragicomic consciousness, so described, is the *ultimate injunction* of what a man should be, Kierkegaard would no longer concur with us, and our ground is somewhat less than firm. Now the issue here must be clearly understood: the question is whether the religious consciousness, as Kierkegaard describes it, is decisively and categorically different in Christian religiousness as contrasted to immanent religiousness. Or, put in another fashion, is paradoxical religiousness higher than immanent religiousness, or is it simply another form and description of the same state of being? The answer to this question is not, unfortunately, solely a matter of clearly understanding Kierkegaard, but the difficulty is that Kierkegaard himself is not clear on this crucial point. His ambiguity in this matter is something that must be noted, and once we have examined the data on this question, it should be apparent that the ambiguity can be dispelled only with the conclusion that the final "existential admonition" of Kierkegaard is unavoidably immanent and humanistic.

In consideration of the spheres of existence some pains were taken to show that the two basic categories of existence, in Kierkegaardian terms, are the aesthetic and the ethicoreligious. That this is true is testified to not only by Kierkegaard's own remarks but, more importantly, by the very manner in which Kierkegaard has described the existing individual as a synthesis. Because of the nature of this synthesis there are but two basic existential possibilities: that of existing in the immediacy of finitude (the aesthetic) or that of existing in the freedom of one's infinitude, by which one is estranged from immediacy (the ethicoreligious). In the light of these two basic possibilities it became clear why Kierkegaard speaks of the ethical sphere as merely transitional. Now then, at this point we face Kierkegaard's Christian contention that the full-blown sphere of religious immanence can be decisively transformed into a higher and final state of being: paradoxical religiousness. This makes the tragicomic consciousness itself a transitional sphere, and suggests that *something else* has entered into human existence other than man's dialectic of finitude and infinitude. It is this something else that is at the heart of the issue, and it is with this that we must come to terms.

In the *Postscript* we have a description of the extraordinary existential transformation which takes place when immanent religiousness gives way to the paradoxical religiousness of Christianity:

> The exister must have lost continuity with himself, must have become another (not different from himself within himself), and then, by receiving the condition from the Deity, he must have become a new creature. The contradiction is that this thing of becoming a Christian begins with the miracle of creation, and that this occurs to one who already is created. . . .[8]

In another striking statement we are told that

> *The paradoxical religiousness* breaks with immanence and makes the fact of existing the absolute contradiction, not within immanence, but against immanence. There is no longer any immanent fundamental kinship between the temporal and the eternal, because the eternal itself has entered time and would constitute there the kinship.[9]

This gives a picture of what happens to the way in which the religious individual exists, and one must take careful note of such phrases as "lost continuity

8. Kierkegaard, *Postscript, op. cit.,* p. 510.
9. *Ibid.,* pp. 507-8.

with himself," "become another," and "breaks with immanence": these describe events which are totally anomalous with Kierkegaard's description of the infinite existing individual. This, then, is what happens, and just as events have their causes, so does what happens have its cause: the something else which enters into human existence. Here we come face to face with "the paradoxical transformation of existence by faith through the relation to an historic fact." [1] This historic fact in which Christian religiousness has faith is not doctrine, nor is it dogma; it is not cluttered with the details and qualifications which go with doctrine. We have here to do with something extremely simple and direct, an existential communication. "The historical fact that God has existed in human form is the essence of the matter; the rest of the historical detail is not even as important as if we had to do with a human being instead of with God." [2] This historical fact is an "existential communication" precisely in the sense that it is to be communicated and appropriated directly into one's existing consciousness without mediation of reason or circumstantial fact, these latter two being instruments of finitude. This is essential, inasmuch as, finitely considered, the proposition that the eternal God has existed as a man in time is absurd. Exactly so: the absurdity of the proposition makes it possible of acceptance only by a willing inward appropriation, and this is called faith.

If this historically and rationally absurd proposition be the something else of paradoxical religiousness, then we must understand why faith in this accentuates subjectivity to the point that the individual loses continuity with both finitude and himself, going deeper into existence than was the case for immanent reli-

1. *Ibid.*, p. 515.
2. Søren Kierkegaard, *Philosophical Fragments,* trans. David F. Swenson, Princeton, Princeton University Press, 1936, p. 87.

giousness. Here we are at the crux of the matter.
Kierkegaard has said that one *must* have passed
through immanent religiousness before he can exist
in paradoxical religiousness.[3] Why? The answer to this
is that the entire task of immanent religiousness is to
seek to ground one's self on that infinite Power which
has constituted it. The God of Religiousness A is the
infinite within oneself which is revealed in the despair of immediacy. For the tragicomic consciousness,
this infinite *is* the God, the only God, the infinite task,
power, and beckoning *telos* whose prodigious weight
presses about him on all sides. Kierkegaard says that
one must have existed in this existential pathos before
receiving the existential communication, otherwise
the revolutionary transformation of the paradox cannot take place. And this is true: if one knows, exists
in, and is conscious of the prodigious weight of God
within one's inner being, then it is incredible, nay,
impossible, to accept the proposition that this God,
whom one *knows* exists within the infinite consciousness, has, to the contrary, existed in that world of
finite immediacy, in that alien, hostile world away
from which one has suffered and struggled. To believe this would, indeed, mean a break with immanence, with oneself, with every certainty upon which
one had relied.

The incredibly contrived, almost crafty rationale
behind paradoxical religiousness is now apparent;
there is no doubt that Kierkegaard is justified in calling this the absolute paradox, it seems just that. But I
have said that the rationale of the absolute paradox is
contrived, and this is where Religiousness B loses its
brilliant shock. It is obvious that the rationale behind
this is contrived not because it is absurd or incredible
(for Kierkegaard would happily welcome these re-

3. Kierkegaard, *Postscript, op. cit.,* pp. 494-5.

proaches as the very genius of Christianity), but because existentially it is false (and this is a reproach which Kierkegaard would not be prepared to deal with). It is false for the following reasons. Kierkegaard has founded his entire religious thought on the dialectical opposition between finitude and infinitude, the temporal and the eternal, as this opposition is revealed to the individual who despairs of immediacy. The existential suffering of infinite becoming is the acute expression of this opposition, and this is immanent religiousness. With might and main, satire and outrage, wit and logic, Kierkegaard has battered down the suggestion that any hope, any sustenance, any eternal happiness can be found in the realm of immediacy and finitude. It is against the background of all this that the historical proposition that the eternal existed in time is an absurdity with revolutionary consequences for the individual. Kierkegaard tells us that the aesthetic individual cannot make this "leap" into the paradox, nor can the ethical individual; no, one must have been religiously immanent *before* this leap can take place. Why? Because otherwise the absurdity wouldn't be absurd. But let us suppose something; let us suppose that an individual has heard the existential communication of Christianity *before* entering the existential pathos of Religiousness A—what would this mean? It would mean that Religiousness A was invalid, was the wrong path, was the absurdly wrong path to take in seeking an eternal happiness. If the individual knew that the essence of Christianity is that God existed in time (and Kierkegaard has told him so), then the task of religious immanence itself becomes absurd; how can he entertain the notion that God is the infinite within him when he already knows that the essential thing is to have faith in the God who existed in finitude?

The rationale here is contrived in the sense that, having taken Kierkegaard seriously as he builds up his stages of existence, we suddenly discover that he has set us up for a colossal surprise. We have become the victims of Kierkegaard's arrangement of his materials; he has ordered it so that we follow him step by step, acceding to his analysis, and then we suddenly discover that he is pointing back to the place where we began. And if we ask, "Why did you not point that out in the beginning so as to save us this long walk?" he will reply, "Why, obviously, you could not possibly see it until you had come this distance." This is very clever, and we must confess that he is right, but the difficulty now is that the cat is out the bag, and the trick will never again be played on anyone. From now on, while Kierkegaard is leading his learners along the road, he will find that they are constantly looking back over their shoulders toward the place of departure, paying little heed to the sights along the way, so that when he suddenly stops and points back, his listeners will not look dumfounded but will wear the smiles of accomplices who knowingly nudge him in the ribs and confide, "We knew it all the time!" In this moment I think Kierkegaard would know deep despair. The paradox of Christianity is seen to be a literary device rather than a final stage of subjectivity. Existentially it is impossible, it is false. The eternal happiness is not conquered in this manner; it remains out over the waters, infinitely far yet inescapably real.

This distinction between Religiousness A and B goes back to sections A and B of Kierkegaard's *Philosophical Fragments,* which was the theoretical preface to the mammoth *Postscript.* These two works show that, as a Christian theologian, Kierkegaard's basic insight was that Christianity must be *decisive.* This one word is essential to the appreciation of his conception of paradoxical religiousness. He had the understandable conviction that if Christianity constituted the greatest single moment in the history of human existence, then it must be decisively different from all else in human history and must demand a decisive response from those whom it touches. This concern for decisiveness is purely Kierkegaardian and is rooted in his own personal. convictions. So it is that when, in the *Philosophical Fragments*, he has dealt with the Socratic method of learning (Section A), he opens Section B with the curious statement, "Now if things are to be otherwise, the moment in time must have a decisive significance . . . ." [4] In this one sentence we have, I believe, the primitive link between religiousness per se and Christian religiousness, between A and B. Why, we may ask, must things be otherwise? They must be otherwise because Kierkegaard refuses to think of Christianity as one among other religions, or even the best or the highest or the final religious truth; no, Christianity must be categorically different, unique, decisive. And Kierkegaard brilliantly constructed his theology upon this concern for decisiveness. But the construction remains only a construction, and, viewed *en large*, the theory of the God-man which crowns it appears as only a curious and heroical crotchet. Existentially it is a failure; to the extent that he was successful in pioneering a profound conception of the possible ways of human existence, so to this extent does his conception of Christianity appear not merely interesting but perplexing. To the degree that his description of the esthetic and ethico-religious personalities is valid for human existence, so is paradoxical religiousness invalid. There is pre-

4. Kierkegaard, *Fragments, op. cit.*, p. 8.

cious little room for choice in this matter: one can very well accept Kierkegaard's analysis of immanent religiousness without accepting his view of Christianity, but one cannot do the reverse. His insights into the immanent possibilities of human existence will remain the profound and permanent contribution which he has made to religious philosophy. His lasting contribution to Christendom will be primarily meditational and devotional, not intellectual.[5]

But we need not, I think, be disturbed over this failing of Kierkegaard's. If he had succeeded in this last task he would indeed be the greatest of all thinkers; we would have to canonize him. His Christian disposition persuaded him that an eternal happiness could be attained by human existence, and this he attempted to depict as the final moment of leaping, breaking with immanence, the moment when the individual no longer *becomes* a Christian but *is* a Christian. The failure of this leap is not disturbing because, as was said a moment earlier, Kierkegaard himself is ambiguous on this point; he is not consistent in his insistence that one can *be* a Christian. And to the degree—any degree—that he suggests the impossibility of making this final break with immanence and with the tension of the tragicomic consciousness, he is reaffirming the inescapability of immanent religiousness whereby one becomes toward this infinite goal without ever attaining it. We find such a suggestion in a short piece which is required reading for any student of Kierkegaard: "That Individual," which was published along with *The Point of View*. Here Kierkegaard speaks of the category of "the individ-

5. For a thoughtful and rather forceful reproach to Kierkegaard for his individual-centered theology note the following two remarks of Karl Barth in his *Church Dogmatics, IV, 1, The Doctrine of Reconciliation*, New York, Charles Scribner's Sons, 1957, pp. 689, 740-1.

ual" which he places in opposition to the category of "the crowd." The distinction is one we already know between the man who is inwardly oriented and him who is outwardly oriented and motivated. But we see just how absolute and final is this category of the individual when Kierkegaard tells his modern reader that ". . . what is lacking to him is that he has not yet rightly become the single individual, which is something I do not pretend to be, although I have striven, without yet apprehending, and continue to strive, yet as one who does not forget that 'the individual' in its highest measure is beyond a man's power." [6] The task of becoming an individual is simply that task of achieving absolute self-identity, of reaching that infinite point of rest which is an eternal happiness, which is the "Christian" state of being. But, lest one think that because "its highest measure is beyond a man's power" this means that it is God and not man who must bring this about, we should read Kierkegaard further when he says, "But this category cannot be delivered in a lecture; it is a *specific ability, an art, an ethical task,* and it is an art the practice of which might in his time have cost the practitioner his life. For that which in God's eyes is the highest thing, the self-willed race and the hosts of confused minds regard as *lèse-majesté* against 'the race,' 'the crowd,' 'the public,' &c." [7] The art of becoming an individual is the immanent art of ever-renewed despair of finitude as one seeks to become the infinite. The ambiguity of Kierkegaard's conception of Christianity's final leap is further intensified by his essay on despair in *The Sickness Unto Death*. We have already noted from this work the final goal of selfhood toward which the religious

6. Kierkegaard, *The Point of View, op. cit.,* p. 130.
7. *Ibid.,* pp. 137-8 (italics my own).

individual strives despairingly, and this goal is that
ultimate goal of faith which is the mark of paradoxical
religiousness. "Faith is: that the self in being itself
and in willing to be itself is grounded transparently
in God." [8] This goal is the eternal happiness and rest
where despair will be eradicated, but the question
is, Can one attain this goal? Is it existentially possible? The entire essay is testimony to Kierkegaard's
belief that such a goal is not possible, it is but the
theoretical suggestion of what *would* be the state of
selfhood *if* despair *could* be overcome, that is, it still
remains the absolute *telos*, the infinite task from which
even death cannot save us.

> For despair is not a result of the disrelationship
> but of the relation which relates itself to itself.
> And the relation to himself a man cannot get rid
> of, any more than he can get rid of himself,
> which moreover is one and the same thing, since
> the self is the relationship to oneself.[9]

Or, again, he says that

> if one might die of despair as one dies of a sick-
> ness, then the eternal in him, the self, must be
> capable of dying in the same sense that the body
> dies of sickness. But this is an impossibility; the
> dying of despair transforms itself constantly into a
> living. The despairing man cannot die; no more
> than "the dagger can slay thoughts" can despair
> consume the eternal thing, the self, which is the
> ground of despair, whose worm dieth not, and
> whose fire is not quenched.[1]

If, then, despair is inescapable, the eternal happiness and completeness of selfhood is unattainable. If

8. Kierkegaard, *The Sickness, op. cit.*, p. 132.
9. *Ibid.*, p. 24.
1. *Ibid.*, pp. 25-6.

despair can be sharpened into the consciousness of sin but can never be eradicated so as to become faith, then Christian religiousness is unattainable: one can become a Christian, one can never be one. As we have said, it is Kierkegaard's own insight into the possibilities of human existence that undermines the possibility of breaking with the tragicomic consciousness, thus making Religiousness B existentially impossible.

What place, then, does Kierkegaard's conception of Christianity have in relation to his philosophy of existence? We need not be disturbed by this question, for it does not follow that this description of the infinite yet impossible goal of existence should be thrown out, thus making Kierkegaard appear foolish. No, the place of Religiousness B is what this discussion has revealed it to be: the theoretical point toward which the religious consciousness yearns but can never exist in. Existentially it has no status; theoretically it has its place. It is not a sphere of existence.

That Kierkegaard believed one could be a Christian (even though he never claimed this distinction for himself) is an understandable consequence of his deep reverence for Christianity as he saw it. But, understandable as this is, it is an unfortunate and fearful thing that he should have asserted that this theoretical break was existentially possible. In all seriousness, Kierkegaard's description of being a Christian is the description of a theoretical possibility of madness, or, in another light, it is the description of death. Its exemplars would be found in asylums, and its nearest prototype is not to be found in the Christian West but in the East, in that final stage of life prescribed by Hindu orthodoxy whereby, after years of meditation and ascetic discipline, the religious hermit achieves complete isolation from the sense world about him and arises to go forth, the beggar-saint, blindly wandering through a world no longer his own. And even for the Hindus, this is but an ideal, an infinite possibility which finds its incarnation only in those obscure and perfect holy men of the past over whose lives the yearning and imagination of the Indian mind have woven a melancholy veil of magic and wonder.

And this was surely the case for Søren Kierkegaard; it was his deep melancholy and his soaring imagination which drove him toward this ultimate affirmation of a deathlike perfection. Because of these two things he had sacrificed much in the world: prestige, respect, security—as well as Regina. He had discovered what it meant to exist as man, what it meant to find inner health, only to be driven farther by the melancholy yearning to go beyond health, to exist as more than a man. I think it deeply significant that in those last years of his life when he had begun his open and vehement attack upon "Christendom," he began to attack more and more bitterly the marriage of priests and the comforts which a woman might bring to the lives of those who claim to have given themselves to Christianity. Toward the beginning of this essay it was said that there is no more poignant symbol of what the world meant for Kierkegaard than the lovely Regina. In the last years of Kierkegaard's life this image of Regina must have returned to haunt him in strange and ever more desperate ways. There is enormous pathos in the vehement way in which he demands, "What I have given up with such suffering, you too must give up!" In this instant, Kierkegaard, in his very existence, was testifying to the fact that he had erred, that he had gone too far in his search for eternity, and that now the temporal world exacted its toll. It was in this state of being, this awful straining against the bounds of existence and sanity, that death met Kierkegaard and took him away. We need not seek an epitaph for this man, he has written his own; and in it the pain, the conflict, the yearning, and the doubts of this life are summed up marvelously:

> What is my sickness? Melancholy. Where is the seat of this sickness? In the power of imagination, and possibility is its nutriment. But eternity takes away the possibility. And was not this sickness hard enough for me to bear in time, that I not only should suffer but become guilty through it? The deformed man has after all only to bear the pain of being deformed, but how dreadful if being deformed made him guilty!
>
> So then, when for me time has come to an end, let my last sigh be to Thee, O God, for my soul's blessedness, the next to the last for her, or let me for the first time be again united with her in the last sigh.[2]

This is the confession of a man whose reach has exceeded his grasp, who lunges toward eternity yet looks back over his shoulder at precious chains that still bind him. The relentless tug of the bright world of finitude was not to be overcome by Kierkegaard or by any of us, for the religious existence does not consist of a colossal break with the realm of sensuousness and finitude but rather it consists of the struggle and conflict suffered by the individual who constantly qualifies his finitude in the light of that nonfinite reality which he has discovered within him. The religious individual who bears this tension is as bifrontal as existence itself; his is the tragicomic con-

2. Kierkegaard, *Stages, op. cit.,* pp. 356-7.

sciousness which sees the humor of what he has
overcome, the pathos of what he has yet to become
and, in the midst of this complete vision, willingly
despairs of what he is so that he may become himself
in a more intense way than before.

Conflict, tension, struggle, becoming: these are the
words that resound through the breadth of Kierkegaard's works. This is not something which one possesses, it is not a thing; it is a way. When he says
that subjectivity is truth, he means that the individual who exists in the tension of subjectivity reflects
the full reality of human existence, its dialectic; that
which reflects the full reality of man's synthetic nature is, in the fullest sense, truth. Thus, truth is a
way, a way of existing, and this truth is the high
point of Kierkegaard's lyrical existentialism. This final
existential admonition is what we have sought.
Whether we call it God, or value, or happiness,
this is what comes into existence for him who is willing to despair of all hope in his world and enter into
the tension and conflict which true existence promises
him. It is almost incredible how often Kierkegaard
returns to this touchstone of his thought;[3] it is something which he must stress over and again, repeating
the simple truth which arises from his understanding
of human existence. This is all that Kierkegaard has
sought to do, "to read solo the original text of the
individual, human existence-relationship, the old text,
well known, handed down from the fathers—to read
it through yet once more, if possible in a more heart-

3. For the most striking expressions of the theme of value
(God, truth, happiness) in conflict and suffering, *vide* the following works of Kierkegaard, all of which have been previously
cited: *Either/Or*, Vol. II, p. 87; *Fear and Trembling*, pp. 119-20,
122, 143, 149; *Repetition*, p. 152; *Stages*, pp. 347-8; *Postscript*,
p. 208; *Training In Christianity*, pp. 117, 154, 189, 192, 207, 218;
Attack, pp. 127, 149, 183, 244-5, 268.

felt way." [4] We have read through this old text with
Søren Kierkegaard and seen him grope toward his God
through the wondrous complexity of that human existence which he knew and loved so well. And as the
reading is finished and the words have ceased to
sound, we are left alone and in silence with the in-
delible impression that somewhere within the reach
of our lives there beckons a great suffering and—
within this—a strange and unconquerable happiness.

4. Kierkegaard, *Postscript, op. cit.,* p. 554.

Part Two

FRIEDRICH NIETZSCHE

THE COURAGEOUS
PESSIMISM

Therefore, since our age furnishes few examples of men who in a great sense are believers, one has reason to be glad that there are some right clever men who are scandalized at religion. If a person, wishing to have something definitely explained, is so fortunate as to find one man who in the seventeenth-century sense is a strict believer, and a scandalized man in the nineteenth century, who both say the same thing (that is, the one says, "It is thus and so, that I know full well, therefore I do not want it," and the other says, "Thus and so it is, therefore I believe it," and these "thus and sos" agree completely), then one can confidently bring his observations to a conclusion. Two such consonant witness are more trustworthy than such as lawyers deal with.

SØREN KIERKEGAARD—*Stages on Life's Way*

CHAPTER FIVE

REMARKS ON PROPHECY

ONE OF THE curious and perturbing facts about prophets is their irrepressible tendency to exaggerate; they are caricaturists of reality. The good or the evil which they attribute to a situation is always more than is actually there. More than anything else, this is the genius of the prophet, his threat as well as his irreplaceable contribution, and it is precisely this genius for exaggeration that has always been little understood or appreciated. Exaggeration is a product of the prophetic imagination, an imagination which looks upon a given situation and judges it according to its final, ideal probabilities. A prophetic judgment is one which has culled out the essential possibilities of a situation and then imaginatively carried out these possibilities to their fruition. This distorted, too-sharp picture of our times is really not "there," yet in fact it *is* "there"; it is there as a warning, as a threat, as an imminent danger of what can happen, what will happen when the fullness of time has come about. It is in this manner that prophets have an imaginative genius, a genius for becoming. Their talent is the talent of the dramatist, but in this case the drama can be as broad as human history itself; like the dramatist they can imaginatively assess and construct possibilities one after another, discovering a beginning, a middle and an end, and then they turn to us and say, "This is what is happening. Do you understand now?" And we say, "No, we do not understand; we do not see this happening." Thus does the prophet deal with reality and possibility, and we with only reality; thus does the prophet see what becomes; we see only what is. If the prophet prophesies the future, this is not because he knows the future better than we, but because he more thoroughly and penetratingly knows the present.

There are but few men who have the prophetic endowment, and few ages which have made use of their judgments. Genuine prophets are, perhaps, a dying breed. The prophet measures himself against his moment of history, and, to the degree that the currents of this history become swifter and more turbulent, the more formidable becomes the task of mastering its dramatic possibilities. If, then, during the turbulence which has marked our past two centuries, there have been those who have taken the mantle of prophecy, we should be grateful, we should listen, for ours is an age of many prophesiers and few prophets. The role is difficult, almost impossible, for it requires not only endowment but, as well, a courage and long-suffering which few men care to endure. Prophetic exaggeration demands the passionate exercise of imagination, dramatization, and idealization of reality; this is the singing lyrical thread that binds together the ecstatic visionary oracles of antiquity with the passionate prophets of our present age. This is a lyrical function which demands not scholarship, not dispassionate objectivity, but passionate involvement and concern for the historical moment. Kierkegaard, Nietzsche, and Camus are all three children of their age, and they are prophets of our time in that weighty and threatening sense in which the giants of the Old Testament were prophets: their judgments inevitably point to us and make us responsible. The words of these men cannot be heard without reaction; reaction must come and one must take sides. There can be no rest once they have spoken.

Of the three Lyrical Existentialists it is Friedrich Nietzsche who has thus far struck most sharply against the sensibilities of his contemporaries. The breadth and clarity of Nietzsche's prophetic exaggeration are astounding; one cannot go through his works without amazement before a mind which betrays an intimacy with the gamut of human existence, with the movements of society from its earliest heavings to its present upheavings. His intimate eye has pondered the dialectics of primitive societies and the earliest rumblings of civilization, the Olympian days of Greece, its centuries of triumph and its centuries of dissolution, the shaggy desert voices of the Old Testament and the tragically triumphant voice of the New, the prelates and monks and ascetics of Catholicism and the somber stoics of the Empire they succeeded, the bright burst and excitement of the Renaissance and the reformations and revolutions which followed it, exploding into the motley veins of modern society with its scientism, progressivism, socialism, statism, totalitarianism, and nihilism, over which and in which he placed himself, watching, brooding, sensing, and judging. This was the vast range of Nietzsche's concern, the field of human existence itself, and Nietzsche gave to it a passionate interest which is unique in the history of human thought.

The uniqueness is in the *manner* in which he thought, the intimate way in which he seized upon these multifarious moments of our history. It was not enough that he should know what Socrates said and his grounds for saying it; no, his understanding was not satisfied until he knew what it was like to *be* Socrates: this was his ultimate goal. His intimate eye sought through to the heart of a man, leaving behind the secondary matters of historical conduct and intel-

lectual pronouncements. What is it like to be a citizen
of Athens sitting in the Theater of Dionysius, watching the masked players unfold the Aeschylean tragedy
to the soaring rhythm of the chorus's timeless comment? What is it like to be Jesus, the prophet from
Nazareth, as he wanders strangely through dusty hills
and desiccated villages, finally turning his melancholy
visage toward Jerusalem? What is it like to be a
Roman emperor, a monk, a Jewish priest, a noble
Athenian, an Italian despot, a German reformer, a
scientist, a proletarian, a Christian, a Philistine?—
these were the questions toward which he leaped,
these were the existential tasks which his lyrical imagination set for itself.

Nietzsche's uniqueness as thinker and analyst is the
shuttlelike alternation of his mind between empathy
and objectivity. His empathic passion seized upon
and reconstructed what it was like to be someone or
to live at a certain time; then, with this image drawn
clearly and permanently, he would stand away at a
distance and form his judgment. This is the method
whose results have been exciting, upsetting, repre-
hensible, and admirable: results which still remain
stuck in the craw of Western thought, awaiting a
painful and plodding absorption. The results of Nietzsche's thought have been *too* intimate, *too* personal,
too clear: the passions they invoke are too strong for
Nietzsche to have been heard, understood, catalogued,
and then forgotten among the convenient pages of
the history of philosophy. For Nietzsche is not
strictly a philosopher; rationality and objectivity have
been trampled underfoot by the impetus of his lyricism: he is, like the other Lyrical Existentialists, a
prophet. His ultimate significance and value must be
estimated from this peculiar point of view: what little
he has contributed to philosophical history must be

measured against the vastness of his contribution to humanity. This is an equation which should be pondered by all novitiates in philosophy.

What we shall want to do is take a close look at the results of Nietzsche's empathic method of thinking; we shall want to understand his criticism of certain kinds of men and the historical or intellectual significance they embody. We need first some basic understanding of the meaning of men and their history. As we turn our attention to Nietzsche's views of time and finitude, the worldly trappings of human existence, the Reader will discover that our first glance at Nietzsche is identical with our first step in understanding Kierkegaard. As with Kierkegaard, we shall first examine the world as Nietzsche sees it and the kind of men whose being reflects the being of the world and little more; and secondly, we shall come to terms with Nietzsche's insight into human existence, into consciousness and the unique reality which is embedded there; and, finally, with a knowledge of what the world is and what man is, we can sketch out the picture which Nietzsche has drafted of the way in which the individual must exist in this world. What we are seeking, then, is Nietzsche's existential admonition, his prescription not of what a man must know, or do, or believe, but of what a man must *be*. What is the world? What is man? These are the questions. The answers will lead us to an understanding of that courageous pessimism which is not only at the heart of Nietzsche's thinking but is the common vision of the Lyrical Existentialists.[1]

1. Citations from Nietzsche are from Friedrich Nietzsche, *Nietzsches Werke*, Vols. I-IX, Stuttgart, Alfred Kroner Verlag, 1921.

Because of the variety of Nietzsche editions both in German and English, the Reader has been accommodated by citations which give the paragraph number of the appropriate work rather than the page number. Although this will, in some cases, necessitate a short search for the desired passage, it is preferable to making the Reader find a Kroner edition of Nietzsche's works —something which he probably couldn't do in the first place.

For the sake of convenience the German titles have been abbreviated; a list of Nietzsche's principal works and their abbreviations is herewith given:

Die Geburt der Tragödie (The Birth of Tragedy)   *GT*
Unzeitgemässe Betrachtungen (Untimely Meditations)   *UB*
    I. *David Strauss, der Bekenner und der Schriftsteller*
       (David Strauss, the Confessor and the Writer)
   II. *Vom Nutzen und Nachteil der Historie für das*
      Leben
      (On the Advantage and Disadvantage of History
      for Life)
  III. *Schopenhauer als Erzieher* (Schopenhauer as
      Educator)
  IV. *Richard Wagner in Bayreuth*
Menschliches, Allzumenschliches (Human, All-too-hu-
  man)   *MA*
    I.
   II. *Vermischte Meinungen und Sprüche*
      (Miscellaneous Opinions and Sayings)
    Der Wanderer und sein Schatten
    (The Wanderer and his Shadow)   *WS*
Die Morgenröthe (Dawn)   *M*
Die Fröliche Wissenschaft (The Gay Science)   *FW*
Also Sprach Zarathustra (Thus Spake Zarathustra)   *Z*
Jenseits von Gut und Böse (Beyond Good and Evil)   *JGB*
Zur Genealogie der Moral (Toward a Genealogy of
  Morals)   *GM*
Der Fall Wagner (The Wagner Case)   *W*
Die Götzen-Dämmerung (The Twilight of the Idols)   *G*
Der Antichrist   *A*
Ecce Homo   *EH*
Nietzsche contra Wagner   *NCW*

When citations are made from Nietzsche's minor essays, the full German titles of these works are given. These essays, as well as the above works, are *opere citato*, referring always to the Alfred Kroner Stuttgart edition. N. B. In the footnotes all Roman numerals refer to primary divisions within the work cited.

CHAPTER SIX

L'INVITATION À LA DANSE

THE MOST GENERAL characteristic of men is not, observes Nietzsche, their fearfulness but their laziness.[1] It is laziness which leads men to hide behind the customs, opinions, and habits of the everyday life, of the crowd. Men prefer to be absorbed in the conventions of the masses rather than shoulder the burden of honesty and openness, rather than bring to life that suppressed conviction that one is, as an individual, unique and inimitable. Every man senses within himself the injunction "Be yourself!" but, rather than expend themselves, men lazily allow walls to build up around them until they are all external crust and accretion with a hollow void within. Through lassitude, men identify themselves totally with the moods, practices, and moments of their history, a history which molds, crumbles, and metamorphoses, a history which soon will be gone even as that with which and in which a man has his being is gone, forgotten in a quiet, meaningless nonexistence. To belong to history, to be indistinguishable from society, means to lose one's being to that which is without meaning or permanence.

But what can a man do against this? Nietzsche's answer is that the man who desires to throw off the fetters of the masses must throw off his complacency and follow the call of his conscience which urges him, "Be yourself! You are not the sum total of all that you do, think, and desire." This is the call of

1. *UB*, III, Sec. 1.

conscience, and Nietzsche remarks that "The soul of every youth hears this call day and night and trembles because of it; for when he thinks about his actual liberation he senses his measure of happiness appointed to him from eternity: a happiness toward which he can in no wise be aided as long as he lies in the chains of opinions and fear." [2] These are the words of the young Nietzsche, the fervent and eager professor of the University of Basel in 1874. These thoughts are at the beginning of the essay, "Schopenhauer as Educator," which Nietzsche later admitted was grossly mistitled; "Nietzsche as Educator" would have been the correct title. And this is not only because we find here an exaggerated idealization of the man, Schopenhauer, an image really of Nietzsche himself, but, as well, because it is as educator that Nietzsche found his characteristic task in life. It is characteristic that he should suddenly turn his attention to the youth of Europe, showing them the possibility of breaking the "chains of opinions and fear." Neither during his earlier years at the university nor during the later hectic years between the southern seas and mountains was Nietzsche ever content merely to inform. Even in his sober study of "Philosophy in the Greek Tragic Era" he could not restrict himself to a scholarly exegesis of pre-Socratic philosophy but soared forth with panegyrics over the "proud" Heraclitus and with utter contempt for the "bloodless" philosophy of Parmenides. Throughout his career Nietzsche was, like Kierkegaard, an evangelical educator; he had a vision which burned within him, and he had to impart it. The vision always had two faces: one a warning, the other an admonition. Only later can we appreciate the admonition, only after we have understood the warning. There are chains to

2. *Ibid.*

break in order that we may become ourselves and not something other. It is this "something other" that we must understand.

Most readers of Nietzsche find themselves disturbed greatly by the vehemence with which Nietzsche has attacked other thinkers. They have the annoying feeling that Nietzsche is avoiding issues and contenting himself with scurrilous personal criticism. It is difficult for Nietzsche's first-contact readers not to be put off by what they feel to be unfair, off-the-center attacks. One quickly concludes that, however exciting his writings may be, they are basically unorthodox and unphilosophical. This, of course, is true, and Nietzsche would heartily concur in this estimate, for he had no intention of classing himself among other philosophers. Whereas Kierkegaard and Camus exempt themselves from this by claiming they are not philosophers, Nietzsche, in his own manner, excludes himself from other philosophers with the claim that all previous philosophers are decadent and that he is the evangel of a new age in thought. He saw his life task as a philosopher in terms of a unique plan: looking to the future he sought to prepare mankind for a moment of "supreme self-consciousness," [3] and looking toward the past, he sought to unmask Christian morality and all its decadent spokesmen.[4] This was the way in which he conceived his life task during the last months of his career, and during that last year, 1888, the five works which he poured forth were largely those of the unmasking kind. Indeed, so much of Nietzsche's thought is critical and analytical in nature that it is not always a simple matter to group together the more positive and evangelical aspects of his writing career.

3. *EH*, "Morgenröthe," Sec. 2.
4. *EH*, V, Sec. 7.

In order to "put together" Nietzsche one must first reckon with the fact that his twenty-two years of writing parceled themselves out into three rather distinct periods. There is the early decade, 1866-76, of positive, rather sustained philosophical writings, marked by a certain scholarly orientation and by a continued interest in aesthetics, culture, education, classical thought, and the significance of Arthur Schopenhauer and Richard Wagner. But thereupon follows a middle period, 1876-82, of writings which could best be called random observations and maxims, in the course of which Nietzsche, in an experimental and somewhat tentative manner, let his mind and wit play upon an almost exhaustive variety of themes. But, beginning with his *Zarathustra* in 1883 and extending through 1888, the mature Nietzsche "finds himself" and launches into the period of brilliant poetic and polemical writings on which his fame and notoriety have largely been established.

Like both Kierkegaard's and Camus', it is true of Nietzsche's career that his mature philosophy is founded upon a kind of aggressive transformation of his earlier thought. And thus one must be as careful in using this early period of his writings as one must be mindful of the fact that his mature writings do not stand alone but incessantly refer back to his first philosophical views. It is clear, then, that Nietzsche's first and last periods of writings are most important to the interpreter's task, and one must remember that a characteristic difference between these two periods is that the early Nietzsche is more affirmative than polemical and that the later Nietzsche is more polemical than affirmative. For scholarly purposes this defines the body of literature within which we have to search for Nietzsche's existential admonition.

So then, this literature reveals Nietzsche to be unorthodox as a philosopher, but we should think twice before terming his personal polemics as "unfair." Nietzsche himself has remarked that in all his attacks on other thinkers, he was attacking not persons but what they represented. Or, as has already been suggested, Nietzsche focused his attention upon certain *kinds* of men and the types of existence they represented. He sought to unmask the falsity and decadence of certain ways of existing: these were the "chains" which he urged men of the future to break so that they might achieve a renaissance, a new level of self-consciousness which Nietzsche saw as the promise of the present age.

What are the chains which one must break in order that he may become himself and not something other? An example would be what Nietzsche saw represented in the life of Socrates, *"eine wahre Monstrosität per defectum."* [5] Nietzsche's categorical rejection of Socrates must be understood in the context of his larger conception of the history of Hellenic culture. After the apogee of Greek achievement in the sixth and fifth centuries B.C., the appearance of Socrates was symptomatic of the incipient decline of Greek culture. Nietzsche draws upon many themes in his characterization of Socrates as decadent but the central thrust of his polemic is that in Socrates we see the death of tragic art and the birth of dialectics, the decline of nobility and the rise of the masses, or, in essence, the loss of men motivated by an authoritative inner strength and the discovery of men who are motivated by external and extrapersonal concerns. The defect in Socrates's nature was that rather than possessing a critical, deliberative consciousness which guided an instinctive, inward flow, the order was reversed so that he was instinctively critical and at-

5. *GT*, Sec. 13.

tempted to create in a conscious manner. This *kind* of man was, to Nietzsche, monstrous; it is monstrous because it means the individual's conduct in this world no longer rests upon an inner integrity and confidence which is self-authenticating, but rather that everything a man does or says must be proved. With this reversal the rightness of a man's thought and action no longer has any foundation within himself as an individual but finds its foundation in that which is beyond and separate from the individual; in Socrates's case this extrapersonal foundation was rationality, but it opened the possibility for any such external sphere—whether this be God, tradition, ecclesiastical authority, dogma, the state, scientific method, or empirical demonstrability—to become a justification for human conduct.

The great significance of Socrates is that he is symptomatic of a general tendency in mankind. In understanding the monstrous defect of Socrates we do at the same time understand the basic defect which Nietzsche sees reflected in a great span of historical personalities. Socrates is both the symbol of and the prototype for a certain kind of defective individual which has not only haunted human history but has dominated it. Socrates becomes an historical prototype because of the striking context into which Nietzsche places him: the hinge between Greece's period of triumph and its period of decline. And within this enlarged vision, Socrates comes to signify not simply a personality, or only a kind of man, but, beyond this, a kind of cultural, moral, and historical symbol, bristling with meanings and colors. For it is quite correct to observe that what Adam signifies for Christianity, Socrates signifies for Nietzsche, the only difference being that this Nietzschean Adam is a complete reversal of the Christian Adam: whereas the

Christian Adam initiated man's fall by choosing inner motivation over an external authority, the Nietzschean Adam causes humanity's decline by choosing external authority over inner motivation. And this is, I think, the precise sense behind Nietzsche's audacious terms, *decadence* and *decline;* he uses these terms within the vast historic perspective of a fall from a higher state of being, a fall under which men now suffer but through which Nietzsche sees the glimmerings of redemption—a redemption which, again, is the opposite of that conceived by the Christian: not Christ but the overman.

In our reading of Nietzsche we must hold on to this pregnant image of Socrates, the Nietzschean Adam; it is part of the myth which Nietzsche has created, a myth perfectly consonant with his classical philological orientation and his intimate eye for types of men in history. Like all myths, it is contrived, but it has the inestimable value of fixing history in a meaningful time span: there was once a time of human greatness; then, through the fall of man, there began the time of decadence in which we now live, but beyond this decadence there lies the hope for a time of redemption when the original greatness of man shall be restored. This is, in its ultimate form, the prophetic vision of Nietzsche, the lyrical vision of the dramatist who has mythologically created a history which has a beginning, middle, and end. The history of mankind has now become a story, and Nietzsche himself has become the storyteller, designating the heroes and antagonists, the climaxes and the preparations, the triumphs and the tragedies. This is not philosophy; it has gone beyond that to something higher and more precious: it is a creative art which has grasped the striving, multifarious moments of history and blended them into a form, a single vision of time which suddenly makes the history of men meaningful. Only the artist and the religious prophet create such visions, and this is, of course, what Nietzsche is.

The Adamic Socrates is, then, a central feature of the Nietzschean myth and is, as well, the central key to understanding the type of decadence which Nietzsche deplores even as the age of Hellenic tragedy and the coming age of the overman describe the renascent self-consciousness which lies at the beginning and end of Nietzsche's myth. Socrates opened the Pandora's box of decadence, and all the many forms of human ill burst into history. What the reader must understand is that even as in the Christian myth we are all part of Adam and share in his sin, so, for Nietzsche, are all men part of Socrates and share his tendency toward decadence. Original sin began with Socrates, and the reaffirmation of this sin turns up time and again in history, and Nietzsche is there to point it out to us. In many forms and in many degrees the Socratic sin is repeated over and again, so that to the extent that we have seen and understood the decadence in Socrates we can understand the same decadence which Nietzsche deplores in all men, and which we have already seen him touch upon when he says that the most general characteristic of men is their laziness; this is the groundwork for the Socratic sin. This is the preparation for allowing oneself to become "something other" than what one is—the Socratic sin of human decadence.

In order to pin down the decadence of Socrates we must see the ancient father of dialectic in the Greek context within which Nietzsche first saw him; that is, in relation to the Greek tragic period and the terms Apollonian and Dionysian. With an intimate empathic eye Nietzsche seized upon a central aspect of the precivilized world: the terror and horror of existing in a world where, without apparent reason, human life and all things precious were cut down by the swords of time, natural accident, and human voraciousness. The terror of existence is the primeval component of human existence itself, and the very real human question arose as to how one could justify and make sense of destruction, change, loss, and death. This is an existential problem, a serious and threatening personal anxiety which demands a solution and relief. It is this basic reality of suffering which gave rise to what Nietzsche calls the Apollonian dreamworld, an imaginary world of Olympian gods who, as giant reflections of mortal men, eternally suffer the same conflicts, pains, and titanic battles as do men themselves. There was a metaphysical solace in this Apollonian vision, but this solace was not complete, for it rested on a theodicy which was thin and pale, a dreamy fancy which faced the empirical reality of life and said hopefully that beyond the rugged mountains of life there was that eternal mountaintop world of the gods just on the farther side of the clouds. The externally projected Apollonian dream was incomplete and unsubstantial because it was only a partial human response to the reality of suffering; it excluded a more basic and elemental response which was the Dionysian. If the Apollonian vision is dreamlike in quality, so then does the Dionysian vision possess the qualities of drunkenness. The Dionysian experience is not the serene and impersonal contemplation of a distant world of perfect forms and beings, but a furious, personal conscious state in which all nice distinctions between forms and individuals crumble before the intoxicated vision of the terrible oneness and joy of existence. Nietzsche calls to mind the awesome Dionysian festivities of

the Greeks when all barriers, all distinctions broke
down in one great, triumphant experience of the oneness of all men with themselves and with their world.
Now the passionate surge of the Dionysian always
finds itself in contradiction to the dispassionate objectivity of the Apollonian myth. Both are real experiences and yet they are in conflict with one another. Thus does Nietzsche in the very inception of
his philosophizing point out, in *The Birth of Tragedy*,
the dialectical nature of human existence. The surprising fact about Nietzsche's first major work is
that in it he has taken up both the task and viewpoint
which we know to be those of Søren Kierkegaard:
the concern for the inner-outer dialectic, for tragedy,
for the corrupting influence of the theoretical thinker,
for the shallow optimism of the aesthetically oriented
philosopher and artist. In *The Birth of Tragedy* Nietzsche's lyrical convictions explode, announcing the ar-
rival of one who, though a stranger to Kierkegaard,
has taken up his mantle and continued his task. In
later years Nietzsche was to comment that in this
first work he should have sung, not spoken.[6]

So it is, then, that in coming to terms with the
nature of Greek culture Nietzsche put his finger on
the dialectical nature of human existence which elu-
cidated the character not only of the Greeks themselves but of men in general. But we must first come
to understand this dialectic in the Greek context
where Nietzsche first placed it. What we have in the
Apollonian and Dionysian experiences is two discreet
human ways of reacting successfully to the fact of
suffering, two contrary and basic methods of overcoming a world which is otherwise unacceptable to us.

Nietzsche sees as the high point of Hellenic culture
the moment when the Greeks found a way of com-

6. Friedrich Nietzsche, "Versuch einer Selbstkritik," Sec. 3.

bining the Apollonian and Dionysian experiences in one simultaneous consciousness: this was the age of Attic tragedy. It is here that Nietzsche displays one of those many special concerns which are native to the Lyrical Existentialists: love for the dramatic and educative possibilities of the theater. This was a love which never seemed to leave either Nietzsche or Kierkegaard and which lured Camus into an active use of the theater as a medium of expression.

The unmatched achievement which Nietzsche saw in the great Greek tragedies was the combination effected between the lyrical chant of the choir and the moving forms of the actors who provided a stylized vision of that tragedy which the choir sang. The Dionysian urge does not express itself in words but in the lyrical rhythms of music, and the Greek choir's lyricism is the expression of this underlying Dionysian spirit. At the same time the old myths of heroes and gods have become the Apollonian players who, with their stylized masques held out to the amphitheater, act out once more the ageless tales of suffering and destruction; the movements of the players become epitomes of human history, summing up the eternal patterns of loss and death which are the lot of all mortals. But the artistic miracle which Nietzsche sees in this combination of music and masques is that within one experience a man sees the changes and destruction suffered by man in history, and yet at the same time he knows that basically life endures and remains unchanged. This is the synthesis of the Apollonian and the Dionysian, of the changing forms of phenomena and the changeless, formless voice of life. Thus does Nietzsche, like Kierkegaard, hold that tragedy is not simple but is dialectic: a combination of outer appearance with an inner experience. In the Attic tragedies the phenomenal hero goes down to

destruction but this destruction is bathed in an overflowing and joyous affirmation of the tragic principle: "We believe in the eternalness of life." [7] In this
affirmation the tragedy is accepted and overcome. In
this experience existence is justified in all its confusion, terror, and pain: life is affirmed.

We can understand from this the general principle
which Nietzsche draws out of this moment of Greek
history, a principle which is no longer Greek, nor
simply ancient, but is to be a guiding principle for
Nietzsche's survey of the whole of human existence:
". . . only as an aesthetic phenomenon can existence
and the world be justified." [8] This illuminating remark shows just how dominating is Nietzsche's concern for human consciousness and its possibilities.
And it hardly needs pointing out just how obvious
are the religious concerns embodied here; for the
problem of suffering, and the justification of existence
in face of this surd fact of suffering, is at the root
of all religious thought. In the miracle of the
Apollonian-Dionysian synthesis Nietzsche has found
a theodicy which he thinks valid for all time. And
one must recognize this as a theodicy even though
the *theos* may be far different from that of Christianity. It is enough that he points to an enduring,
eternal reality called "life," but we must not with
Nietzsche (as is already the case with Kierkegaard)
eagerly conclude that this is either a Christian or non-
Christian principle. Basically it is neither, nor is it
even a principle, rather it is an experience given
within the consciousness of the individual.

What the Reader must bear in mind is the somewhat surprising fact that this extraordinary first work
of Friedrich Nietzsche is essentially colored by re-

7. *GT*, Sec. 16.
8. *Ibid.*, Sec. 24.

ligious and theological concerns; the former concern is obvious, and the latter is no less obvious in those passages where he bemoans the death of those divine myths upon which the tragedies depended,[9] and praises the marvelous ability to see wonder in the myths of old.[1] This must be borne in mind simply because when the Reader confronts the colossal pronouncement that "God is dead," he should recognize the tone of sadness which underlies Nietzsche's requiem for the Christian god; this is not a sadness for the Christian god himself, but a sadness for the anguish which men must now undergo before, from the depths of their being, they have sensed and brought forth new gods. In the depths of the Greek soul Nietzsche saw the glimmerings of an awesome and powerful experience which had come to light in the Dionysian voice of tragedy. This was the strange power which he gropingly gave the name "music," and it was this same haunting lyrical reality which he faithfully served up until that ultimate moment when his spirit forsook the outer world of Apollo and, sinking unreturningly into an ultimate intoxication, found its home and rest. It was out of this oblivion in the early days of 1889 that Nietzsche's mind reached forth blindly and fatefully to conclude one of his last letters with a new but not strange signature: "Dionysius."

We have, then, the context within which Nietzsche first framed his attitude toward Socrates. For Nietzsche, the supreme importance of the Attic tragedies was that as aesthetic productions they created within the spectator a dialectical consciousness through which he could both see the world's awesome reality for what it was, and still accept this reality joyfully

9. *Ibid.*, Sec. 10.
1. *Ibid.*, Sec. 23.

and confidently. Obvious in this viewpoint is the conviction that every man must recognize the world for
what it is, but accompanying this is the conviction
that the world "as it is" is unacceptable and unjustifiable. This basic viewpoint is the same that the reader
immediately discovers in Kierkegaard, and, like Kierkegaard, Nietzsche claims that in order for the individual to exist in face of this world's unhappy
reality he must bring into play some resource which
is inimical to the world, a resource within the individual himself.

The Apollonian reveries which blur out the sharp
realities of existence are but empty deceits unless
they are supported by the surging inner Dionysian
consciousness. Of paramount importance here is the
fact that even though this is a dialectical experience
in which both elements have a necessary part, still
Nietzsche sees the Dionysian element as basic and
creative; the Apollonian representation of this experience is secondary and derivative. This is how it
should be, and this is precisely the defect which
Nietzsche saw in Socrates: in the father of dialectic,
reason did not guide and give form to an unquench-
able inner drive, rather, reason was basic and was
guided into creative actions. What this means is that
in Socrates the dialectical consciousness attained by
the Greeks was destroyed; concern for form, measure, distinction, in short, for rational perfection, became dominant; an external concern for Apollonian
niceties became all-important, and the unique passion
which gave personal authority and inner certitude to
the individual—this dried up and vanished. Socrates
epitomizes the loss of the Dionysian, and this is the
Socratic sin which initiates the fall of Western culture.

Nor did Socrates alone exemplify this first step

toward Grecian decadence: Euripides, as dramatist, betrays the great height from which he has fallen since the earlier period of tragedy. Under his hand, the myths, which once brought the gods before the eyes of men, now lost their entrancing magic, and the reality of everyday life, of the masses, now crept in. The chorus was no longer the singing witness of a joyous vision, but was a spectator and a conscious instrument of the dramatist's rational designs. The spectator no longer found himself at stake in the drama, he was no longer an anxious participant in a spectacle, indeed, a ritual, which united chorus, players, and auditors; no, now he was a spectator pure and simple: everything was "out there," detached and unengaging. As the spirit of music died, so died the myths which this spirit created and sustained. The myths now came to be dogmatized as if "out there" apart from the individual they had significance. And Nietzsche says to Euripides: "And since you abandon Dionysius, so, as well, has Apollo abandoned you." [2] Here Nietzsche has put forth the extraordinary insight that religious myths have religious value only so long as they remain myths, wondrous and entrancing; the moment they become accepted as realities and asserted as dogmas, they have lost all religious value. Why is this? Simply because of the dialectical nature of myths: myths are not true or real in themselves; they have truth and reality only to the extent that they offer expression to some vital inner demand which the individual bears. If the demand is gone, and if the myth now becomes history, then all is lost: both myths and men will have fallen into a state of decadence.

Such is the decadence which Socrates symbolizes: the state of mind which turns confidently outward

2. *Ibid.*, Sec. 10.

and impersonally contents itself with the sounds and patterns of the phenomenal world. It is hardly an exaggeration to say that the whole of Nietzsche's later thought finds its rootage in this general insight, and this is why the Adamic Socrates is a central symbol for Nietzsche. Nietzsche's critique of democracy, journalism, and mass appeal is all found in this insight: the Socratic attitude means that a man is no longer to be respected or judged for what he is as an individual, but rather for what he does or has; estimation of human value is no longer personal and private, but impersonal and public. A new ideal man has arisen, and Nietzsche sees in this a complete reversal of earlier personal and social values. Here, as well, is Nietzsche's critique of statism and socialism, the attitude which turns confidently outward to the abstractions of state, racial destiny, or economic patterns and there finds a reason for existing. Here is his critique of that basic optimism of science which accepts the phenomenal world as an all-sufficing reality whose truths are, *ipso facto*, "good." Here, moreover, is the ground for Nietzsche's condemnation of Christianity, a religion whose priests are deceitful figures in whose hands are delivered their followers' souls, and whose God is a great vacuum sucking up the independence and integrity of countless individuals. This insight is basic to Nietzsche's thought in precisely the same way in which it is basic to Kierkegaard's: it involves a lucid recognition of what the world is and of its insufficiency for the spirit of man, and it involves an approval of any efforts to assert one's independence against the external environment as well as a scathing denunciation of all attitudes which lead one to forsake one's inner integrity for the sake of a person, an idea, or a hope. The whole of Nietzsche's critique of the Western world's decadence is largely a tirade against aesthetic attitudes and ways of living, taken in the Kierkegaardian sense.

Putting together the voices of Nietzsche and Kierkegaard, we can hear them uttering the same thought: "In order to become yourself and not something other, you must break the chains of the aesthetic life by despairing of this world as all-sufficing and asserting the force of your own will." Let the Reader not be perturbed that Nietzsche, the great "yea-saying philosopher," should seem difficult to characterize as a despairer of the world; there is no difficulty at all here. Indeed, Nietzsche, in a far more radical manner than Kierkegaard, has despaired of the world: the tenet that "God is dead" is a categorical denial of any meaning or purpose in nature or history. Nietzsche's insistence on an honest appraisal of reality is simultaneously an insistence that we give up seeking gods or hope or security in the world about us; the world cannot gratify such demands, and we must not blind ourselves to this fact. Whereas Nietzsche expresses simultaneously this notion of facing up to the world's reality, yet refusing it, Kierkegaard enjoys plotting this out into stages as if there were a deliberate sequence of events. For Kierkegaard this has no more than a pedagogical value, the actual discovery and despair of one's world being a sudden and confused human event.

Albert Camus, who is more of a master with the written sentence than either of these two thinkers, has succinctly expressed this general point in the following line: "Few people understand that there is a refusal which has nothing in common with renunciation."[3] Precisely so: to refuse the world for what it is does not mean that one gives up and flees it; ra-

3. Albert Camus, *Noces*, Paris, Gallimard, 1947, p. 34.

ther, it means that one lives in it under different terms, that one's relation to his world is transformed. This insistence upon the world's lack of meaning is not only found in Nietzsche's early work on Greek tragedy, but is a fundamental theme growing ever stronger in the course of Nietzsche's writings and finding, perhaps, its most lucid statement in a work written during the last year of his productive life.

What alone can be our doctrine? That no one gives man his qualities—neither God, nor society, nor his parents and ancestors, nor he himself. . . . No one is responsible for man's being there at all, for his being such-and-such, or for his being in these circumstances or in this environment. The fatality of his essence is not to be disentangled from the fatality of all that has been and will be. He is not the result of a special purpose, of a will, of a goal; nor is there through him any possibility of attaining an "ideal of mankind," or an "ideal of happiness," or an "ideal of morality." It is absurd to wish to attribute his essence to any kind of end. . . . One is necessary, one is a piece of fatality, one belongs to the whole, one is in the whole—there is nothing which can judge, measure, compare, or sentence our being, for that would mean judging, measuring, comparing, and sentencing the whole. . . . *But there is nothing other than this whole!* That no longer is man to be held responsible, that the mode of being may not be deduced from a *causa prima,* that neither sensorily nor as "spirit" is the world a unity—this *above all is the great liberation,* only with this is the *innocence* of becoming re-established.[4]

4. *G,* VII, Sec. 8.

Such is the world to which Nietzsche says, "Yea." It is a world in which no place has been prepared for man; the individual stands alone and free in "the innocence of becoming." This is the same lucid vision of the world which the young Camus had when he said, "The earth! In this great temple deserted by the gods, all my idols have feet of clay." [5] Neither Nietzsche, nor Camus, nor Kierkegaard has any delusions about the world. Their uniqueness as thinkers is that they have seen their world in its full reality of change, death, disillusionment, and confusion, yet they have accepted this reality as a challenge, as an invitation to existence. They accept the world in the same way in which Nietzsche fancied the Greeks could accept life's tragedies with an inner welling joy. Something abiding within them as individuals responded to the challenge of an arenalike nature and history; in fact, it was the very forbidding and foreign aspect of this world which awakened this response of courage. They *needed* this denuded vision of the world and struggled to keep alive their awareness of its threat, without which their existence as individuals would become meaningless and banal. Thus are conflict and struggle the leitmotiv of their thought and lives: each of them sought out that "seventy-thousand-fathom" depth which revealed not only the truth about the world but the truth about himself, namely, that his being was not defined or swallowed up by the world, but that it was ultimately free and responsible. They understood that a serious and honest understanding of the world was the first step in learning to exist as an individual.

Kierkegaard claimed that the advantage of his way of thinking over that of other philosophers was that he accepted the negative as well as the positive facts

5. Camus, *Noces, op. cit.,* p. 92.

about reality; that is, he felt that he was dealing with the whole truth about the world and not the half-truth. This, of course, was precisely Nietzsche's attitude as well, and it is made amply clear in his remark that

> For thousands of years all that philosophers have dealt with were concept-mummies; nothing really living ever escaped their grasp. These honorable concept-idolators kill and stuff when they worship; they threaten the life of everything they worship. Death, change, old age, as well as procreation and growth—these are, to them, objections, even refutations. Whatever exists does not become; whatever becomes does not exist.[6]

The identity of this view with that of Kierkegaard is exact, and Nietzsche has nothing but contempt for all philosophers who deal only in half-truths about reality. His scorn lances straight through to the person of the philosopher himself, alternating between the accusations of laziness or cowardice. Why should the history of philosophy be a series of half-truths about reality? For only one reason, says Nietzsche; because the philosophers themselves were not men enough to face up to the full and awesome reality of their world. They blinded themselves to this reality, they lied to themselves, sensing that if the world really was without meaning or permanence they could not bear to exist in it. The value of Albert Camus' small work, *The Myth of Sisyphus*, is that it deals with precisely this problem: "If this world is basically absurd, then is suicide the logical answer or is there still some reason to go on living?" Camus, as do all the Lyrical Existentialists, answers yes, and it is this question and the answering yes which stand at the thresh-

6. *G*, III, Sec. 1.

old of the thought of all three thinkers. Kierkegaard despaired of the world and then, in repetition, regained it in a transformed manner; Nietzsche, as well as Camus, despaired of a world of hope, permanence, goodness, and meaning, but in and through this despair he discovered the source of these yearnings: his own abiding uniqueness as a conscious being. And this discovery redeemed and justified the world.

What this means, then, is that when Nietzsche says "yes" to life, this does not imply simply an acceptance of the world, but, more fully, it implies an acceptance of existence itself, acceptance of the fact that one shall, as an individual, exist in such a world. The shortcoming of previous thinkers is not merely that they did not accept the whole of the world's reality but, more importantly, that because of this half-blind error they could not see or accept the fact of the existing individual's own unique place in this world. Thus, Nietzsche sees himself as a corrector of the falsity of previous philosophical and religious ideas; in his role as unmasker of Christian morality and its decadent spokesmen, he was striking out against what he saw as lies and delusions about the world, lies which corrupted and weakened the individual rather than allowing him to develop that unique power which waited within him. The ancient nobles accepted the full truth about the world and existed accordingly; they were not philosophers, they accepted this truth unconsciously and naturally. But philosophy and the millenia of decadence were given birth in the conscious and contrived attempt to falsely contemplate the world impersonally and objectively; thus does the very nature of philosophy rest on an untruth. But finally Nietzsche sought to inaugurate a third stage, a kind of renaissance or re-establishment of that ancient and natural way of accepting the world,

only in this case it is a highly conscious and sophisti-
cated state of mind, armed with all the weapons of
modern science. This third stage is really the destruction of philosophy as we know it, and we enter into a
new and more difficult discipline which demands not
only our intellects but a painful and passionate response of our whole beings. Nietzsche proclaims the
end of that totally false separation of body and spirit
which, "especially since Plato, has lain over philosophy like a plague." [7] This is the end of that decadent
age of bloodless philosophy where

> Truth must dwell only in the palest, most abstract
> generalities, in the empty shells of the vaguest
> words, as in a box spun of spidery silk; and next
> to such a "Truth" now sits the philosopher, as
> bloodless as an abstraction and wrapped up in a
> cocoon of formulas. [8]

The Nietzschean evangel that God is dead does **not**,
after all, have anything to do with God, but it does
have everything to do with the world in which men
live. That God is dead means that this world is both
complete within itself and meaningless within itself.
It means that men have come to realize that not only
has the "twilight of the gods" arrived but it is also the
time of the "twilight of the idols," those man-made
idols of Christianity, philosophy, modernism, statism,
Philistinism. If God is dead, then the world stands
transformed; it has now become neither better nor
worse, rather is it now seen for what it is and what
it always has been despite the veils of indolence,
cowardice, and sickness which have blinded the eyes
of man to its reality. If God is dead, then mor-

7. Friedrich Nietzsche, "Die Philosophie im tragischen Zeit-
alter der Griechen," Sec. 10.
    8. *Ibid.*

tality is the lot of all men, their spirits are grasped tightly in the hands of finitude, their days are entangled fatefully in the mechanism of time. The earth no longer holds up a deceitful and smiling face, nor does human history display a progress or purpose into which a man can throw himself and find justification. No longer dare a man seek for fulfillment in the myriad roles which society offers him.

> To the question "For what purpose are you living?" they would quickly answer with pride, "In order to become a good citizen, or scholar, or statesman." And thus are they something which never can become something else, and why are they just this? Alas, is there nothing better? Whoever views his life as a point in the development of a race, or a state, or a science, and thus wishes to belong body and soul to the history of becoming—such a one has not understood the lesson propounded him by existence and must learn it over again. This eternal becoming is a lying puppet show before which man forgets himself, the bona fide dissolution which scatters the individual after all winds, the endless game of nonsense which is played before us and with us by the great child, Time. Heroic honesty involves ceasing, one day, to be its plaything.[9]

To cease being the plaything of time: these are the chains which Nietzsche invites us to break. No longer are we to seek hopelessly in this world for truth and happiness; these are the fraudulent, playful promises of the world. This must cease, and in this cessation we shall see the falsity and unhappiness of our world. But it does not end there: along with this

9. *UB*, III, Sec. 4.

naked vision of the world there follows a wondrous discovery.

> . . . There steals upon him something inexpressible in comparison to which happiness and truth are but idolatrous imitations: the earth loses its heaviness, the events and forces of the earth become dreamlike, a transfiguration spreads over him like summer evening. It is, for the visionary, as if he had just begun to awaken and as if only the clouds of a fleeting dream still played about him. These, as well, shall one day be blown away: then it is day.[1]

I know of no finer passage than this, expressing Nietzsche's conviction of the joy which follows despair of one's world. For Nietzsche, to awaken to the reality of the world meant to awaken to the reality of oneself. Two realities appear simultaneously: the self-conscious individual and the world in which he exists. The dialectic of existence is there. It has been said that this transfigured consciousness, faced with a world which looms empty and threatening, responds to this threat as if to an invitation or challenge. This is the crux of Nietzsche's understanding of the world: it is a dialectical understanding in which the individual plays his fated role.

It seems to have been little noticed and not at all understood that one of Nietzsche's favorite and recurrent images is that of the dancer. It was he who said that he would have nothing to do with a God unless he could dance. But what is the significance of dancing? Why is it such an important image for Nietzsche? The answer to this should not now be difficult to find, for the analogy is as simple as it is eloquently expressive: the beauty and skill of the

1. *Ibid.*

dancer is that, in dancing, he shows his studied independence of the pull of the earth. Dancing is a gay mockery of gravity; it does not deny the earth, nor does it scorn it; in dancing, the earth is used by man, and in every graceful leap away from the earth we are dimly conscious that the wishes of gravity are being thwarted. Dancing is difficult, it is unnatural; if one gave in to the world one would never rise from the earth. To dance above the pull of the earth is a struggle and an accomplishment; every movement is a frivolous or graceful testimony to man's freedom and will. What is the dancer other than a symbol of that dialectical truth about human existence which Nietzsche has championed? The world stands before us, and we must come to understand and feel it for all that it is. And out of the depths of this understanding and feeling for our world there comes the call to dance, the invitation to freedom, the first taste of the joy of existence.

CHAPTER SEVEN

DANGER IN THE STREET AND
IN THE HEART

WE HAVE NOW MANAGED to ramble our way through an essential portion of Friedrich Nietzsche's thought: his understanding of and attitude toward the world. In these ramblings the Reader may have noticed how two complementary themes echo unceasingly through Nietzsche's words: movement away from the world and movement toward the individual. The former theme is what has first occupied us, and our perusal of it has, at every turn, shown us that whenever Nietzsche has pointed out a vacuum in the world, the individual is there to fill it. If the world is empty of meaning, then all points to the individual, all depends upon him. And so, again, we come to a crucial area in the philosophy of Lyrical Existential-ism: the unique nature of the conscious individual. It is crucial because, on one hand, the dominant scien-tism of the modern world tends largely to condemn the "archaic" notion of freedom and uniqueness on the part of the individual, and, on the other hand, be-cause Lyrical Existentialism has, in the face of this condemnation, offered the only persuasive and hope-ful defense of the individual. I have chosen my word carefully here when I say "persuasive"; these three thinkers do not offer proof of individual freedom. There *is* no proof. And it is arrogant nonsense on the part of anyone to claim to have proved or disproved the reality of human freedom. If one has come to understand the viewpoint of Lyrical Existentialism on this matter, he will appreciate that, in respect to proof or demonstration, the notion of individual freedom must remain and will remain problematical, but at the same time the viewpoint of Lyrical Existentialism should have persuaded him that this is of small moment. The uniqueness of the individual will continue to remain a conscious fact, witnessed to and acted upon, but it will never be decisively proved in the public square or the private laboratory or in Positivist tracts. This is only as it should be. It is both the genius and the limitation of the scientific attitude that human freedom should be denied.

If in nothing else, the Lyrical Existentialists can be of value to us in making persuasively clear both the value and limitations of science. Intellectual crises arise in ever-swifter cycles these days, and doctrinaire scientists and their apologists find themselves in the same ludicrous position as did their opponents, the Biblical literalists of a half century or so ago. The Biblicists, in fearful and half-blind arrogance, clung to the conviction that the Bible must possess complete truth or none at all, that if one jot or tittle of the Bible were proved untrue, then the whole Biblical structure would crumble. In their desperate certainty, they demanded absolute dominion or none at all. Dogmatic scientists and their philosophical spokesmen are now in the identical difficulty: they hold the untenable conviction that science must have absolute and unquestioned dominion, else its entire structure would crumble, that the scientist must have both the first and last say in all human matters, lest science itself be called into question. Again: complete dominion or nothing. This nonsensical attitude indicates the obvious fact that such scientists do not as yet have a complete understanding of science, and their dogmatism in this respect is as great a disservice to science as it is to mankind, even as the dogmatism of the Biblicists has been as great a detriment to the Bible as it has been to society as a whole. Once scientists understand the nature and limits of their science—even as Biblicists have gradually appreciated the nature and limits of the Bible—the atmosphere will be much clearer for an understanding of the elusive and precious uniqueness of each of us as individuals. Perhaps then, even our philosophers may leave off from their anxious conviction that they have the world in a box and turn once again to the service of their fellowmen rather than their scientific elect.

Once this healing wind has blown the atmosphere clear again, I believe that Friedrich Nietzsche and that thought which has been called Lyrical Existentialism will stand forth as the clearest guide which the past century has offered for those who would honestly come to terms with the new and undeniable truths of the modern age and yet not be destroyed by them, nor let them destroy what is precious in the past. What should be clear at this point is that the Lyrical Existentialists are decidedly modern in their acceptance of the value of scientific method and of its appraisal of our natural and historical environment. Their peculiarity is to have assented to this disenchanted and demythologized world, yet refused it as a measure of their own uniqueness. They are "modern—yet. . . ." And this is the genius of their way of thought which will eventually come to be appreciated. They have seen the nature and limits of our world, yet they have not given in to it; rather, they have responded to this modern predicament with a renascent discovery of the uniqueness and freedom of the individual, a discovery which is a complement to (and not a contradiction of) a balanced scientific world-view that understands its relativity, not its absoluteness.

In understanding how Nietzsche sees the vacuum of the world filled by the presence of the individual, we shall confront a rather famous expression, *will to power*, a Nietzschean expression which is essential to his description of the free role which the individual can play in relation to his world. There has not always been complete understanding of the meaning of *will to power*, but I hope the Reader will not be too surprised if he is told from the outset that if he has come to some understanding of Kierkegaard's term *inner teleology*, he has already come most of the way in comprehending this Nietzschean expression which, despite its peculiar characteristics, is basically the same.

What does it mean for the individual to separate himself from his world? What does it mean for him to set himself at a distance from his environment? By what power does he do this, and in what way does this endow him with more power, more freedom, more self-determination? As a suggestion of an answer, let Nietzsche give us an analogy.

> There is a lake which one day refused to allow itself to drain off and so threw up a dam at that place where hitherto it had flowed out. Since that time the lake mounts up ever higher. Perhaps just this kind of renunciation will endow us with the power with which the renunciation itself can be endured. Where man no longer flows out into a god, perhaps from this point on he will mount up higher and higher.[1]

There is a dialectical principle implicit in this analogy: the exercise of independence is reinforced by

1. *FW*, Sec. 285.

more independence, the individual's affirmation of his own unique power creates a greater reserve of power. At first glance it is disturbing that the term *power* should be used to describe what is a conscious moral act rather than a physical act; nonetheless, "power" is the proper term. If we are speaking of an action which effects a change and transforms our conscious relation with the world, then a force is present and active, there is a power proceeding from the individual. To despair of the succor of the world, to cease flowing outward toward an external certitude and redemption—this renunciation brings to bear the unique reality of the individual, and it is a powerful and active reality: something is taking place within the conscious life of the individual.

In his thinking about the nature of man, Nietzsche is possessed by a single-minded goal: to pin down the unique reality of the individual qua individual, to suggest that characteristic and basic fact about the individual which can in no way be touched upon by an empirical analysis of man. In this light, his concern is identical with that of Jean-Paul Sartre, who, in his *L'Etre et le nèant,* contends that the Freudian empirical analysis of the individual in terms of a composite of drives (e.g., "sex drives," "hunger drives," etc.) is a superficial external analysis which can in no way explain or account for the basic source of these drives inhering in the existing individual. Nietzsche, as does Sartre, points to the basic existential constitution of the individual, which explains the multifarious drives presented by the individual to any objective observer, whether he be psychologist or historian. The following citation from *Thus Spake Zarathustra* should fully bear this out and, as well, make clear that the "characteristic and basic fact about the individual" is his will to power.

And Life itself spoke unto me this secret: "Behold," it said, "I am *that which must ever overcome itself.*"

Indeed, you call it "will to procreate" or "drive toward an end," toward something higher, farther, richer: but all this is one and one secret. . . .

Whatever I create and however much I may love it—soon I must become the opponent of it and of my love: thus my will wills it.

And you also, the Knower, are but a path and footprint of my will: truly, my will to power treads upon the feet of your will to truth!

He who shot at the truth with the word "will to existence" missed it entirely: such a will does not exist!

For whatever does not exist cannot will; but how could anything in existence still want existence!

Only where there is life is there also will: but not "will to life," but—thus do I teach you— "will to power." [2]

In these words we find the central fact of existence to be a will to power, and this is characterized as a ceaseless overcoming of oneself. "Self-overcoming" and "self-surpassment" are terms which we have already encountered, and the above citation recalls to us again the important Kierkegaardian themes of despair and repetition. Indeed it should, for we are dealing with the same insight into human existence. That we may have no doubts about the fundamental nature of this Nietzschean concept, we should note another instance where he says that

2. Z, II, "Von der Selbst-Ueberwindung."

Physiologists should think twice before putting down the instinct of self-preservation as the cardinal instinct of an organic being. Above all, a living thing seeks to *discharge* its strength. Life itself is will to power; self-preservation is only one of the indirect and most frequent results of it.[3]

If we are to understand this term, we must first off recognize that it is in no wise simple, rather it is both a complex and penetrating Nietzschean concept. Obviously we have to do with two factors: will and power; what is the nature of willing, and what kind of power is Nietzsche speaking of? It is clear that in will we are dealing with a kind of activity, and in power we are to understand some kind of condition or state of things. Let us take the next few pages to feel out Nietzsche's understanding of these words.

What is called *willing*, is, says Nietzsche, a quite complicated act and has nothing of the simplicity which this one word seems to imply, nor which its advocates or opponents imply in their use of it.[4] Rather, willing is a complex event involving three general elements. First of all, willing involves a number of sensations. There is the sensation of going away from a condition and the simultaneous sensation of going toward a different condition. And, very importantly, there are complex muscular and organic sensations which always accompany willing, even in those cases where we make no overt physical movement: we will something, and a physiological response immediately is sensed. But secondly, besides this complex of sensations, there is the element of thinking involved in willing. A ruling thought is

3. *JGB*, Sec. 13.
4. The following argument is largely a paraphrase of *JGB*, Sec. 19.

present in every act of will, and this guiding, pur-
posing thought is integral to willing; you cannot
subtract it from the process and still have something
called willing left over, for without it there would not
be any willing. But there is yet a third general
element which combines with this complex of sensation and thinking, and this is emotion. Here Nietzsche
displays his brilliance as an intuitive psychologist; the
emotion which he finds inherent in willing is the
emotion of command, the emotion of supremacy in
respect to something which will obey. It is from this
emotion, he notes, that the idea of the so-called
freedom of will is derived. Underlying this term
freedom is that emotion which says "I am free, 'he'
must obey."

This is that consciousness of direct, rigid attention
fixed exclusively on one thing and nothing else, that
inward certainty that obedience will follow. Nietzsche
says it is this emotion which we feel within us, for
when a man wills, he commands something within
him which he believes will respond in obedience. The
crucial thing here is that the commanding and obeying persons are the same: it is oneself. Not only do
we experience the emotion of command, but, as well,
as the obeying party, we feel the constraint, pressure,
and resistance of obeying this command. In all this we
see the great complexity of willing, and understand
that, for Nietzsche, there is no such thing as the will
but rather there is only the complex action of willing.
Willing is an event, not a thing, and one of the significant facts about Nietzsche's description of this event
is its duality: the commander and the obeyer, the
thought and sensations which point both toward and
away. In this description we are probing the heart of
Nietzsche's understanding of the self-conscious individual. This duality which Nietzsche sees is the **nature**

of self-consciousness itself, the mirror in which we see ourself at a distance as if it were another self. This is that dialectical reality in which "I" reject "myself" in order to attain a more preferred state of existence: the commander and the obeyer are set at antipodes to one another, yet both are part of the dialectical reality which is at the center of human existence. Nietzsche's description of the centrum of individual consciousness is neither less nor more than that same description which came from the pen of Kierkegaard. And when Nietzsche speaks of *will*, he is simply pointing to the human fact that "I" can change "myself," that "I" can overcome "myself." In this decisive insight we find the source of his passionate concern for becoming and self-surpassing. And it is this same insight which, in the present century, moved Camus to say that "man is the only creature who refuses to be what he is."

Thus, the Nietzschean doctrine of will has to do with an inner willing and always refers to a particular conception of the self-conscious individual. We *are* part of this world, and we must honestly recognize the reality of the world and our organic place in it— *yet*, as self-conscious creatures, we are conscious of a separation from this world and from this self *as they are*. There is a void within the individual which pulls away from what is and *becomes* something else. This is the cutting edge of human willing which, within itself, creates the possibility of surpassing what one is. There is the world of which we are an integral part; there is the inner reality which is not a part of the world and all that is; and, finally, there is the self-conscious existence of the individual in which these two conflicting realities inhere. This is the tense arena of conflict in which the will plays its unique game of becoming.

Both Nietzsche and Kierkegaard possessed a rather helpless attraction toward metaphysics. Outside of a few metaphysical sallies in the *Fragments* and the *Postscript*, Kierkegaard satisfied this need within the withered bosom of Christian dogmatics—a satisfaction which ultimately harmed rather than enhanced the genius of his thought. But by Nietzsche's time this bosom was dry, and Nietzsche gratified his penchant for a well-rounded picture of reality by doctrines of the *eternal return* and a metaphysics of the will to power —this, too, was a gratification which added a charming, though harmful, overtone to his philosophizing. It is in this metaphysics of the will to power that Nietzsche's doctrine of inner willing takes on an expansiveness which Kierkegaard never ventured nor cared to venture. And even though this is a secondary aspect of Nietzsche's thought, we must say a word about it, lest the Reader come to perplexity about the basic identity of Nietzsche's and Kierkegaard's views.

Nietzsche knew very well that to claim the will to power to be the ultimate principle of life was a contention which threw him directly into the problem of freedom-causality. If there were such a will, then this meant two things: (1) that the will was a causal agent and (2) the will was free in its activity. Thus it is a free causality. Nietzsche did not shy away from these implications; rather, he affirmed them in a radical manner by suggesting[5] that if the entire instinctive life and all organic functions could be traced back to the will to power, then it would be warranted to speak of all active force—mechanical as well as organic—as will to power.

This is a modified Schopenhauerean viewpoint which has quite good grounds for argument, even though Nietzsche is not at pains to argue it with any

5. *JGB*, Sec. 36.

great clarity. The upshot of this bit of metaphysics is the claim that all entities in this world (be they individuals, organisms, or composites of mechanical or physical elements) find their active presence in the world by virtue of their own will to power, which is a free, causative force. Thus would Nietzsche endow all things in this world with an essential freedom, and thus would he point to this will to power as the primary explanation of reality, relegating empirical, reactive causes to the class of secondary explanations. "The world seen from within, the world defined and designated according to its 'intelligible character'—it would simply be will to power and nothing else." [6]

But this is, as I say, a secondary matter and, in the end, is little more than a bone thrown to the history of philosophy. The fact that the will to power is, for Nietzsche, the assertion of a pocket of freedom in this world and that this freedom finds its cardinal manifestation in the individual—this is what is important and what constitutes the center of Nietzsche's concern. Willing is a unique action that is part of the very nature of the individual. It is part of him, because self-consciousness itself implies willing.

So then, if we have some picture of the place which willing has in the dialectical fact of self-consciousness, then we may ask about "power." It has already been said that this was a condition or state of things, and our discussion of willing has already made it clear that this power is not external but is an inner state of being. Of course, it is possible that an external personal or social power might accompany this, but this is purely secondary and incidental—a point which will be taken up in the following chapter. We ask, then, What kind of inner power is Nietzsche speaking of?

6. *Ibid.*

The answer is, I think, obvious, and it is driven home as a certainty when Nietzsche himself aids us by calling will to power the "instinct of freedom." [7] Will to freedom: it is as simple as that, and yet it is not simple at all unless one has grasped the Lyrical Existentialist conception of that freedom which consciously sets a man apart from his world. And this freedom is power; it is power felt, experienced, lived in: the power of separateness, integrity, and self-determination. To understand the term "will to power" is to see it as a redundancy: inner willing *is* this power, and this power *means* inner willing. We have to do with a state of being, a way of existing, which Nietzsche would urge us to intensify. Selfhood, responsibility, freedom, self-determination, aloneness, integrity—all these terms are but the varying expressions of this state of being. And it is not a state of being which is static; inner freedom for the individual is not an achieved state, it is a state of becoming. Freedom creates and wants the possibility of more freedom: it grows and ceaselessly consolidates itself against the environing world. How far does one go? How much freedom is required? Already we perceive the existential admonition which Nietzsche holds forth to us: "It is a ceaseless, infinite task, this willing of inner power; your task is not to achieve, rather, it is to become."

The will to power is that ceaseless "dying away from immediacy" which we found in Kierkegaard. In Kierkegaard we found the two basic categories of existence to be the aesthetic, which unreflectingly feeds upon the fortunes of the environing world, and the "ethicoreligious," which, in opposition and freedom, pushes itself away from this leechlike dependence and defines itself in terms of its difference and conflict with the world. In Nietzsche we find the same

7. *GM*, II, Sec. 18.

two categories of existence. There is that bovine life which seeks above all "the universal, green-meadow happiness of the herd, with security, safety, comfort, and ease of life for everyone." [8] This is the idyllic dream of one mode of existence and is, curiously enough, as exact a description of mid-twentieth-century American life as may ever be formulated. But there is, for Nietzsche, that second mode of existence which, in its demand for integrity and freedom, completely negates this idyll of the masses.

> We opposite ones, who have opened both eye and conscience to the question where and how the plant, "man," has hitherto grown to its mightiest height, hold that in every case this has taken place under opposite conditions, that for this end the dangerousness of his situation must be increased enormously, his powers of invention and of being incognito (his "spirit") had to develop into subtlety and audacity under long oppression and compulsion, his life-will had to be increased to the unconditioned power-will. We believe that severity, violence, slavery, danger in the street and in the heart, secrecy, stoicism, the art of the tempter and every kind of deviltry—that everything evil, terrible, tyrannical, predatory, and serpentine in man serves just as much for the elevation of the species, "man," as does the opposite of this. [9]

Such a bombastic passage makes quite clear how an individual's "instinct of freedom" inescapably finds its world to be an arena of combat. All that is solid, respected, "good," and reasonable in the world pales into nonsense before the inner demand of freedom.

8. *JGB*, Sec. 44.
9. *Ibid.*

"Good" and "evil" are neutral, insignificant words which possess no intrinsic value. The individual, as he wills greater inner power, crosses indiscriminately across society's moral frontiers, using what he can where he can in a world whose so-called values and dis-values no longer hold meaning except as they are endowed with meaning by the individual himself.

The world does not hatch meanings and values for us as a chicken hatches eggs. The meanings which we use and the values which we maintain have always been of the same fabric as man himself, and have been spun out of those men who have risked the creation of a further step in civilized history. Values are not "there" in our environment; if they exist at all, they will exist in the hearts of those men who struggle against the world and themselves in order to insure them. The values of our world urge us to habit and conformity: they are the chains with which lazy men gently bind themselves. It is our will to power which would have us tear loose from these fetters and exist freely and for ourselves before all that environs us. What Nietzsche envisions is a state of being in which a man stands above history, ignoring its precepts and values and possessing its moral heritage; and in this state of separation he recreates as "man" his own unique relation and destiny in the world, dispensing with all intermediaries, acting as if no man had hitherto done this, *knowing* that no man hitherto has done this or could do this for *him*.

I have said that it is as man—not simply as individual—that Nietzsche would have us recreate our relation with the world. And it is in deepening the meaning of this that we touch upon the full significance of the will to power. In this passion for freedom the individual draws his strength from a reality which is not his alone but is his as a man. Freedom and selfhood find their ground in a power which is the common possession of all men. In the struggle to disentangle one's existence from the world and its history, the free man is seeking to rediscover his uniqueness as man, which history has obscured. He knows what history has to say about him, he knows that the voice of tradition is only

> . . . the old false adornment, frippery and gold dust of unconscious human vanity, and that even beneath such flattering color and overpainting, the terrible, original text *homo natura* must once again be recognized. This means to translate man back again into nature; to master the many vain and fanciful interpretations and subordinate meanings which hitherto have been scratched and daubed over the eternal, original text, *homo natura;* to bring it about that man shall henceforth stand before men as already—hardened by scientific discipline—he now stands before the *rest* of nature—with fearless Oedipus eyes and stopped-up Ulysses ears, deaf before the luring calls of old metaphysical birdcatchers . . .[1]

And then we know that Nietzsche has reached a rock bottom of honesty when he speaks these quiet, revealing words:

> . . . this may be a strange and mad task, but that it is a *task*—who can deny it! Why have we chosen it, this mad task? Or, asked in another way, "Why knowledge at all?" Every man will question us about this. And we, so pressed, who have already asked ourself this question a hundred times, have not found and cannot find any better answer. . . .[2]

1. *JGB*, Sec. 230.
2. *Ibid.*

The task is self-authenticating. In living it, in pursuing it, in existing with it, one finds its justification. There is no "better answer"; once we have abandoned the voice of history and the formulations of religion and philosophy, there is left only an inner certainty —nothing else. Few words reveal, as do these, the humanity of Friedrich Nietzsche. Once the bombast is done and the echoes have ceased, the man stands before us in the humility which becomes any honest thinker and says, "In the end I know it is true, but this I can't communicate to you. You must discover it for yourself."

The individual who wills greater power and freedom for himself views the resultant conflicts and sufferings in this world as welcome and expected events. He says yes to them in the same triumphant way that the Greeks said yes to the tragedy which unfolded before them in the amphitheater. With a joyous knowledge and freedom, he rises above the tragedy of this world for precisely the same reason as the Greeks: he has become conscious of that unique reality within him which is unconquerable, enduring, and untouched by the world and its history. The Dionysian reality which Nietzsche found in Attic tragedy is the inner reality which makes possible that assured and intensely conscious distance which the free man puts between himself and the world as he wills himself greater power. It is because of this Dionysian reality that the dialectic of self-consciousness is not static but becomes. Self-consciousness is not complete in itself, it ceaselessly calls its *self* into question, willing to surpass itself in the light of something beyond. What must be made emphatically clear is that if we understand in what way Nietzsche is an atheist, we must also understand in what way he has replaced the God of external history with an ultimate reality within the individual. Jean-Paul Sartre provides the most apt contrast on this point: Sartre is atheistic in a total manner; this is to say, not only does he deny any objectively given ultimate law or being, but he denies as well any subjectively given ultimate— neither in man's world nor in his self-conscious existence is there a meaningful stability. Thus, Sartre's world is totally meaningless, and existence, in all its aspects, is absurd. Nietzsche, on the other hand, denies any objective God and, hence, sees the objective world as humanly meaningless, *but* he passionately counters this with the affirmation of a reality within man which is ultimate, which is redeeming, which is eternal. No, there is nothing given in the world itself, says Nietzsche, which is final, saving, and enduring; there is no God or principle to which man can cling and find sustenance for his being. The world must be recognized for what it is and drawn away from, and in this creation of distance from the world one has already begun to rely upon that inner Dionysian reality which is his ground of uniqueness. "Have you understood me? *Dionysus* versus *Christ.* . . ."—these concluding words of *Ecce Homo* are not expressions of a deranged mind but are explosive summations of Nietzsche's thinking. The question "Have you understood me?" is seen now in a poignant light, for, indeed, he was not understood. If Nietzsche, rising above the restricted horizons of his time, saw and affirmed the loss of "God" and the rejection of Christ, he did not stand content with this affirmation. He understood, as we are now gradually beginning to understand, that the loss of God-consciousness is the paramount tragedy of modern times, that the foundations of modern civilization had been shaken, and that we had set foot into an age of nihilism. But his genius was to have seen this very

nihilism, this incipient fall into darkness, as the dawn-
ing of a renaissance. The loss of God is not the loss
of meaning; it is the rebirth of the possibility of noble
individuals who courageously and creatively face their
world without intermediaries, without the weakness of
referring their judgments to outside gods or laws. Out
of the loss of Christ there arises Dionysus; out of the
death of the gods there arises human freedom; out of
the rejection of the world there arises the affirmation
of the unique and lasting reality which is embedded
within the being of all men. Even though the earth
has become deserted by the gods, we are not lost, we
are not in darkness; rather, we now, in a great reversal of attitude, can grasp the possibility of self-
discovery. Dionysus versus Christ: in this portentous
phrase the movement of the Nietzschean myth has
come full circle. The age of decadence, of human
weakness and godly intermediaries, has come to a
close. The age of rebirth, of human strength and
freedom, has now dawned.

It is not enough to say that Nietzsche is an atheist; he
is far more than this. It is not enough to see him only
in the light of his negations and criticisms—this
would be dishonesty to ourselves as well as to Nietzsche. What is precious and enduring in the life of
Friedrich Nietzsche is the positive and prophetic
manner in which he pointed the way to a kind of existence which makes the religious tragedy of modern
times a religious renascence. For him who has eyes to
see and ears to hear, it cannot be stressed enough that
Nietzsche is a religious prophet, and it is in this that
he is of one voice with the Lyrical Existentialists. It
is the genius and value of the Lyrical Existentialists
that they have, both as individuals and as thinkers, reacted positively and passionately to the profoundest
problem of our time: the religious twilight in which

men have lost all feeling of ultimate rootage in existence. As modern men have stared at darkening skies,
watching the old guiding stars blink out one by one
into nothingness, Nietzsche and Kierkegaard and
Camus have spoken the one word of comfort and
guidance: "Look elsewhere. There are yet other stars,
brighter than you could imagine and as lasting as the
human heart itself."

Little more need be said about Nietzsche's understanding of the human consciousness and the dialectical existence it reflects. The truth about human existence is that it *is* a dialectic, that it *is* in tension, and
Nietzsche urges us to affirm this dialectic which we
are. "What says your conscience?—Become who you
are." [3] This is the task. This is the existential admonition. The tension and conflict must be willed to
greater tension and greater conflict. In this there is
freedom, there is power, and there is joy. For such an
existence there will be both "danger in the street and
in the heart," and there will be neither surcease nor
rest in the task of becoming, for it has no end: one
will never *be* that eternal, all-embracing reality
which burns within. Each of us exists, troubled and
incomplete, and the only honest response to this is to
become. This is the admonition which is religious despite the loss of God. A new kind of religious man is
portrayed here, of a noble religiousness which ranks
higher than any other form of existence.

It is not the works, but the *faith* which is decisive
here and determines the order of rank—to make
use again of an old religious formula in a newer
and deeper sense: it is some kind of certainty
which the noble soul has about itself, something
which cannot be sought, nor found, nor per-

3. *FW*, Sec. 270.

haps even lost.—*The noble soul has reverence for itself.*—[4]

There is no better answer than this.

4. *JGB*, Sec. 287.

CHAPTER EIGHT

THE NOBLE MAN RESURRECTED

FOR THE LYRICAL EXISTENTIALISTS, the greatest sins are not those of commission, nor of omission—but those of submission. This follows inescapably from their understanding of the nature of the world and the nature of the individual. The whole tenor of their writings is dominated by the conviction that no man must ever let himself drift, giving up his freedom to an intermediary which takes on the responsibility for his basic choices. And who among us will deny having seen, in himself and in others, that this inner laziness, this tendency toward relinquishment, is a dominant trait of men? Who will deny the compelling lure of an objectively stable role, position, profession, set of beliefs, or pattern of conduct which no longer needs be questioned and in which one finds identity and fulfillment?

"Who are you?" asks one man to another. The reply: "Why, I'm Charlie Murphy . . . (now comes the outward reach for inner security) . . . from Minnesota Mining." Or, "My name is Horace Bane. I'm the minister down at the First Baptist Church." Or, "Joe Wilks, Department of Philosophy, University of Chicago." Or the less fortunate: "I'm Mort Abernathy. Live just down the street there: second one on the left."

All of us are lost souls, attempting pathetically to find a place, a permanence in this world, a fixed significance "out there," even though it be but a house "down the street there" where an old man eats, sleeps, draws his pension checks, and tries not to think too much about death. The quiet and melancholy fact about mankind is that all of us gravitate easily and naturally into the ruts, pigeonholes, and slogans of life. Submission is the course of life which all of us or any of us are wont to follow. This is the simple, primeval —almost negligible—truth about human existence which Lyrical Existentialism first posits.

But thereupon follows a second observation which becomes a judgment: Those who have submitted have never existed fully as men. This is not a moral judgment; it is best called an existential judgment, or, taking the word in its deepest sense, it is a religious judgment. The central contention of the Lyrical Existentialists is that the most fundamental distinction between individuals is in terms of what they *are*, of the kind of existence they represent. Social, moral, physical, genealogical distinctions are secondary and nonessential facts about individuals in this world; the primary and serious matter is what kind of individual one is. This dominant existential concern makes for some interesting and much misunderstood attitudes on the part of these three thinkers. It accounts for a state of mind which can never accept political and social issues as ultimately important; a fact which often makes possible the accusations of "reaction" and "conservatism"—an inevitable accusation inasmuch as it is before the great revolutionary hopes for final justice, freedom, totality, and peace that they react most vigorously in condemning those movements which mistakenly seek what is ultimately a religious fulfillment in the shifting, destructive arena of history. If all three have been bitter opponents of socialism, it is not because they are heedless of the need for human justice, but because they believe that questions of human justice are not ultimate questions in human life and that such ideologies which posit them as ultimately important are not only destructive of what is precious in the individual but are, in their visionary fanaticism, destructive of the possibility for a relative justice and freedom in any society.

In an age when Utopian Marxism has borne its fruits, the political wisdom of these three thinkers is finding its confirmation. Given their understanding of the world and their concern for individual existence, the political wisdom of the Lyrical Existentialists consists in recognizing that a relative justice and freedom are the sole attainable possibilities in this world and that anything reaching beyond this toward absoluteness will inevitably destroy both what it seeks and the individual as well. This, indeed, is the tragic situation in which the twentieth century now finds itself and which has found one of its most lucid analysts in Albert Camus.

But this existential concern has spawned another attitude which is equally open to misunderstanding: moral relativity. When Kierkegaard says that a choice is made right by the vigor with which one chooses, when Nietzsche says we must go beyond good and evil to create our place in this world, when Camus denies all absolute moral values in face of a century which is almost totally social-minded—these amoral convictions are but expressions of that more basic understanding of the individual as the sole creator and guarantor of a moral action, and the natural-historical world as the humanly meaningless scene in which eternal gods and immutable natural laws have ceased to play a part. As in the case of their political attitudes, this moral relativism would seem to be a more profound appreciation of the nature and value of morals than is any viewpoint which is idealistically, rationally, or empirically oriented.

Thus, also, does this existential concern create attitudes about history, about science, about the body-mind problem which—if only superficially understood—appear to be outrageously shortsighted and *démodé*. For the casual observer these three thinkers seem to be enigmatic and difficult-to-pigeonhole antimoderns. For the casual observer they are simply unsystematic, confused pamphleteers who have only partially come to terms with the budding modern world-view. That such is our verdict upon these thinkers is inevitable, given the mentality of our age, but such a verdict becomes itself a judgment upon the confident superficiality of our age. As has been said repeatedly, the Lyrical Existentialists are profoundly and wholeheartedly "modern" in their appraisal of nature, history, and the "animal" man, *yet* they are not content with this, nor do they remain there. It is their prophetic genius that they have *seen through* the modern world and discovered its limited insights and its destructive possibilities. That they have been misunderstood and condemned by their contemporaries is testimony to the fact that they are more than "modern," they have prophetically seen the impasse toward which the modern world moves and have attempted to provide a meaningful response to this. It is in this sense that all three of these thinkers felt deeply that they were "children of their age" and at the same time recognized that their anxious pleas were "out of season." What more melancholy recognition of this is there than Nietzsche's observation that "some are born posthumously"? The imaginations of the Lyrical Existentialists had already ridden out the storms of modernity, with its dreams of Utopia, totality, and conquest of nature and history; and, in its aftermath, they have seen that the only preoccupation worthy of the minds and hearts of men is that finite, confused,

and suffering being, the individual. All things point
to the individual, his place, meaning, and destiny in
this world. What *is* an individual? Their answer to this
is simultaneously the formula for what he must become.

Friedrich Nietzsche proposed what can best be
termed an "inner asceticism," something which Camus
was later to call an *ascèse*. Asceticism, pure and simple,
means an external withdrawal from the world in order
that one may destroy the world's control over one's
spirit by the conscious disciplining of thought, conduct, and body. Inner asceticism is a withdrawal from
the world solely in terms of a conscious attitude; one's
mode of conduct may remain unchanged. What is
ascetic in this case is that in existing consciously in
the world as a free, utterly responsible individual,
one welcomes each moment of experience in the environing world as a further confirmation and enhance-
ment of this freedom. Thus, traditional asceticism
moves away from the world and the flesh; inner asceticism moves toward the world and the flesh, accepting them in their full reality, but rejecting them
in their inadequacy. This suggests rather clearly how
this attitude is both irreligious and yet religious in intention. Asceticism, discipline, control, authority, command, willing—these are the words which are central
to Nietzsche's description of the individual's task, his
inner asceticism. As he sees it, all individual achievement involves discipline and struggle against the
world and oneself.

That is the first preparatory schooling for spiritu-
ality: not to react immediately to a stimulus but
to gain control of all inhibiting, excluding instincts. Learning to *see*, as I understand it, is al-

most what unphilosophical terminology calls a strong will; what is essential here is precisely *not* to "will," to be *able* to suspend decision. All unspirituality, all common vulgarity comes from the inability to resist a stimulus—one *has* to react, one follows every stimulus.[1]

The very possibility of learning to observe our environment or ourselves depends upon a discipline of ourselves within this environment. There is an ascetic cruelty in this; there is a deliberate suffering which is required not simply in order to see but in order to *know*.

> Finally, one should consider that even the seeker of knowledge functions as an artist and glorifier of cruelty in that he compels his spirit to perceive *against* its own inclination and often enough against the wishes of his heart—namely, to say no when he would rather affirm, love, and adore. There is no doubt that every instance of taking a thing deeply and fundamentally is a violation, a deliberate injuring of the basic will of the spirit which incessantly reaches out toward appearance and superficiality,—indeed, in every desire for knowledge there is a drop of cruelty.[2]

This inner asceticism, this art of cruelty, finds its ultimate task not simply in disciplining one's perceptive relation with the world but in refashioning one's very being as an individual—what Nietzsche calls "giving style" to one's character. This is an art, the existential art par excellence. Obviously one cannot, by some mystical fiat, become another person, a "new man";

1. G, IX, Sec. 6.
2. JGB, Sec. 229.

but what is possible is the reshaping of what one is. This is the art of enhancing one's strengths and of re-evaluating and reshaping one's given weaknesses until even they become necessary and integral parts of one's character. This is the art of creating a second nature out of one's first nature, the transformation of what one is into what one wills to become. This is the art of will to power which surpasses the "givens" of individuality and goes beyond. In this effort of self-mastery the individual refuses to drift submissively with the tides of his environment and personal history but, instead, consciously places his being under his own surveillance and responsibility. It is such a person as this who has pushed himself away from the world and, simultaneously, discovered an inner world of freedom and absoluteness. "It will be the strong, mastery-seeking natures who taste their subtlest joy in such control, in having such constraint and completeness under a single law." [3]

That there is a joy in such self-mastery goes without saying; it is precisely in this tense consciousness of selfhood—and only in this consciousness—that the Lyrical Existentialists can speak of happiness. For Kierkegaard, or Camus, or Nietzsche the inner medley of happiness and suffering sounds louder with every push away from the world and into freedom. There is a rightness, a belonging,—as Kierkegaard says, a truth—in this subjective condition which brings us happiness; a happiness which we control, guarantee, and which only we can know. Such a free individual, says Nietzsche, is an artist who finds his joy in all stylization, be it of himself or of any aspect of nature. This term "stylization"—which later was to become equally important for Camus—is a strikingly apt expression for Lyrical Existentialism's conception both

3. *FW*, Sec. 290.

of art and of inner asceticism. It is appropriate because it gives a precise expression to the fundamentally dialectic viewpoint which understands and accepts the "is" of this world, *yet* acts upon it and transforms it. Stylization means to start with the candid recognition of what one is, where one is, and what one has, and then to transform this "given" in terms of what it shall become. Whether we speak of the art of existing or the arts of objective expression, stylization is the central process entailed. In one word it tells us of what the world is and what the individual is in his unique role of freedom. And in one word it reveals to us the integrated conception which Lyrical Existentialism has of the individual's task in himself and in his world: in being true to himself as an individual, he is also, in the highest sense, true to his world. Such an integrated conception is beyond being modern; it has set foot upon a new ground where both man and his world find their places and justifications.

In this stylizing activity the individual is constantly giving something to existence; there is an overflowing into existence which Nietzsche, at all points, marks as greatness. A power comes from within, and in its outpouring we have a picture of that master morality which, "in its fullness, imparts itself to things—it transfigures, it beautifies, it *rationalizes* the world. . . ." [4] This is the master morality, the noble morality of the individual who has mastered himself and, thereby, overcome the world. Such a morality has

> . . . reversed its roots in a triumphant yea-saying to itself—it is self-affirmation, self-glorification of life, it employs sublime symbols as well as practices, but only "because its heart is too full

4. *NCW*, "Epilog."

for itself." All *beautiful* art, all great art, inheres in this: the essence of both is gratitude.[5]

Gratitude is the expression of a life which has met existence on its own terms and with its own resources. There is no intermediary here between man and his world; his acceptance of its challenge is not due to God's having created and sanctified the world. No, simply for what it is, the noble individual meets the world and accepts it in gratitude. It is the arena which invites him to dance, it is the raw material which awaits his overflowing vitality which will stylize and transform what it encounters. Throughout his works Nietzsche reiterates the conviction that gratitude— which he sees to have been the prime trait of the Greeks—is the essential attitude of all genius and greatness in an individual.[6] But this superabundance, which discharges itself gratefully into the world, must be understood as the outcome of one's will to power, as the result of that tense inner asceticism which has created a pocket of freedom in the midst of the world. This freedom, this whole, integral being which gratefully gives itself to existence and thereby stylizes it —such a being draws this freedom, this warrant for stylization from some source which is unique, which is its own, which is not of his environing world.

Such a spirit which has *become free* stands in the middle of the Whole with a joyous and trusting fatality, in the faith that only the particular is objectionable, that all is redeemed and affirmed in the Whole—*he no longer negates.* But such a faith is the highest of all possible faiths: I have baptized it after the name of *Dionysus.*[7]

5. *Ibid.*
6. *G*, X, Sec. 44.
7. *Ibid.*, Sec. 49.

The Dionysian faith is Nietzsche's answer to the twilight of our gods and idols. In the dialectic, world-man, God no longer is the absolute power, the hidden support of the world. Yet man does not stand alone and lost, for Nietzsche points to a hidden support which lies within men themselves: the source of their uniqueness, and the possibility for their freedom. Such a source and possibility will become no more than this unless the individual himself wills it to be so. The Dionysian power within a man comes into existence only under a certain condition, and this is an inner, conscious condition in which the individual bears the dual consciousness of being part of the world, yet not a part of it. The world has become stark and two-dimensional, but at the same moment the individual has received an extra dimension and glorification. This extra dimension is the Dionysian power, the "absolute telos" toward which one moves in the rebellious consciousness that one must stand free and separate from the world.

In his earliest thinking about the Dionysian experience Nietzsche was concerned primarily with the passive, receptive nature of this event, the inner aesthetic experience of the spectator which transformed tragedy into a joyous affirmation of life's eternity. This early passivity was influenced largely by Nietzsche's study of Attic tragedy and his interest in the achievements of Richard Wagner. But as was previously remarked, this early passive conception of the Dionysian experience was, in later works, transformed into an aggressive event. It is with Nietzsche's notion of the will to power that the Dionysian faith becomes a positive conception not only of what a man is but, most importantly, of what a man must be. It is the Dionysian faith which undergirds one's will to power, making possible the inner ascetic activity which stylizes and transforms itself as well as all that it meets. Nietzsche's existential admonition lies precisely in this task of inner asceticism. The result of this ascetism is the attainment of wholeness and integrity; the individual becomes "hard," complete; all that he is, in his given capacities, talents, and weaknesses, becomes artistically enhanced, molded, trimmed, and integrated into a oneness in which every facet of his being contributes its necessary part. If any one word sums up the goal toward which this aceticism moves, it is integrity: this is the infinite task, the suffering of one's constitutional duality in the light of the goal to integrate into one being. Such a goal of completion and rest is, perhaps, never to be attained; nonetheless it remains the only goal worthy of human existence.[8]

8. In respect to the will to power and its central place in Nietzsche's existential admonition, it is advisable at this point that we make reference to Walter Kaufmann's *Nietzsche*, New York, Meridian Books, 1956. With its great background of scholarship, this admirable work has quickly assumed the position (at least in the Anglo-American world) of being definitive.

Scholarship, however, is not necessarily equivalent to understanding, and Mr. Kaufmann's critical achievement must be balanced against an interpretation of Nietzsche which is somewhat whimsical. Mr. Kaufmann's position in this central area is summed up in his claim that "Nietzsche's doctrine differs from 'irrationalism' inasmuch as it does not oppose reason to the basic principle of his philosophy: instead reason is pictured as the fulfillment of the will to power; . . ." (p. 203). As we shall point out, the grounds which Mr. Kaufmann adduces for this claim are highly questionable. It is right and proper to say that Nietzsche is not, strictly speaking, an "irrationalist," but it is quite another matter to claim that reason is the "fulfillment of the will to power." Nothing could be so misleading. Mr. Kaufmann betrays here a basic misunderstanding of Nietzsche, stemming apparently out of a failure to grasp the notion of the will to power as an inner asceticism whose activity is one of stylization.

Mr. Kaufmann's treatment of this area of Nietzsche's thought (pp. 197-204) is founded on an unfortunate equation of "reason, intelligence, or spirit" (p. 200). This makes possible the citation

It is, of course, a curious fact that Nietzsche's existential admonition points to an ascetic task which no one can presently achieve. Nietzsche frankly admits that no one today can exist in such a fashion,

---

of references to the latter two terms as being positive examples of Nietzsche's affirmation of rationality. Thus, in his exposition of this, all but one of the citations become deceptive. This one exception is Nietzsche's remark in *Morgenröthe* that ". . . if the degree of *venerability* should be established, only *the degree of reason in strength* is decisive. . . ." (*M*, Sec. 548). Beside the fact that Nietzsche here speaks of *Kraft* (strength) and not *Macht* (power), and beside the fact that this was written somewhat before the birth of his notion of will to power, the citation itself is an inconclusive remark referring to a sociopolitical use of strength and not to an inner personal power.

As a striking example of Mr. Kaufmann's approach to this central aspect of Nietzschean interpretation, we should note his claim that for Nietzsche "the lack of reason, intelligence, or spirit is a lack of power" (p. 200). Moreover, the unequivocal statement is made that a proper evaluation of "spirit" (*Geist*) is "so vital a point in Nietzsche's philosophy that one cannot overlook it without misapprehending Nietzsche's thought" (p. 199). Perhaps so, and in support of this Mr. Kaufmann makes the following paraphrase of *G*, IX, 14:

> In human affairs, too, Nietzsche points out, it is reason that gives men greater power than sheer bodily strength. Foresight, and patience, and above all "great self-mastery" (which, under unfavorable circumstances, also makes possible dissimulation)—that is, according to Nietzsche, of the very essence of *Geist* (p. 199).

This seemingly conclusive Nietzschean affirmation of "reason, intelligence, or spirit" as signs of power was so obvious to Mr. Kaufmann that a paraphrase was all that was needed rather than a direct citation. However, a direct quotation of *G*, IX, 14 throws quite another light on Mr. Kaufmann's paraphrase.

> The species do *not* grow in perfection: the weak prevail over the strong again and again, for they are the great majority—and they are also more *intelligent*. Darwin forgot the spirit (that is English!); *the weak have more spirit.* One must need spirit to acquire spirit; one loses it when one no longer needs it. Whoever has strength dispenses with the spirit. . . . It will be noted that by "spirit" I mean care, patience, cunning, simulation, great self-control, and everything that is mimicry (the latter includes a great deal of so-called virtue).

but he looks forward to some future time when such
men will appear who are equal to this task. These are
the "overmen" who are yet to come. That the upshot of Nietzsche's thought should be an admonition,

---

This is Mr. Kaufmann's own translation, taken from his *The
Portable Nietzsche*, New York, The Viking Press, 1954. Even
the most cursory comparison of this citation with the paraphrase will show that Mr. Kaufmann has taken a Nietzschean
tirade *against* intelligence and spirit (the devious weapons of the
weak who form the herds of history)—he has taken this tirade
as a Nietzschean affirmation of reason as a fulfillment of the will
to power. This is but one example of the manner in which
Mr. Kaufmann interprets this aspect of Nietzsche's thought, and
this extensive footnote would need to become a long critical
essay in order to clear up the confusion which the Kaufmann
book creates in its line of interpretation and its use of citations.
The interested reader should check Mr. Kaufmann's quotations
and paraphrases against the German texts. Except for the inconclusive citation already mentioned, none of the quotations from
this section of the Kaufmann book (pp. 197-204) even serve to
suggest the rational bias which is attributed to Nietzsche.
Perhaps the confusion here is best understood as a reflection
of our Anglo-American philosophical climate. Mr. Kaufmann
seems to be in such haste to save Nietzsche for the history of
philosophy that he runs roughshod over the insurmountable evidence of Nietzsche's a-rationalism and his strong antirationalistic
attitude. Any reader of Nietzsche should be on his guard when
Nietzsche says in one of his last works that one of the innova-
tions of his *The Birth of Tragedy* was that "Socrates was for
the first time recognized as the instrument of Greek dissolution,
as a typical *decadent*. 'Rationality' *against* instinct. At least
'rationality' as a dangerous, life-undermining force!" (*EH*,
"Die Geburt der Tragödie," Sec. 1) Most certainly this remark
does not mean that Nietzsche is fundamentally antirational; it
does, however, point up the essentially a-rational character of
this thought—a-rational in the precise sense that rationality is
not a determining factor in the development of the individual's
will to power.
This failure to appraise correctly Nietzsche's attitude toward
reason is possibly due also to a too-simple interpretation of
Nietzsche's Apollonian/Dionysian dialectic. One suspects that
underlying Mr. Kaufmann's interpretation is the notion that if
Apollonian forms are the fulfillment of the Dionysian surge,
then this is equivalent to saying that rationality is the fulfillment
of the will to power. This is an obvious temptation. True,

and that simultaneously he should tell us that we "modern men" shall not achieve it—this is the surprising eschatological tendency of his thought, a tendency which we now understand to find its place in

---

indeed, that Nietzsche did come to speak of the Dionysian in the same terms as the will to power (G, XI, Par. 4), but by "Apollonian" he never signified anything other than artistically stylized forms—something quite different from rationality. Mr. Kaufmann recognizes that by "Will to Power" Nietzsche means an inner power, and he also divines the place of asceticism in this activity. But, unfortunately, he equates asceticism with rationality, an equation which is no more correct than is the similar equation with intelligence or spirit.

The inner asceticism wrought by the will to power attempts to take what is "given" (i.e., an a-rational first condition) and stylize it into an integrated whole. That this is a whole does not mean it is a rational whole; rather, the goal is to fashion one's own given contradictions and disproportionalities into a whole which is instrumental to one's increasing will to power. One's personal character as well as one's external creations are, at their zenith, the most artistically wrought forms for the expression of that inner reality which is the Dionysian. Rationality has no place in this, for rationality creates its own rules; but the Dionysian expression is subject to no external rules or intermediaries: it creates its own forms. This artistic task of inner asceticism is obviously denied when Mr. Kaufmann says that, for Nietzsche, ". . . the truly rational man need not go to war against his impulses. If his reason is strong enough, he will naturally control his passions" (p. 203). Such a remark not only makes rationality an external arbiter of the will to power, but, moreover, makes Nietzsche an incredibly naïve rationalist. Mr. Kaufmann suggests that the success of this asceticism depends on one's reason being "strong enough." Such a suggestion bears no relation to the thought of Friedrich Nietzsche; rather, Nietzsche would say that the ascetic task depends solely upon one's *will* being "strong enough."

These few remarks may be sufficient to indicate the folly of attempting to rationalize Nietzsche. Out of the thousands of maxims and fragments written by Nietzsche, one might think that some clear evidence might be brought forward to buttress Mr. Kaufmann's viewpoint. But such is not the case. This is so, because the Kaufmann viewpoint fails to understand Nietzsche at the point where no interpreter can afford to misunderstand him: in understanding the will to power. If this point is lost, then the genius of Nietzsche's thought is lost. Nietzsche's

the historical "myth" which Nietzsche conceived. But this eschatological tendency does not at all appear curious if one but reflects upon this identical quality in the thought of the other Lyrical Existentialists. Kierkegaard's goal of becoming a Christian, of becoming an individual, was not presently realizable either by Kierkegaard or his contemporaries: it was, rather, an unrealizable task which beckoned to us and would find its fulfillment only in a later time. So also for Camus, who stakes everything on a *renaissance* which may some day come. The very character of Camus' thought is shaped by this straining toward a goal which is not yet attainable. So, then, if we say that Nietzsche has a doctrine of the *overman*, we must also say the same for Kierkegaard and Camus. These identical tendencies are simply the reflection of identical ways of thinking. This projection of the fulfilled task into a future time is, in part, an expression of Nietzsche's conviction that the struggle for inner integrity is, in itself, the supreme task for any individual whether or not there is a final end to it. The conviction that there can be a time when men attain perfect integrity is simply another way of saying, as does Kierkegaard, that this inner task does have meaning and does move toward a goal even though it remains infinitely beyond our grasp. For both men, the goal of this inner striving is an "impossible possibility." But this eschatological projection is, as well, an expression

---

a-rationalism is a function of his vision of the inner ascetic task, and it is in the light of this task that he, like Heraclitus, can embrace the irrationality as well as the rationality of this world: "The affirmation of flux and destruction, the decisive element in a Dionysian philosophy; the yea-saying to contradiction and war, to becoming, with a radical rejection even of the concept 'being' . . ." (*EH*, "Die Geburt der Tragödie," Sec. 3)—such is the attitude of a thinker whose thought was not only beyond good and evil, but equally beyond rationality and irrationality.

of the way in which Nietzsche—as well as his two fellow thinkers—was sensitive to his social, cultural environment. Nietzsche was profoundly antimodern in his rejection of the nihilistic impasse toward which the modern world lumbered. He knew that an appreciation of individuality awaited the breakdown of all the many futile attempts to find external idols and ideologies to fill the vacuum left in the world by the discovery of God's absence.

Nietzsche understood that the possibility of healthy, creative individual lives depended upon surpassing the nihilism and despair of the modern era. And it is precisely in this sense that we must understand his *Uebermensch*, for this does not mean a superman, who is but an intensification of what he is and of what his age is, but rather an *overman* who has surpassed his own original nature and his own cultural heritage. Thus does this ideal image of the overman possess cultural as well as subjective connotations. The two go together: to the extent that we have individuals who shape their lives freely and courageously, so shall we have a new society which reflects their presence. We need not overly trouble ourselves with the presumed *mystique* of the overman; it is better that we simply recognize this term as a powerful dramatic image which fits neatly into Nietzsche's mythological conception of human history and, at the same time, suggests admirably the goal of overcoming what one "is" in light of the task of becoming.

Certainly there has been much confusion about the overman. On one hand, there is the misapprehension that this implies a superman which is simply the magnification of what man is, an individual who is bigger, stronger, wiser, more courageous, and more daring than present-day men can possibly be. On the contrary, Nietzsche's ideal individual embodies a rejection of such concepts of progress and amelioration of man and represents a kind of individual which has surpassed, transcended, and overcome the decadent type of man in terms of a reorientation which is inner and free.[9] On the other hand, there is the misapprehension related to this former one which believes somehow that the overman is a higher phase in the evolution of the human species. But this evolutionary notion is rejected by Nietzsche with equal clarity.[1] The overman is in no wise an evolution from our present situation but rather a revolution in which decadence is overthrown and the ancient noble morality is again reinstated. This will be the return of the Dionysian faith, and, whether we speak of the overman of the future or the noble man of the past, we are dealing with the same existential admonition and with the kind of men who embody it.

The overman, then, is the noble man resurrected. And the prime characteristic of such an individual is the manner in which he freely and gratefully accepts his own nature and that of the world, eagerly giving himself to the task of stylizing these givens of existence. The noble man transforms himself and his world in terms of his own inner demand to do so. The world is his oyster, for no matter what his situation he knows that neither the world nor his own psyche and soma can dominate him: he knows his inner resources, and this is the wellspring of his freedom. Such a man is honest, says Nietzsche; he takes pride in the fact that he can make promises—and always fulfill them. Why? Because he knows the solitude of total responsibility; being free, he is also responsible: there is no permanence, no guarantee of anything in human life other than the guarantee

9. *Vide EH*, IV, "Also Sprach Zarathustra," Sec. 6.
1. *Vide ibid.*, IV, Sec. 1.

which he himself asserts. Nothing is more certain than this: that freedom is a burden, even so, it is the one burden, the sole burden which human destiny offers the individual. In the ultimate meaning of the word, it is the only thing of which man can truly say, "It is *mine*."

This is the kind of power which the noble man wills for himself, this is the ascendency, the mastery, which he holds over himself and over his environment. This is not an external power of domination; no man can or need have such power. The environing world is not an unsubstantial, pliable, and secondary reality which awaits man's domination; it is a brutal, hard, sure fact which the individual meets and must reckon with. The noble man has accepted his world for what it is and would be the last to entertain the naïve dream of conquering nature. He knows he cannot do it, and, more importantly, he does not have the sickly compulsion to destroy nature in order to have a visible sign of his uniqueness. This futile dream is of the essence of decadent thought which despairingly seeks for the security of gods and idols "out there" in the world, apart from oneself. Rather, the power willed by the noble man is the power of freedom, the power of existing in this remorseless world in terms of one's own unique and separate reality. The noble man has already overcome the world by the fact that he has called it into question, struggled with it, and tinted it with his own reality. He transforms all that he touches, he stylizes all that he must live with, humanizing, civilizing, shaping his character as well as his environment in terms of an image which is not a final image of his nature but which is his own image in the sense that it symbolizes his difference, his revolt, his protest against the fixed world that was given him. This is his conquest of the world, this is the result of his will to power.

And so it is that the kind of "masters" envisioned by Nietzsche are not masters over society or history. This kind of dominance is incidental; it is a possible but not necessary result of one's will to power. The noble man may be a king or he may be a slave; his external social circumstance has no bearing upon what is essentially an inner achievement. Nietzsche's philosophy is not the overture to a new society in which aristocracy once again reigns supreme; it is the overture to a new kind of individual in whom the ascetic task is the supreme concern.

One final word must be spoken about the will to power, and this is to note the almost biological manner in which Nietzsche describes it. The Dionysian reality which underlies the power that the individual wills is a reality which must be reckoned with. Even as the world is a surd fact which the individual ignores only at his own peril, so also is the inner Dionysian surge a fateful and inescapable fact of human existence. Nietzsche alternately speaks of this as a metaphysical principle and as a biological principle. It is a vitality which can be immediately expressed or else it can be repressed and bottled up until it either explodes or seeps outward in perverted, sickly forms. Again, as with Kierkegaard, a conception of health is at stake. The Dionysian instinct will not be denied; whether we wish it or not, it shall determine what we shall be. One can accept it and cultivate its transforming power, or one can deny it and suffer the effects of this denial. This is why Nietzsche is so insistent in his condemnation of those who deny their instincts.

> I call an animal, a species, an individual corrupt when it loses its instincts, when it chooses, when it *prefers* what is to its disadvantage. . . . I see

life itself as instinct for growth, for duration, for gathering of forces, for power: wherever the will to power is lacking there is decline. My contention is that all the highest values of mankind *lack* this will, that decadent values, *nihilistic* values, hold sway under the holiest of names.[2]

Nietzsche's use of the perplexing word "instinct" is nothing other than a characterization of the Dionysian reality in biological terms. And if this palpable inner force is not cultivated and vented, it becomes a negative, destructive, decadent force in human life. Instinct then turns upon life itself, creating a sickly, subterranean vengeance against the individual and his world. Nietzsche's extensive meditations on guilt, bad conscience, and the morbid psychology of religion, idealistic philosophy, and pessimism are actually descriptions of the way in which the imperative surge of the Dionysian reality has been denied, thus issuing in sickness and degeneracy. It is in this light that we must understand Kierkegaard's equally extensive discussion of anguish and despair, for Kierkegaard sees that the imperative of one's inner *telos* is so awesome and infinite, that the inner ascetic task is so colossal, that one despairs of existence itself and has a sickness which endures unto one's death. In like fashion, Albert Camus' ironic story, *The Fall*, is a masterful description of this identical sickness: that of a man who is destroying himself through his yearning for innocence and freedom and wholeness.

The instinct of freedom is a wondrous primeval force in human existence. It is something "given" in human experience, even as the reality of the world is "given"; it is a reality to which the individual must be responsive. He has the awesome task of willing, af-

2. *A.* Sec. 6.

firming this power within him; he bears within himself the staggering imperative that he realize the impossible possibility of becoming free, of becoming an individual, unique, autonomous, and within the solitude of total responsibility. Such an existence is the ideal existence; it is the existence of the overman, a way of life yet to be attained. But in the meantime, during this long, tortured interval between dawn and high noon, men's lives lie entangled in the net of values which urge them to deny this foreboding possibility of freedom. And this is their sickness, their degeneracy. "This *instinct of freedom*—it is already apparent—when forced into being latent, this instinct of freedom, repressed, downtrodden, imprisoned within itself and finally only able to find expression and release on itself: this, and only this, is at the beginning of "bad conscience." [3] The power that can create nobility is the same power that can effect degeneracy. The difference here is "only that the material upon which the constructive and tyrannical nature of this power is unloosed is man himself, his entire, old, animal self—and not upon the *other* man, *other* men, as is the case with that grander and more spectacular phenomenon." [4] The Dionysian reality is a two-edged sword, not to be denied. To thwart it means self-destruction; to affirm it means the power of selfhood.

The willing of this inner power is the essential ascetic task of the noble man or overman—both ideal Nietzschean types which never have existed nor will exist. This is the difficult inner labor which makes them what they are. But there are other noble qualities flowing from this; they are the more noticeable traits which stand as signs of this inner becoming. The two

3. *GM*, II, Sec. 17.
4. *Ibid.*, Sec. 18.

most crucial traits of character in the noble man which remain to be mentioned are his moral relativity and what Nietzsche calls his *pathos of distance*. The importance of this latter has not always been appreciated.

The moral relativity of the noble man is a more obvious quality inasmuch as the inward orientation of his life means that there can be no fixed, abiding external values which he will blindly follow. *Unabhängigkeit* is a condition which means much to Nietzsche, and the nobleman, in his independence and autonomy, will always run roughshod over the artificial moral distinctions which guide the lazy and passionless lives of the herd. In the eyes of the herd, the noble man will always appear as a paragon of evil, as an irresponsible and immoral culprit. This is as it should be. And in one of his finest analogies Nietzsche says, "But it is the same with men as it is with trees. The more he strives toward height and brightness, so much more strongly will his roots strive earthward, downward, into darkness, depth—into evil." [5] For Nietzsche, as for Kierkegaard, the "right" moral choice is not dependent upon an external standard but upon the *manner* in which one chooses. The ethical distinction between good and bad has no meaning for Nietzsche except as it may refer to the passion, honesty, and freedom with which one chooses. Even if it were conceivable that there was an invariable and perfect moral standard, this would be meaningless to the noble man. Even though his every action *might* conform to such an objective standard, still he would make his choices in independent disregard of this standard; the presence or absence of moral standards is of no moment to him: rather, it is a threat, a constant temptation which would take away the one

5. Z, "Vom Baum am Berge."

thing that is precious and indigenous to him—his freedom. So then, even as morality is a threat to the noble man, so also is he a threat to morality. The noble man is a dangerous man: his sphere of reference is beyond good and evil. He has overcome this temptation within himself, he has surpassed it. He stands apart, at a distance, ever questioning himself and the world.

"The first thing by which I decide whether a man has 'intestinal fortitude' is whether he has a feeling for bodily distance, whether he everywhere sees rank, grade, order between men and men, whether he *makes* distinctions. . . ." [6] This statement introduces us to a highly important notion of Nietzsche's: the pathos of distance. This intriguing term is an essential character trait of the noble man and, it is obvious, of Nietzsche himself:

> During my days at Basel my whole intellectual regime, including my daily schedule, was a perfectly absurd abuse of extraordinary powers without any kind of compensation for the strength drained from me, without the slightest thought for this loss and its replacement. I lacked that subtle egoism, that protective shield of an aggressive instinct. This was a feeling of equality with any and all men, a "selflessness," a forgetfulness of distance—something for which I shall never forgive myself. [7]

It should be apparent that a pathos of distance is, like the trait of moral relativity, an inevitable consequence of the will to power. And it is equally apparent that this suffering of distance is, by and large, the same dying away from immediacy that is so im-

6. *EH*, "Der Fall Wagner," Sec. 4.
7. *Ibid.*, "Warum ich so klug bin," Sec. 2.

portant to Kierkegaard. Both men feel that the creation of distance between one's own being and that of
the immediate world is simply one way of expressing
the discovery of an inward orientation in freedom,
which is to say, an orientation in that unique reality
which is one's own: the absolute telos, the Dionysian
reality. This is that dialectical nature of the kind of
existence which Lyrical Existentialism depicts for us.
This is that tragicomic consciousness which laughs
at what is below it and weeps at what is yet to be
achieved. This is at the base of Nietzsche's recurrent
images of heights and mountains upon which the free
spirit sits, roaring with divine laughter, as he gazes
down at the sober, serious puppetry of other men;
yet this same mountain dweller, in turning to himself,
thinks of his pain, his struggle, his war, his need of
hardness for the task which is his.

Nietzsche limits the meaning of pathos of distance
to human relationships, and even though Kierkegaard
broadens this suffering of distance to include the
world, this primarily means the world of men, their
history, their ideas, and their values. It is this very
trait of aloofness, of distinction, which Nietzsche sees
as the mark of the noble man, and at the same time, it
is the trait which is most offensive to the masses, to
the democratic minded, to Christians, to all those who
lazily refuse the inward task or who bitterly fight
against it. One immediately thinks of the writings of
Camus, against which the cry was constantly raised,
"How dare you stand so aloof from our age and the
answers we have given to our problems!" This is not
an age of men who can bear such inner tension, says
Nietzsche.

> The cleft between men and men, station and
> station, the multiplicity of types, the will to be

oneself, to stand out—that which I call pathos of distance, is characteristic of every strong age. The strength to withstand tension, the tense distance between extremes becomes smaller and smaller today; the extremes themselves finally blur themselves into similarity.[8]

"Tension" is the revealing word here, for it is precisely a tension which must be borne by him who wills this inner power in face of the world's brute reality. This is an inner asceticism of stylizing oneself and one's world, and the individual himself is the bearer of the tense struggle of these two realms. For Nietzsche, the distinction between an individual and all other individuals is valid only if it is *suffered* for, and thus it is a *pathos* of distance which inner asceticism creates between man and men. This means, as well, that the noble man is hidden from other men; no man can understand or participate in the inner task which is his own. He is, as Kierkegaard suggests, incognito. And Nietzsche himself underscores this with the remark that "every profound spirit needs a mask, indeed, a mask continually grows around every profound spirit, thanks to the constantly false, which is to say *superficial*, interpretation of every word, step, or movement that he makes." [9]

So then, the pathos of distance—like all Nietzsche's central concepts—points to a description of what the world is, what the individual is, and what existence should be like in this dialectical situation. When it was said that Nietzsche draws his "should" from an "is," this meant that once one has understood and fully accepted the dialectical fact of existence, then one knows there is no other way of existing honesty ex-

8. *G*, X, Sec. 37.
9. *Ibid.*, Sec. 37.

cept in terms of this inner tension. Once this en-
lightenment comes, one *knows* how he must exist;
whether one exists in this way or not is another matter:
in either case he cannot forget or refute this inner
knowledge. He will either lapse with it into sickness
or exist in terms of it and find health.

The noble man is the bearer of this inner knowledge; he knows and accepts the fact that his existence
must be the tense arena wherein two realities meet
and struggle. He knows as well that he is the sole
guarantor of this struggle; he is alone with it; in a
sense, it is all that he possesses. In fact it would be
profoundly true to Nietzsche to say, in definition,
that man is struggle. Without this struggle he would
not be a man; there would be no individual existence
at all except for the dialectic which constitutes it. And
this struggle takes the form of an ascetic task—a
shaping, a molding, a stylizing, a creation by which
man has affirmed his own inner uniqueness in face of
his world. The theme of struggle, conflict, suffering,
and war is the single theme echoing through Nietzsche's works from beginning to end. For Nietzsche,
the good existence was the one of tension and ceaseless self-overcoming, and the goodness of this was that
it honestly reflected the full dimension of human
reality. This is why art meant so much to Nietzsche,
for art in its myriad forms is the most splendid sign
of man's stylization of reality. The creation of art, of
culture, of civilization itself depended upon just such
a struggle, the struggle of noble individuals who
feared neither themselves nor their world. These are
individuals who know the world for what it is, its
meaninglessness, its hostility, its inhuman permanence. They are profoundly pessimistic about the
world and its history, yet this has become to them not
a tragic vision but rather an invitation, a challenge to

live in terms of the ground rules of existence. This is the challenge which Nietzsche sought to accept.

> Henceforth alone and terribly mistrustful of myself, I then—not without inner resistance—took sides *against* myself and for all those things which hurt and struck hard against me. Thus did I again find the way to that courageous pessimism which is the opposite of all idealistic falsehood and is also, so it seems to me, the way to myself—to my task.[1]

A courageous pessimism is the kind of existence which arises out of Nietzsche's understanding of ourselves and our world, and it is this term (better than "yea-saying philosophy" or "Dionysian philosophy") that best sums up Nietzsche's thought. His existential admonition means that from within ourselves we draw the joyful courage to face a world which we greet with the deepest pessimism. If there be optimism in Nietzsche, it is an optimism not about the world but about man. In men and in men alone is our hope. And that man should surpass himself and become more than he is—this was Nietzsche's hope, the hope which he left to posterity.

That Nietzsche's wondrous intellect should have become lost in the dark recesses of madness is one of the great personal tragedies of modern times. One could fancy that it was somehow a kind of justice, and that the last act of that dying God whom Nietzsche scorned was to strike out and destroy the mind which, more than any other, had spawned murderous blasphemies. Had that hand not reached out, it is impossible to foresee what uncharted seas Nietzsche would have explored in later years. Even at the time of his incipient insanity his mind possessed an almost

1. *NCW*, "Wie ich von Wagner loskam," Sec. 2.

overwhelming clarity and honesty and incisiveness. One cannot read the works of that last year of his life without having the terrible feeling that it is unbearable for a mind to be so penetrating and so courageous; no human heart could contain this tension for long. And so it was. The last months of Nietzsche's productive life were a monument to the human spirit and the heights it could scale. But then it was over, and Nietzsche was gone; only the body remained. For a while the body continued to function, and it sat in Nietzsche's Turin apartment writing letters to all of Europe. In the margin of one, there were scribbled a few disconnected sentences, and in a concluding line was written "—from time to time there is magic." Indeed, moments of magic were studded through all his remarkable works; the still-functioning body had written a final memorial to the spirit and career of a great and noble man.

Part Three

ALBERT CAMUS

THE TENDER INDIFFERENCE

Today, on the contrary, where in Europe only the herd animal is honored or dispenses honors, where "equality of right" can all too easily turn into equality of wrong, by which I mean into a common war upon all that is unusual, strange, privileged, upon the higher man, the higher soul, the higher task, the higher responsibility, the feeling of creative power, and mastery—today, the term "greatness" belongs to those who wish to be noble, autonomous, different, solitary, and self-sufficient; and the philosopher reveals something of his own ideal when he asserts: "The greatest shall be he who is the most solitary, the most hidden, the most exceptional, the man who is beyond good and evil, the master of his virtues, of the superabundance of his will; precisely this shall be called greatness: the ability to be just as many-faceted as one is whole, just as broad-reaching as one is complete within." And asked once more: Is such greatness possible today?

FRIEDRICH NIETZSCHE—*Beyond Good and Evil*

CHAPTER NINE

THE ENDOGAMOUS COCOON

THERE WAS once a time, long ago, when men, in describing themselves and their works, used the only basis of comparison they knew: the implacable grandeur of the world. They gazed at sights as brilliant as the sun, as flashing as lightning, as blazing as fire. And sounds, for them, were the sounds of thunder and avalanche, the roaring of the lion, the patter of rain, or the quiet melodies of the nightingale. And so also were the feel of moss, the smell of spring, and the taste of honey the wondrous standards to which men and their works could be compared. But gradually this wonderment before the world began to fade—so imperceptibly that one hardly noticed—and men began to live in forgetfulness of this world which did once stand them in good stead. The wondrous standard to which all things came to be compared was that of the works of men. And this transformation has become our heritage. The very sun itself blazes like an atomic blast, and the once serene stars now have the myriad brilliance of New York at night or Brussels at Christmas. And what sound could be more awesome than the roar of a cannon, the blast of a steam whistle, the driving of a locomotive—or more gentle than the hiss of a radiator, or the rustle of a skirt, or the sigh of a mattress? And our smells are those of smoke, perfume, and nervous sweat; our feelings those of metals and plastic; our tastes those of weary tongues smitten by our foods, tobaccos, and alcohols. Slowly and inexorably we have "civilized"

ourselves with words and concepts and ideals which
are but the recapitulation of our own images and
works. Thus we have spun about ourselves with ever-
tighter strands the cocoon of modern culture, a cocoon in which men are lost within themselves and
within their own dreams and failings. The proud
achievement of modernity has been the creation of a
culture which is endogamous and a poetry which is
incestuous. And it is within this ingrown culture that
the pathos and the poison of an unhappy society
fester and spread. Our present time suffers under a
restricted vision which can no longer know the
measure of man, his stature, and his place in this
world. Man has no measure but himself, and thus he
has no measure at all. He is lost and confused. If one
is a believer in evolution and human progress, then it
must be confessed that the crowning event in this
age, which so prides itself on its science, is man's discovery of his own nothingness.

It is a matter of the loss of perspective, a perspective which cannot be regained without a revived
consciousness and renewed understanding of that environing world which embraces our lives. Our unprecedented knowledge of the world-in-part has resulted
in an unprecedented ignorance of the world-as-a-
whole, and this loss of perspective of the whole means
that we undertand neither ourselves nor our world.
These are the two sides of the same coin.

And so it is that the perplexed generations of the
mid-twentieth century have heard a voice which they
understand only dimly but nevertheless are powerfully drawn toward, as it is with certain sounds that
prod old memories which we cannot bring to consciousness but which we know are enormously important events in our personal past. Such has been
the voice of Albert Camus, and such is the half-

awakened response he has received. We feel that
there is something terribly important in what he is
saying to us, yet we fail to grasp it. And what we fail
to grasp is precisely that old, primeval perspective,
which we have lost decisively though not irremedi-
ably. In almost simple terms Albert Camus speaks of
what the world is and of what we are, and in this simple vision we suddenly see a returning meaningfulness
in the task of existence. The genius and the difficulty
in what Camus tells us about the measure of man are
that he states a contradiction. The measure of man, he
says, is the stone of this earth, and yet he contradicts
this by adding that nothing in this world is to the
measure of man. Contradiction? Yes. But in this contradiction is the tense recognition of man's inescapable
finitude, helplessness, and death as well as his passionate need and demand for freedom, creativity, and
duration. In this contradiction we discover the continuation of the voices of Kierkegaard and Nietzsche.
Albert Camus is not the consummation of this attitude
nor is he the final spokesman for it; rather, he is the
continuation of this vision into the present time. He is
the Lyrical Existentialist of the mid-twentieth century.

To have expressed this contradiction about human
nature is to have expressed a truth about it. Man, as
part of the world, is no more significant than the low-
est common denominator of it, the very stones themselves; yet the existence of man is neither defined by
nor exhausted by the things of this world: he is more
than this world, and in this quality of "more than"
he is without measure, he is limitless and free. This
dialectical view of human existence is the fundamental
characteristic of Lyrical Existentialism and finds in
Camus its ardent spokesman. The significance of Albert Camus is not that he has probed more deeply into

this dialectic than did his predecessors; indeed, after Kierkegaard there was little more for any man to add to this basic concept; rather, it was a question of living in terms of this insight and, perhaps, of broadening its significance. This was done by Nietzsche in terms of far-ranging historical and cultural insights that Kierkegaard never dreamed of. And the peculiar genius of Camus has been the sensitive and honest way in which he has given social and poetic perspectives to this vision of human existence. If Kierkegaard has given us an existential psychology, if Nietzsche has given us an existential myth of history, then Camus has given us a poetic insight into the meaning of individual existence as it is caught within the ruthless and soulless forces of social convulsion. And this is, without a doubt, the unhappy image of the twentieth century: that of millions of individuals dominated, torn, and destroyed by social and political forces which they may understand but cannot control. The absurd and seemingly insane situation of present society is that one group of well-intentioned men is willing to murder the rest of mankind not because of any immediate personal hostility but rather because of a higher imperative which transcends all these individuals. And even though we may lucidly foresee the imminent possibility of destroying human society itself, we admit that there is nothing we can really do about it. Let no one doubt that this is insanity, and that we live entrapped in the midst of a social insanity. Like Pilate, we can all wash our hands in innocence of any cataclysm, and the highly comic possibility lies before us of the human race destroying itself, yet no one being guilty of it. The inane and oft-repeated conviction that men, through science, will conquer and control the world is now seen in its true light:

the result of our science is that we have lost control of our world, and human society is now dominated by inhuman forces which cannot be placated. The question which afflicts our age, and which will remain the only question worth answering, is whether we shall discover peace or destruction.

Into the welter of our present history Albert Camus has projected his voice, and it is one of the few voices of sanity that are to be heard. If human society has gone wrong, then it is because individuals themselves have gone wrong, and the judgment of Camus shoots through our present confusion to remind us that a sick society is the reflection of sick and limping individuals, that something is wrong with us, and that only in us can the transformation begin. Everything points to and proceeds from the individual, and it is in individual men that the works of Camus find their focus and justification: in the victimized and oppressed individual with his anxiety and confusion, and in the murderous and oppressing individual with his equal portion of anxiety and confusion.

Albert Camus is, confessedly, a child of his times. He is part of the present moment, has shared its frenzy and hope, and has partaken of its anxiety. As a writer, he does not stand above his history but, rather, within it, and his judgments are directed not at others but at himself and his fellow men. If there is guilt, then he accepts his own part in it, and in this acceptance he makes guilt a common possession of every individual. If there be any one word which sums up the tenor of all his works, it is *confession:* his writings are the confessions of a sensitive and enormously perceptive individual. In these confessions we see ourselves and our implication in the common turmoil of our age. And if there be any one word which sums up the quality of the man himself, it is *honesty;* in being unbearably honest with himself, Albert Camus has done a work for us which we should do ourselves. In such a man we discover that his guilt is our guilt, his doubts and anxieties are our own doubts and anxieties. And thus we learn of ourselves through him.

Finding himself part of a murderous history, Albert Camus has confessed for us the responsibility which each man has for this history. And his words have broken out of the endogamous cocoon of our history and reminded us again of what it means to exist as an individual in this vast and incomprehensible universe which is our world. He has reminded us of the way in which each of us is far, far less than he thinks himself to be and how, in another way, each of us is immeasurably more than he believes he is. With quietness and fervor, he reminds his generation of that lost perspective by which a man knows what he is and what his world is. Through him we learn again of finitude, helplessness, and death in face of a world which is strangely beautiful and strangely oblivious to our humanity. And through him we learn as well of the freedom, the courage, and the rebellion which we can throw in the face of the world in asserting what is precious and irreducible in our own nature. Like Søren Kierkegaard, Camus has read through once more the old text of the individual human existence-relationship, and, like Kierkegaard, he has read it through in a heartfelt way. In him we see that balanced, deep-probing perspective of Lyrical Existentialism cutting into the diffused problems of our times. And underlying this is the conviction that once we have come to understand and accept our world for what it is, we shall be able to understand and accept our own peculiar individuality for what it is. Everything rests with the individual: in understanding ourselves, we shall understand our task in existence; and in understanding our task we shall have taken the first step toward the renaissance which Camus quietly awaited.

CHAPTER TEN

THE DARK BREEZE

EVERY BEGINNING implies an ending. The one implies the other even as dawn implies the sunset. This is a simple—and perhaps pathetic—fact about human experience. And the most poignant and significant illustration of this fact is human existence itself. The ending that we call death waits upon the event of birth, and birth is the initial step toward death. The two events are inextricably bound together, each implying the other.

The writing career of Albert Camus gains its singular character from the way in which it began: with an overriding preoccupation with the fact of death. The whole of Camus' early writings could be called a meditation on death. This consciousness of mortality floods through the early novel, the essays, and the plays, investing itself with poetic forms and dramatic faces and showing us at all times the groundlessness, the absurdity, of a human life which ultimately drops into the black quietude of nonexistence. The forms and faces of these first works are those of anguish, the anguish of the single individual who has suddenly discovered that he—and all men—are held at bay by a destiny which cannot be escaped. This is the first step in becoming conscious of finitude, and it is precisely this step which Camus first takes as he begins his writing. Once the individual has understood the fact of his death—if, indeed, this *is* something which can be understood—the nature of his finitude comes to take on meaning. The recognition grows that this world which lies about him is an arena of failure, disappointment, and incompleteness; it is a realm which has no regard for his aspirations toward wholeness, finality, and joy. Rather, it is a hostile place, which never has and never shall take heed of human hopes. The vision of finitude is a vision of the world as sovereign, a majestic, inscrutable power before which the individual stands in his moment of fretful and futile struggle and then, like a candle, is snuffed out. Camus has given us a vision of human finitude which, in its lucidity and honesty, has an almost unbearable intensity, and, more than anything else, his first writings appear as a succession of explosions, the explosions of a human consciousness in anxiety and revolt before a world which does not hear. But these explosions, although they involve a despair of the world, do not mean that the individual has despaired of himself or of the validity of his own anxious demands and aspirations; they remain the one thing that he can cling to, the one thing that is his and gives his life meaning. And thus, he does not flee the world nor deny it; he revolts against it, affirming his own unique meaning no matter how futile this struggle may be. It is in understanding this revolt that we shall see how a man may accept the sovereignty of this world over the finite and mortal individual that he is and yet find a joy not only in himself and not only in his revolt but, beyond this, an abiding joy in the sovereign and unmatchable beauty of the world itself.

For example. A young man visits an ancient North African village nestled on the Mediterranean coast. Above the city in the hills are the ruins of a bygone civilization. The village is Tipasa, and the ruins are those of Rome. It is spring, and on the hill the young man strolls among the ruins. The brilliant Algerian

sun flashes over the sea, turning it silver, and presses
down over the lush vegetation of the hillside, sucking
out the odors of absinthe and aromatic herbs. The heat,
the smells, the dancing colors of the hillside assault
the senses and draw the mind outward toward the
heady richness of an exuberant earth, and in the midst
of this scene the young man sees the remnants of
temples of a once-mighty empire, temples which now
are only fallen stones, once cut and polished by the
hand of man but now gently being absorbed back
into the earth from which they came, aided in this by
the embrace of scented, brilliant flowers which gayly
accompany these remnants of man's pretentiousness as
they return to dust. The temples and public buildings
which were once built to withstand an eternity are
now seen in their proper measure: stones becoming
dust. Rome is gone, and the myriad flowers remain
as always, triumphant and resplendent. In the hills of
Tipasa there is found a symbol for the finiteness of
man and the remorseless beauty of the world.[1]

Or Djémila. Here the ruins are those of an entire
city: the streets, the columns, the temple, and the
forum with its triumphal arch. But, again, the triumph
is not that of men. The city is dead, and the young
man moves through it conscious only of the silence
of these ruins. On this day there is an inhuman, over-
powering wind which sweeps through the fallen
stones, and as the sun bears down ever more intensely
on Djémila the wind grows in force and violence.
And, caught in this bath of sun and wind, the young
man slowly feels the strength drawn from him. His
eyes burning, his lips parched, his skin drawn dry and
tight, and his ears pounded by a buffeting louder than
the beat of his heart, he is overcome by the wind and

1. Albert Camus, *Noces*, Paris, Gallimard, 1947. This is the
section entitled "Noces à Tipasa," pp. 13-26.

sun. He is no longer an individual, distinct and in possession of himself, but he has become part of this indomitable, inhuman roar that swirls about him. "Soon, scattered wide to the four corners of the world, oblivious, oblivious of my self, I am this wind and in this wind, these columns and this arch, these warm-bodied stones and these pale mountains around the desolated city. And never before had I at the same time so felt my detachment from myself and my presence in the world." [2] Here at Djémila it is not only a civilization which falls before the invincible force of this world, it is the individual himself who espies his own helplessness and mortality, his own destructibility as a part of nature's eternal cycle of nascence and death. And this death, *his* death, is now a conscious certainty which denies his every aspiration to endure, to find a beauty or a peace which will give everlasting security. Every wonder that he has known and tasted is now threatened; it is almost ready to be taken from him. To realize this, to recognize this certainty of death, is not to lose one's taste for life's wonders; rather, the very precariousness of them now makes them precious and irreplaceable. Hope in the future no longer makes sense; our conscious world now focuses upon the present in its richness which can never be exhausted. In this experience the young man has recognized his approaching death for what it is, and he has no choice but to hate it; but this hatred is a refusal, a revolt: it is in no wise a despair of life.

Few people understand that there is a refusal which has nothing in common with renouncement. What is the meaning here of the words "future," "improvement," "position"? What is the meaning of progress of the soul? If I obstinately

2. *Ibid.*, p. 35.

refuse all the "later"s of the world, it is because it is also a question of not renouncing my present richness. I do not like to believe that death opens into another life. For me it is a closed door. I do not say that it is a step which must be taken, but that it is a horrible and filthy adventure. Everything that is proposed to me endeavors to take away from man the weight of his own life. And before the heavy flight of the great birds in the skies of Djémila, it is exactly this certain weight of life that I demand and receive. To be whole in this passive passion, and the rest no longer belongs to me. I have too much youthfulness within me to be able to speak of death. But it seems to me that if I should, it is here in Djémila that I would find the exact word which, between the horror and the silence, would speak of the conscious certainty of a death without hope.[3]

The discovery of mortality not only refocuses one's consciousness on the richness of the present moment but, in addition, it calls into question all the bywords, virtues, and values which would make us live for that unknown, nonexistent world called the future. In a word, it is hope which is denied by this consciousness of finitude; whatever causes us to hope results in our abandonment of the one tangible reality given us: the present. In Djémila the discovery of death's reality is simultaneously the loss of hope and all traditional values founded on hope. Out of this simple, inescapable fact of death we see already how Camus' mind begins to establish an essential morality. It is from such elementary yet ultimate human experiences that Camus gathers the foundation stones for his thought. Thought and art, proof and human drama

3. *Ibid.*, pp. 36-7.

are here fused into a single instrument.

But let us follow the young man through one more scene. The young man is, of course, Camus himself, and this time he is strolling through a burial cloister in Florence. It is a dreary, rainy afternoon, and he moves slowly through the cloister walk looking at the inscriptions on the burial stones. Each inscription extolls the virtuous attainments of him who now lies dead. Here is an affectionate father and faithful husband, over there lies both the best of husbands and an excellent businessman, and there lies a young woman praised not only for her many virtues but also because she spoke French *si come il nativo.* "But none of all this touched me. According to the inscriptions almost all of them were resigned to death— doubtlessly so, because they had accepted their other duties." [4] Children are in the cloister, playing hop-scotch over the burial slabs. Gradually evening begins to fall, and the young man sits down, his back resting against a column. A priest passes by and smiles at the young man. In the church an organ plays, and its muted sounds mingle with the shouts of the children.

> Alone, against the column, I was like someone who has been seized at the throat and who shouts out his faith like a dying word. Everything within me protested against such a resignation. "You must," said the inscriptions. But no, and my rebellion was right. Step by step I had to follow this joy which, indifferent and engrossed, erred about like a pilgrim on earth. To anything beyond this I said no. I said no with all my strength. The burial stones taught me that it was useless and that life is *"col sol levante col sol cadente."* But even today I do not see what futility subtracts from

4. *Ibid.,* p. 80.

my rebellion and I feel very well what it adds to it.[5]

This is human revolt, and it is a revolt not only against death, not only against all the surd limitations which the world places upon us, but it is a revolt against all human values which would urge us to accept death, finitude, and suffering as right and good. To say that these things are inevitable does not mean they must be accepted and welcomed. And to say that a revolt against these inevitabilities is futile does not mean that such revolt is wrong or without meaning. Indeed, it is the most meaningful attitude a man can have, for it is a painful and courageous honesty about oneself and one's world. Behind the no there lies a yes, and in this simple yet ultimate experience of conscious rebellion a human judgment is shouted forth which scores not only the absurdity of the world outside us but, as well, the absurdity of all apologies for this world. At stake here is a conscious way of existing in this world, a way of existence which is "true" because it reflects honestly the essential character of man and the character of the world in which he exists. These few experiences of a young man's travels through North Africa and Europe are the sources out of which Camus shall build a moral philosophy and an existential admonition which echos, in the mid-twentieth century, the now-stilled voices of Søren Kierkegaard and Friedrich Nietzsche.

The sudden lucid vision of the world in itself and by itself is an experience of what Camus calls the *absurd*. And it is the description and discussion of the absurd which is undertaken in *The Myth of Sisyphus*,[6] Camus' first effort at the philosophical essay.

5. *Ibid.*, pp. 80-1.
6. Albert Camus, *Le Mythe de Sisyphe*, Paris, Gallimard, 1942.

The primary datum for this essay is a personal experience which has become an increasingly frequent personal event in this century: the breakdown of our normal, habitual rhythm of intercourse with the world, and the consequent discovery of the meaningless, cyclical pattern of these habitual activities, a pattern which presumably is moving toward something with a sure progress but which now is seen to be a purposeless, never-completed circle about which the individual turns until the inevitable moment of death ends his turnings.

What happens is that the scenery crumbles. Get up, streetcar, four hours at the office or factory, eat, streetcar, four hours of work, eat, sleep, and Monday, Tuesday, Wednesday, Thursday, Friday, and Saturday with the same rhythm—for the most part this cycle goes along smoothly. But one day the "why" arises and everything begins with this fatigue colored by surprise. "Begins" is very important here. The fatigue is the final moment of the activities of a machinelike life, but at the same time it touches off the stirring of consciousness. It awakens it and provokes what follows. What follows is either the unconscious return to the cycle or the final awakening. Eventually, there comes at the terminus of this awakening the consequence: suicide or readjustment.[7]

The experience of the absurd is an undeniable datum of modern life, and, as such, it has undeniable consequences. Once the individual has discovered the absurdity of the habits, obligations, and necessities which his social role forces upon him, then the question must be faced: Is life still worth living or is suicide the only honest and courageous action? The ex-

7. *Ibid.*, p. 27.

perience of the absurd has posed for the individual a
question which is ultimate.

To be clear about this. What is this experience, what
is this sudden, awful feeling that reflects the absurdity
of existence in this world? It is that same feeling already experienced in Tipasa, in Djémila, in Florence
by the young man. It is the sudden discovery which a
factory worker may have had yesterday as he rounded
the same corner for the thousandth time and walked
toward the factory gates. It is the unexpected feeling
which a clerk may have at lunch today as he sits in a
noisy restaurant. It is the discovery in all of these
cases that the meaning of what one does today does
not and cannot depend on tomorrow, on the future. Tomorrow *is* today, its drudgery repeated, and
is not today a tasteless yesterday warmed over and re-
served for more times than can be remembered? To
live for later, for the future, is to live for an illusion,
for something which does not exist and which serves
only to blind our eyes to the ever-present banality of
the present moment, the never-changing now, which
is all we know and all we shall ever know. In truth,
the scenery crumbles; the stage now stands bare, its
deceptions vanished. The world of nature now looks
thick and strange to us; it has lost the forms and meanings which we had learned to spin about it. The trees,
the stones, the buildings are now seen for what they
are: unique and unaccountable things "out there," forever distant and estranged from this conscious being
which I am. Nature has re-become itself before our
eyes; we see the world as it is—with no human conception added to it. Other men even, they too are
seen in their opaque, strange reality. We know our
own consciousness, but as we look about us in the
crowded café we see beings who gesture, whose
mouths and eyebrows move, who make sounds that

are but sounds. We see human life about us uninterpreted; the habitual, frenzied intercourse between ourself and others is now at a standstill. Strange puppets
now gyrate before us, unexpectedly and erratically,
with no observable purpose or justification. And at the
crest of this experience of the absurd is the climactic
discovery that the puppet show, the frenzy, the
dreams, and the struggles are rendered doubly and
finally meaningless by the certainty that anyone at a
given moment may cease to exist and that everyone
at an ultimate moment *will* cease to exist. The certitude of death hovers over and tints every individual
moment with absurdity. And the question then comes:
Is it worth it? Why act, why live, why do anything
at all if this vision of the meaninglessness of existence
is, in itself, destined to be taken away from us? Our
conscious estrangement from the world is, at every
moment, threatened by an ultimate estrangement: the
destruction even of this, our anguished consciousness.

This is the experience of the absurd which Camus
would have us face up to. The absurd, he says, is
not the world, nor is it our own consciousness,
rather the absurd is the *contradiction* between the
anguished demand of our consciousness and the indifferent silence of the world. The world, in itself, is
not absurd; it simply is what it is. The absurd is this
strange, disjointed confrontation of man with his
world. The experience of the absurd is simply this: a
revelation of the unbridgeable chasm between the
yearnings of the individual and the indifference of the
world. This is a definitive revelation about the nature
of the world and the individual. It does not matter that
all men have not had this experience; that one man
alone has had this experience is enough. It is enough
that one man *knows*, that one man has seen his true
situation in existence. One individual is enough to pro-

vide laboratory data for this subjective science; all subsequent experiences are only corroborative cases. And of course Camus is not dealing with one case only, with his own experience; he is speaking from a vantage point in the mid-twentieth century from which he can survey more than a century of such frequent experiences. The experience of the absurd, he says, is "in the streets," it is an inescapable fact of modern experience and it permeates our society and our literature. There is nothing new in this, nor does Camus claim that he has discovered anything new about the absurd. This is ground long since explored by many others: Dostoevski, Kierkegaard, Husserl, Shestov, Jaspers, Heidegger—to name but a few. But what Camus does claim is that no one has thoroughly analyzed all the questions and consequences posed *by* the absurd experience.

It would be enlightening for us to reflect now on what possible difference Camus' discussion of what the world is has from that of Kierkegaard and Nietzsche. The most obvious difference is this: Camus looks about him—in the streets, as it were—and observes that this vision of the world is simply happening whether individuals wish it or not. Camus sees this experience as an almost inevitable event in contemporary society. Kierkegaard and Nietzsche, speaking from an earlier and somewhat less frenetic moment in history, do not see this as an accidental experience which can happen to any man; rather they stress that only the individual who *wills* this experience can have this transformed vision. For them, such a vision is not fortuitous; it is the product of the individual's passionate assertion of himself against the world. "Despair!" says Kierkegaard. "Push away from the shores of finitude!" And Nietzsche exhorts, "Break the chains! Become who you are!"

The difference between this attitude and that of Camus is significant perhaps only to the degree that it indicates the tremendous increase in personal anxiety and breakdown that characterizes our urban industrial society of the twentieth century. For all three of these thinkers, there is first of all some given experience which makes possible this new relationship with the world, and then, secondly, an individual effort is required to realize this possibility. Kierkegaard urges us to "Despair!" only in the face of some ultimate personal disappointment. Nietzsche exhorts the youth of Europe to escape their enchainment to the external world because of what he points out as the obviously derisory and human-all-too-human nature of these chains. And, in another way, Camus, after pointing out the probability of conscious reactions against the demands of society, then asserts that one must choose whether to live in terms of this discovery of the world or not. For all three thinkers the problem is to exist in this conscious revelation, to affirm and reaffirm this truth about the world and oneself.

What is enlightening here is that the peculiar way in which Camus almost casually accepts the absurd experience is a distressing testimony to the truth of the Kierkegaardian-Nietzschean prophetic warning to modern civilization: the more modern men turn outward with an ultimate faith in the value of the external world, the more will they become sick, and the more frequent and violent will be the breakdown of individual relationships with the world. Kierkegaard's "crowd" has now come of age, pressing down on each of us as individuals; Nietzsche's age of nihilism has now come to fruition, and men may now discuss nonchalantly and without passion the several possibilities of destroying all human life. Camus stands at the harvesttime of a season of misguided and melancholy

plantings; what for Kierkegaard and Nietzsche was a
warning and a prophecy is for Camus a terror and a
reality. That the fullness of time has now come for
these fearful prophecies is, for Camus, a final vindica-
tion of the insights of Lyrical Existentialism.

If the experience of the absurd is a definitive and
revealing vision of the nature of the world as distinguished from the nature of individual consciousness,
then our first task, says Camus, is to hold on to this
vision and not deny it. To deny the absurd is not to
overcome it; if we are threatened by the absurd, the
sole honest course is to struggle against it. This is precisely what Camus means when he says that "there is
a refusal which has nothing in common with renouncement." In revolting against the absurdity of existence in this world, one has not renounced the truth
of the absurd; one has simply refused it. Such revolt is
the only honest and lucid answer which can be given
the question: Is life worth living if it is absurd? Suicide is renouncement, a surrender which gives final
assent to the absoluteness of the absurd; revolt is a
constant struggle against the oppressive absurdity of
existence-in-this-world. But suicide can take place not
only as a physical act; it may as well be a mental act.
This is what Camus in *The Myth of Sisyphus* calls
"philosophical suicide," and this is the charge which
he levels against those aforementioned philosophers
whom he calls "existentialists." In Dostoevski, Kierkegaard, Husserl, Heidegger, and others he finds an attempt to escape the truth of the absurd either through
asserting a transcendental Being who somehow recon-
ciles this contradiction or through absolutizing and accepting the absurd itself as a kind of God.

Kierkegaard himself is caught within this accusation, and Camus recognizes in his dialectical religiousness the desperate mental effort to escape the truth of

the absurd with a mad leap which embraces the most radical expression of absurdity: the God-man. Kierkegaard, says Camus, could not hold out under the tension and did not realize that the absurd vision of the world is not an ill which must be cured but rather an ill which must be lived with. This desire to be "cured" has been spoken of in Part One, Chapter Three and is an essential part of Kierkegaard's melancholy imagination. The Dane's inability to maintain his balance on the sharp blade of the absurd is a fact; but one must, as was done in Part One, do justice to the greatness of Kierkegaard's thought by honestly taking account not only of his personal temperament and family background but also by recognizing the courageous manner in which he drove his insights home within a social and intellectual climate which was radically different from these insights and which was immeasurably more restrictive than the climate of contemporary France in which Camus has written. One must not forget that for Kierkegaard to have thought and written as he did is almost a miracle in itself; and in making short shrift of Kierkegaard, Camus does, in this early essay, betray not only a limited appreciation for the genius of Kierkegaard, but, as well, he betrays an unbecoming, albeit youthful, arrogance.

Confronted with the fact of the absurd, Camus maintains that we must ceaselessly reaffirm the truth of this, lucidly recognizing our inner demand for unity, coherence, and meaning, and recognizing at the same time the difference of the world from us and its indifference to our demands. One must hold out against the temptation to deny the world by a mystical and unreal absolutizing of one's own spirit; and one must resist, as well, the temptation of denying oneself and absolutely accepting the world in its irrationality. The former leads to madness and anarchy; the latter leads to spiritlessness before the tyranny of the world. In both cases one has denied one part of the absurd experience: either the world or oneself. Suicide, whether physical or philosophical, is not the answer to the absurd; an obstinate, honest lucidity is. And in this obstinacy, Camus says that we have discovered not only a revolt, but also a passion never before known, and a freedom never dreamed of. In revolt, we assert our freedom against the encroachments of the world, and this constant assertion is a vibrant inner passion. As we have seen all through Lyrical Existentialism, revolt, freedom, and passion are but different ways of describing that tense consciousness of what it means to exist fully as a man.

But Camus as a thinker is, like his two forebears, most convincing when he is thinking not along rational lines but along existential lines, i.e., in terms of examples of living men. More than Nietzsche and even more than Kierkegaard, Camus creates dramatic types which illustrate, more immediately and positively than argument could ever do, the personal reality of his ideas.

In *The Myth of Sisyphus* he has depicted four types of individuals who, ideally, live in terms of the absurd. These are not moral types, and Camus places no moral coloring upon them; they are simply absurd types. Don Juan, for example, fully accepts the single reality of the erotic moment, the sensual delight, ever sought and ever renewed, without meaning, without higher purpose. The actor is another absurd type: an individual whose thirst for the present moment is satisfied through reliving the lives of others; quantity of experience is what he attains, and the richness of this experience is, like that of Don Juan, lucidly accepted as momentary and quickly forgotten. Or the conqueror. Here is a man who has recognized that history is never complete, never given a final meaning; yet he gives himself to the struggles, to the transient victories and defeats of this history, savoring the action itself—nothing more. And finally, Camus suggests in *The Myth* that the artist appears to be the most absurd of all men, for he is, ideally, the high priest of the absurd. The artist has no other task than to describe existence in this world; he mimics it, and through this mimicry one lives an experience not once, but twice. The single function of this creator is to fix his vision of the world for what it is; he must add nothing to this vision. If the world is irrational, it must be depicted as such; if man is a being who hopes for unity and meaning but cannot find it, then he must be depicted as such. If the artist is to be true to himself, Camus suggests that he must serve the one truth he knows: his vision of the absurd contradiction between himself and his world.

These four "absurd types" are simply sketches, and are put forth by Camus as suggestions of possible ways in which one very well might live in terms of a consciousness of the world's absurdity. But more ambitious examples of this are given us in Camus' first novel and first two plays. Martha, the heroine of *The Misunderstanding*, Caligula, the astounding hero of the play which bears his name,[8] and Meursault, the unfortunate little functionary of the novel, *The Stranger*[9]—these three characters, in different ways, reflect a life which has been struck by the absurd vision of the world and are attempting to live in terms of this vision. Jean-Baptiste Clamence, the hero of *The Fall*,[1] is actually a fourth example, but the moral com-

8. Albert Camus, *Le Malentendu, suivi de Caligula*, Paris, Gallimard, 1944.
9. Albert Camus, *L'Etranger*, Paris, Gallimard, 1942.
1. Albert Camus, *La Chute*, Paris, Gallimard, 1956.

plexity of his character is such that he will be treated separately in the next chapter.

As we look at these heroes of the absurd, the Reader must bear in mind the warning made a moment ago about the lack of moral coloring in these examples. Many are the readers as well as critics of Camus who have gone astray at this point. In these plays and novels Camus is functioning as an artist rather than as a philosopher. He takes the fact of the absurd as a starting point, then, as a creative dramatist, he develops these dramatic incarnations of the absurd vision toward their denouements. Here Camus the artist is experimenting with certain ideas of Camus the philosopher. As an artist, Camus presents his characters without recommendation, without a *parti pris;* they are simply *there* as individual dramatic facts, uninterpreted even as all living facts come to us uninterpreted. The thought and art of Albert Camus work together, each complementing the other without necessarily encroaching on the integrity of the other. This is the difficult and unique role which Camus chose for himself; he does, as a Lyrical Existentialist, hold these two activities of thought and art with a greater balance and tension than did either Kierkegaard or Nietzsche. The following remark illustrates just how conscious Camus is of this dual role:

> This leads to a singular conception of the art work. Too often the work of a creator is thought of as a series of isolated testimonies. But this confuses the artist with the man of letters. Profound thinking is in a state of continual becoming; it weds itself to one's experience and there takes shape. In the same way, the single creation of a man strengthens itself through the successive and multiple visages of his works. Each one comple-

ments the others, corrects them or overtakes them, and contradicts them as well.[2]

This singular credo is a lucid recognition of the fact that all human thought and art find their source in the groping, uncertain, ever-changing existence of the individual. No creation is final; all creation is relative. So then, when we speak of Camus as a philosopher we recognize a thinker who refuses to give any finality, any system, to his thought; his thinking will, as he says, correct, surpass, and even contradict its previous moments. The reason for this is almost disarmingly simple: the ideas with which Camus is concerned are those which answer the question: How can I honestly exist in this world in terms of what I know and only in terms of what I know? Thinking has importance here not as something valuable in itself but solely as a practical aid to the continual task of existing. For Camus, as for all the Lyrical Existentialists, thinking will find its "proof" only in the existence of the individual himself; to "prove" one's ideas by something external to one's existence—rationality, efficiency, conformity—is a dangerous forgetfulness of the primary crucible in which all ideas must be tested: the fitful, relative life of each of us as individuals who shall exist for threescore years and then be gone.

So then, in comparison with traditional philosophers, Camus travels light: he uses only the amount of philosophy he can live with, and he lives with only that philosophy which can be so used. All else is secondary. The primary question is whether life is worth living, and, if so, how? "The rest, whether the world has three dimensions, or whether the mind has nine or twelve categories—this comes afterward. These are

---

2. Camus, *Le Mythe de Sisyphe, op. cit.*, pp. 154-5.

games: first of all one must answer." [3] Camus answers by living in terms of his ideas, and his ideas find their incarnation in himself and in the lives which he, as an artist, creates. This is the importance of his art in relation to his thought. Thought leads to what is primary: life itself. And through art one can find the working out, the demonstration, of the consequences of our ideas.

This, then, is how we must view Camus' dramatic creations and, in this particular instance, his "absurd types." They are living experiments with the way in which ideas may be developed when they are made existential. The idea of the absurd, when brought into existence, takes sometimes startling directions, and it is in examining these varied directions that we shall come to a *primary*, that is to say, an existential, understanding of the absurd vision, in terms of its pitfalls as well as its benefits. Søren Kierkegaard knew very well the morbid as well as the healthy directions that could be taken by the discovery of the world's meaninglessness, and his pseudonymous works are rife with existential speculations on the morbid and healthy development of the religious consciousness. In the same way, we find in *The Misunderstanding*, *Caligula*, and *The Fall* morbid effects of the absurd vision, and in *The Stranger*, as well as some later works, we discover a healthy direction taken by this same vision. It is from such "experiments" as this that Camus' thought was to take its direction, its confidence, and its power.

Martha, the austere and bitter heroine of *The Misunderstanding*, has come into the realization that the humdrum life of an innkeeper which she leads is futile and meaningless. And, with death awaiting her at some obscure moment in the future, she has no intention of spinning about in the tedious circle of hopeless daily

3. *Ibid.*, p. 15.

routine. With no meaning in the present and no hope in the future, she takes action to break through the absurd walls which surround her. With the reticent cooperation of her mother she has embarked on the plan of murdering any guest at the inn, provided the guest be both rich and unattached. From the morose Slovakian interior of Europe she looks outward, longing for the openness, the freedom and abandon of the sea. With one more victim she and her mother will have gained enough money to realize this yearning, this liberation from an absurd existence. The guest arrives, he is apparently both rich and alone, and, for Martha, the decision is foregone that he must be murdered. But this is only the plot of one situation in the play. There is another situation. It is this: a young man has left his mother and sister in the interior of Europe and has sought his fortune in the coastal lands of Europe. He has found it, and he is now a wealthy young man, married and happy, returning to Slovakia to announce his success to his mother and sister—and to take them with him back to the sea. His mother and sister are the same innkeepers in question, and Jan, the son, leaves his wife in another inn and registers in the fateful inn under an assumed name. He wishes to observe them for a while and then gently break the news to them of his identity. The irony created by these two situations is obvious, and it is not unexpected when the sister and mother unknowingly poison the son, rob him, and throw his body in the river. But what *is* unexpected is Martha's reaction to the discovery that she has murdered her brother. In this reaction lies the power of the play and its character as a drama of the absurd. For the mother, this discovery is too much, and, rejecting Martha, she follows her son in death by drowning herself in the same river. But Martha is adamant; she clings tenaciously to her lucid vision of life's absurdity, and refuses to allow the horror of her deed to change what she feels is the essential rightness of her desire for liberation. Before committing suicide, the mother hears Martha's obstinate self-justification:

> He was given everything that life can give to a man. He got out of this country. He knew other places, the sea, free individuals. But me, I stayed here. I stayed, petty, gloomy, bored, stuck in the middle of the continent, and I grew up with the dullness of the land. No one has kissed my mouth, and even you have never seen my body unclothed. I swear to you, Mother, such things must be paid for. With the silly pretext that a man is dead, you cannot back out just when I was about to receive what is owed me. Can't you realize that death is unimportant for a man who has really lived? . . . But consider me! You are standing in the way of everything and are taking away from me those things he has already enjoyed.[4]

With her brother dead, Martha still sees no reason why the ironical outcome of her action should be any obstacle to achieving the desperate desire which drove her to the murder. Quantity of experience is all that matters in this oppressively absurd world of hers. This is all that anyone can have, and Martha holds that it is only just that she receive the same richness of experience which her brother has already known. Oppressed by the meaninglessness of this life, Martha, nonetheless, obstinately demands that life heed her yearnings; with a blind passion, she refuses to forsake this demand and lay all her hopes in a God who is outside of this history that she is part of.

4. Albert Camus, *Le Malentendu,* etc., *op. cit.,* pp. 81-2.

Oh! I hate this world in which we are reduced to God. But I have suffered an injustice, I have been wronged, and I will not bow down. And deprived of my place on this earth, rejected by my mother, alone in the midst of my crimes, I shall leave this world unreconciled.[5]

This is the absurd vision. Martha's despair of the world is total.

The final word of despair in this upsetting and dire drama is the word of advice given by Martha to Jan's wife, who is horrified and overwhelmed by the blatant, unrepentant confession of murder. Martha has no course left but suicide, but before taking this last step, she gives her final and absolute indictment of existence in this world. Her advice to Jan's wife is this:

Pray to your God that he make you into a stone. This is the happiness which he holds for himself, the only true happiness. Be like him: make yourself deaf to all cries and join the stones while there is yet time. But if you feel too cowardly to take part in this blind peace, then come join us in our common abode. Good-by, my sister! You see, everything is easy. You have to choose between the stupid bliss of stones and the slimy bed where we await you.[6]

Between death and stultification there lies but the inescapably absurd life of hopeless anxiety. The play concludes with this cry of bitterness and despair. For Martha, the absurd vision was final, and there was no recourse but to give in to the stony implacability of the world or flee the absurd in death. Here ends Camus' first experiment with the absurd. Martha's des-

5. *Ibid.*, p. 85.
6. *Ibid.*, p. 95.

perate attempt to mold the world to her purposes ends in failure, and this failure means that life is not worth living. Martha was right and yet she was wrong. At this point the ways of human existence become entangled and obscure; there is no clear and easy justification or indictment of this bitter heroine. If there be an indictment, it comes from her mother who, in discovering the identity of her victim, discovers as well a forgotten love for her son. The mother dies because she knows she has destroyed the one thing of meaning and love in her life, her son. Martha dies because she has failed to force her demand upon the world. There is a difference here: the mother has discovered something more than the absurdity of this world, whereas Martha has discovered nothing beyond this absurdity. Martha dies unreconciled to the world and to her own existence in this world; everything is utterly negated. But the mother, although unreconciled to the world outside her, dies with the belated discovery that between the unhappy creatures of this world there can be a love which redeems the absurdity of the world of human history. Within herself, the mother has discovered a meaning which could have held the world at bay. Despite the bleakness of this play, we suddenly realize that Camus' first experiment has shown results.

Martha is defeated in her plan to strike back at the absurd; hers is a drama of frustration. But in Caligula we find an entirely different situation. He does strike back, and the astounding manner in which he does this makes *Caligula* one of the most extraordinary plays ever written. Caligula too has discovered the hopeless, limited character of human existence in a world which is as senseless as it is implacable. He has discovered that "men die and they are not happy." [7] Once he has realized that human life is not cradled in

7. *Ibid.*, p. 111.

the providential hands of the world but, rather, is blindly crushed by these hands, he takes action that only an emperor could take. Caligula *assumes the function of the world*, that is, he, instead of the world, creates arbitrary finitude and suffering over men. If it is true that the world is a place in which unhappy men die, then Caligula intends to live in this truth, and every human deception and lie about the worth and meaning of existence will be brought down. "It's simply that everything around me is a lie, and I intend for everyone to live in the truth. And, by God, I have the means to make them live in the truth. . . . They are ignorant, and they need a professor who knows what he is talking about." [8] Caligula is the professor of the absurd. Indeed, what is astounding about him is that he is the incarnation of the world!

The birth of Caligula's consciousness of life's absurdity is the death of his sister. Theirs was a relationship of incest; he loved her and lived with her as his wife. And then, by death, she is taken away from him. This is the senseless, brutal act for which Caligula holds the world to account. Even he, an emperor, is helpless before this absurdity. And Caligula yearns for the freedom and power to break loose from the chains of finitude. As he puts it, he wants the moon; this simple wish expresses quite exactly his consciousness of the futility of human desires. Every word and every action of Caligula is haunted by the dreadful sense of the absurdity of existence, and Caligula sets himself the task of aiding this absurdity by making it apparent to all men. This is a labor of love, a labor of truth.

"Tomorrow there will be a famine." And so it is: Caligula closes the public granary, and the people starve. Capriciousness of the world? No, but it

8. *Ibid.*

amounts to the same thing: the capriciousness of Caligula. Caligula addresses all patricians as "dearie" and orders them to change their wills, leaving everything to the state. He rapes the patricians' wives or else sends them to the public houses. He kills indiscriminately and joyfully. "Do you love me?" he asks a patrician. "Why, of course, Caesar. There is nothing that I would not do for you!" "Wonderful," says Caligula; "take him away, guards! This man is going to give his life for me. What a marvelous sacrificial act of love!" In the middle of the night the patricians of Rome are aroused from slumber and summoned to an audience with Caligula. He performs for them a brief and ludicrous dance and explains to his audience that he had an "artistic emotion" which he wished to express, and he mentions also that anyone failing to appreciate the beauty of the dance would be decapitated. Executions, famine, extortion, and immorality: these are the decrees of Caligula. The emperor reigns freely and gleefully over an empire which is suddenly learning the meaning of arbitrariness and absurdity.

Caligula has pushed the absurd to its utmost limits. He has seen and accepted the absurdity of life and is attempting to act logically in accordance with it. Behind the apparent madness of his actions is the quiet conviction that he is, after all, doing the only honest and logical thing possible. This reign of the absurd is, of course, short-lived; revolt seethes in the hearts of the outraged patricians, and Caligula's assassination is plotted. Caligula is quite aware of what is afoot and bemusedly watches the preparations. His pedagogy is not working; these men wish to kill him for the wrong reason: they believe that life is meaningful, and that Caligula has destroyed this meaning. But at least one of the patricians desires to kill Caligula for the right reason. And the right reason would be one which recognizes the truth of life's absurdity and *yet* finds grounds for destroying Caligula. Cherea, Caligula's friend as well as enemy, explains to the emperor why he will gladly kill him, and in this explanation we see that Cherea also recognizes the absurdity of the world but goes beyond this. Cherea has discovered, even as the mother of Martha belatedly discovered, that this world *is* absurd but that there is more to human existence than this. When Caligula asks him why he does not approve of the obvious logic of his reign, Cherea replies:

> Because I want to live and be happy. I believe that no one can do either the one or the other by pushing absurdity out to its utmost consequences. I am like everyone else. Sometimes, in order to feel free, I wish for the death of some loved one, I covet women whom the laws of family or friendship forbid me to covet. If I were logical, I would either have to kill or seduce, but I don't think that these vague ideas are important. If everyone tried to carry them out, we could neither live nor be happy. And once again, that's the important thing.
>
> *Caligula:* Then you must believe in some higher idea.
>
> *Cherea:* I believe that some actions are more beautiful than others.
>
> *Caligula:* I believe that they are all equivalent.
>
> *Cherea:* I know that, Caesar, and that is why I do not hate you. But you are a disturbance, and it is necessary that you disappear.[9]

In this strange dialogue we see the degree in which Caligula is right and yet wrong. He is right in his recognition of the meaninglessness of the world; he is

9. *Ibid.*, p. 179.

wrong in his blindness to the meaningfulness of the existing individual. There is the world, and there is the individual: Caligula has given in completely to the world. And this is why he must disappear.

And disappear he does. The play concludes with his assassination. It is worth while making one more citation: the mirror scene in which Caligula himself finally discovers that the way he has chosen is somehow not the right way. This is the moment just before the conspirators burst into his chamber. Caligula stands before the mirror and, significantly, sees only himself: the suffering, confused individual whom he has forgotten.

> Everything seems so complicated, and yet it is so simple. If I had gotten the moon, if love sufficed, everything would be different. But where can I quench this thirst? What heart, what god could have the depth of a lake for me? . . . There is nothing either in this world or the next which is to my measure. But I know, and you, as well, know (*weeping, he holds his hands out to the mirror*) that all that is needed is for the impossible to come about. The impossible! I have sought it to the limits of the world and in the confines of my being. I reached out my hands (*crying*), I reach them out and it is you that I meet, always you in face of me, and to you I am filled with hatred. The path I took was not the right one; I ended with nothing. My kind of freedom is not good.[1]

At the last, Caligula has made the simple and pathetic discovery of himself. If there were only the world before him, then any demand, any freedom, any impossibility would be justified. But this simple truth is

1. *Ibid.*, pp. 210-11.

complicated by the fact that there are also men who stand before him, individuals like himself, who in their own groping way want to "live and be happy." Too late, Caligula discovers that there is something more than the absurd. And Camus' second "experiment" ends before a mirror: the world is no longer there; we see only ourselves.

The Stranger is a simple, classic tale, and in it we find a drama which takes us beyond the absurd and brings us to a balanced viewpoint of the world and the individual. In *The Misunderstanding* and in *Caligula* it was this balanced perspective which was at issue and which came to light only belatedly and tortuously, but in *The Stranger* this perspective emerges in an affirmative, almost triumphant manner. *The Stranger* is a perfect example of the way in which art complements thought in the work of Camus. It is truly a work of art, and, as such, it is far less "speechy" than the two plays, but at the same time, this lack of rhetoric does not lessen the power and clarity of the perspective Camus is concerned with, rather it enhances it. This is to say that to the degree that Camus writes more completely as an artist, so does his writing become a more effective expression of his ideas. There is no mystery in this: the essence of Lyrical Existentialism is the conviction that ideas are effective and important only to the extent that they are existentially embodied. Ideas, if they are important, must be translated into existence by living them and must be communicated to others by making others relive them. It is courage and passion which help us in the first task; it is poetry and fiction which help us in the second.

Meursault, the central figure of this tale, is a victim of circumstances. He eats, sleeps, works, meets others, has conversations, makes love, gets into scrapes, just

as any of us do. He also kills a man: something which
few of us do, but which we very well might do, given
the same circumstances that were given Meursault.
The murder of a man makes all the difference, for it
introduces into the story the necessity to judge Meursault. Meursault's trial is an interesting one; the trial
does not concern itself with whether or not he killed
the man—this is a fact over which there is no issue—
rather, the trial concerns whether Meursault's past life
shows himself to be such a person as would be capable
of deliberate, premeditated murder. This is quite a
different issue, and in order to determine this, we
must look through Meursault's past from another
viewpoint, that of legalistic morality. The trial, then,
is a recapitulation: after having followed Meursault
through the humdrum events of his daily life, we now,
from a different viewpoint, are made to see that this
life was not, after all, so banal or innocent as we first
thought. In living Meursault's life along with him, we
have felt only innocence; in reliving his life through
the perspective of moral absolutism, we now feel guilt.
And before the trial is out, Meursault too comes to
recognize that, looked at in this way, he *is* guilty. Yes,
he *did* send his mother away to an old people's home;
yes, he *was* sleepy and benumbed during the wake
and during the funeral of his mother; yes, he *did*
sleep with a girl that same weekend, and struck up an
acquaintance with a man of criminal background and
did some favors for him and carried a revolver in his
pocket and strolled out on the beach where he could
not avoid encountering the man he murdered; yes, he
did all these things, and they all seemed normal, almost
inevitable at the time, but now in the courtroom they
are neither normal nor inevitable; each little event links
with the other in a chain of evil intent, of monstrous,
irrefutable criminality. The trial teaches Meursault

something about himself and about life. "It was as if familiar paths, traced under summer skies, could lead just as well to prison as to innocent sleep." [2]

In the name of the French people, Meursault is condemned to be guillotined. The trial is over, he is placed in a cell, and long months drag by while Meursault wonders if an appeal will be granted him. He dares not let himself even hope for such a possibility, so great could be his disappointment. There is really only one thought coursing through his mind: it is his probable death. How, really, can he accept it, how can he reconcile himself to it? This is Meursault's only task now, and it haunts his cell through the quiet nights and the dimly lit days. He no longer thinks about the trial; this is but a fact in his life. He did something, he was said to be "guilty," and now he must "pay" for it. Nor does he think over his past life. He is cut off from the gentle, meandering movement of days with his friends, with Marie and Celeste, with Salomano and Raymond, with yet others. There is now only the present moment and this moment is weighted with the thought of his mortality. Meursault the quiet and indifferent little man, is not anxious before this thought; he is simply troubled—and a little scared. He knows that "this is how things are," and he views the loss of his past and the imminent loss of his future without illusion or rancor.

The prison chaplain then arrives. On three occasions already, Meursault had refused his visits. This time the chaplain is determined to speak to him. Meursault, in his own simple way, does not really understand the chaplain when he talks of God, sinfulness, and the need for forgiveness. He tries to explain to the chaplain that with a sentence of death hanging over him, he doesn't have time to acquire an interest

2. Camus, *L'Etranger, op. cit.*, p. 138.

in something which never has interested him. The priest is talking of hidden beings and worlds and feelings which mean nothing to Meursault, who sees only what is immediately before him. The priest rumbles on, becoming steadily frustrated by the indifferent, almost unperturbed state of mind of the prisoner.

This conversation with the chaplain, which concludes *The Stranger*, is among the most intense, explosive, and, at the conclusion, the most beautiful scenes to be found in the writings of Camus. And in order to grasp the story in all its power, we must understand the peculiar situation which develops in this scene. This is Meursault's moment of justification. During the trial he found no justification, nor did he himself aid in his defense. During the trial, Meursault sat somewhat amazed at the theoretical possibility that he was about to be considered guilty. He did not understand what this meant, for he was, indeed, a "stranger" to this way of looking at things; he was a stranger in this world where absolute moral valuations are placed upon the chartless, confused course of human life. Meursault is not a thinker; he is simply a man. But his significance as a man is that he embodies in his every word, thought, and action the truth of life's absurdity. Meursault does not *know* that human life spends itself within a world without unity or higher meaning; he does, however, *exist* as if this were so. He is a living, unconscious witness to the incompatibility of human life with such fancies as gods, eternal moral laws, hope, purpose, and the afterlife. Meursault is a victim of circumstances which have thrust him into the machinery of these higher valuations, and he has found no justification before them. Innocence has been turned to guilt, insouciance has been turned into criminal intent, an accidental event has been turned into a cosmic crime. And Meursault stands lost and alone amidst the movement of this higher machinery which he neither understands nor can relate to his own life. The cosmic machinery says that Meursault has been defeated, that he should bow down before it, abject and penitent. But Meursault, the stranger, does not bow down, he has not been crushed, in fact, he is totally untouched and indifferent to the machinations of "justice." And when the chaplain enters the cell, Meursault is once again confronted with this strange other-world of values and necessities. As the priest drones on, urging him to bow down before this strange world, the tides of revolt gradually gather themselves within Meursault. No matter how hopeless his present situation, no matter how decisive his defeat at the trial, no matter how little he has to hold on to, still he knows he was right, that the life he led was justified, and that the priest who stands before him is attempting to take away from him the certainty he possesses.

> He seemed so certain, didn't he? But not one of his certainties was worth a single strand of a woman's hair. He really wasn't even sure he was living, inasmuch as he lived like one already dead. Of course it looked like my hands were empty, but I was sure of myself, sure of everything, more sure than he, sure of all I had, but I held on to this truth even as it held on to me. I had been right, I was still right, I would always be right. . . . Nothing, nothing at all was really important, and I knew very well why. Out of the depths of my future, during this whole absurd life I had lived, a dark breeze blew toward me across the span of years which had not yet come, and all along its passage this breeze laid low all of those

ideas which people had urged me to accept during these past years which seemed no more real to me than those years yet to come.[3]

The "dark breeze" of death hovers over all and equalizes all. All men are suddenly on the same level; all will die and be forgotten. Meursault alone is not condemned: the priest, as well, is a condemned man, just as is Marie, or Celeste, or the judges, or the attorneys. All men are condemned to death; this is the absolute condemnation which so equalizes human life that it is nonsense to cast down upon any man an absolute judgment. Any human life, summed up, is marked by the absurd. And any human life which is forced into the mold of eternal value judgments becomes a life of guilt, of sin, of failure. Meursault himself is testimony to the fact that human life is crushed and distorted when pressed under the mold of immutable principles. In this terrible outburst Meursault has, in his own way, given living expression to his certainty that this world is an indifferent, heedless arena which has not prepared a cradle of eternal laws and values for the children of men, but which veils its eyes to the fretful meanderings of the individual in his journey from the womb to the grave. The individual human being is a groping, relative creature, and he can live and find happiness only in a world which recognizes his relative nature. Meursault knows very well what the world is, and he knows what human life is like in such a world. And from this knowledge he has gathered an understanding of human morality which the priests and the judges have yet to discover.

The priest leaves the cell, and Meursault is spent and empty.

3. *Ibid.*, pp. 169-70.

With him gone, I was calm once again. Exhausted, I threw myself down on the bunk. I think I must have fallen asleep, because I awoke with stars above my head. Sounds of the countryside came into me. Odors of the night, of earth and salt cooled my temples. The marvelous peace of this slumbering summer poured into me like a tide. . . . So near to death, Mama must have felt herself free and ready to live everything over again. No one, no one at all had the right to weep over her. And I too felt myself ready to live everything over. As if this great anger had left me purged of evil, empty of hope, before this night teeming with signs and stars, for the first time in my life I gave myself up to the tender indifference of the world. Feeling that it was so much like me, so fraternal, I knew that I had been happy and that I still was.[4]

In this moment, Meursault has gone beyond a vision of the world's absurdity. He is no longer obsessed with the rancorous feeling of what the world is not. Without illusion, he has come to terms with the world for what it is and with himself for what he is. He has refused the world without renouncing it, or, put in another way, he has accepted the world without surrendering to it. There is a balance here, a tense truce between the individual and his world. Meursault has discovered the relative importance of his world and the relative importance of his life. The absurdity of this world is no longer seen to be a fact of absolute importance. Meursault can accept the fatality of this life, even as he can accept and forgive his fellow men. He no longer can place an absolute demand either upon the world or upon men. And with this wider

4. *Ibid.*, pp. 171-2.

vision of the human condition, he knows that he was always right and always shall be, and he feels happy, even as he has always been happy. He has found his justification.

The meditation upon death that marks Camus' early writings is not a futile preoccupation. Once we have realized the certainty of our death, a gamut of anxious questions comes to obsess us as to our actual significance and place in the scheme of this universe. A reassessment takes place, and Camus' only concern is that this difficult reassessment of ourselves and our world be carried out honestly to its ultimate consequences. These experiments have shown us that the desperate constriction of the mind before the absurd is only a first, startled stage in this reassessment; we must get beyond this. We may despair, because of the discovery that we have no absolute place or guarantee in this existence; at this point we have only lost an illusion about the world. To stop here and go no farther will mean personal sickness and social disorder, as Kierkegaard and Nietzsche have already shown us. The second step is to push away from this world; one must cease despairing of the inability of the world to conform to our demands. It is not simply a matter of not *thinking* of the world as absolute, but, more importantly, of not *feeling* that our existence is providentially guaranteed by the world. Once we have taken this second step, the ways of the world are felt to have only relative importance, and we simultaneously discover the relative importance of our own destiny. This is the discovery of finitude and uncertainty. The old certitudes and confidence and ease have passed away. And so the question arises: "Who can now guarantee this life of mine?" And the answer follows: "No one but myself."

CHAPTER ELEVEN

THE DOVES OF AMSTERDAM

THE MOST GENERAL characteristic of the Lyrical Existentialists is that they never view a problem *sui generis;* no problem is, for them, an isolated fact. Rather, they are convinced that all problems must be discussed only in terms of relationships. This conviction profoundly colors the whole of their thought; it underscores what is the decisively modern character of their way of thinking. In terms of broad philosophical distinctions, we can say that they are not "substance" philosophers, but rather that they fall within the category of what can be called "process" or "relativistic" philosophers. This is to say that they would deny that anything in this universe of human experience exists in and for itself. Whatever exists, they would say, has its existence as an individual fact only in terms of its relationship to other individual facts. If they were physicists, they would be relativity physicists. And they *are* psychologists and moral philosophers, and, as such, they are psychological relativists and moral relativists.

This is a broad and most uninteresting way of summing up a trait which the Reader has encountered again and again in the course of these pages. Repeatedly, we have seen in Kierkegaard, Nietzsche, and Camus the espousal of relative views of the world, of the individual, and of morality, and the abandonment of all absolute views. What is obvious is that no one of these men—despite his overriding preoccupation with the individual—thinks of the individual as an isolated, solitary fact: this would be a *fictitious* individual. The *existing* individual (which is the only kind of individual ever known to us) is an individual-existing-in-this-world. This not uncommon hyphenation is simply a direct way of expressing the relative, contextual view of individuality. In Kierkegaard we found varying stages of individual existence, and these were distinguished solely in terms of the way in which the conscious individual was related to his world. In Nietzsche, the bovine existence was distinguished from free existence by the type of relation which the individual had with his environment, and already we have discovered in Camus this same distinction. In all three instances, we have a characteristic movement *away from* absolutism and relaxation *to* relativism and struggle. As seen by the Lyrical Existentialists, absolutism in thought and feeling inescapably implies a relaxation and laziness; in the same way, relativism in thought and feeling inescapably implies an awakened, intense struggle on the part of the individual. This moral observation about the nature of personal attitudes is at all times linked with the argument that all absolute and final attitudes are either deceptions or lies.

Certainly this entire viewpoint entails a disparagement of the traditional Western preoccupation with rational thought. Rationality is not rejected, however, it is devaluated to a status of relative importance. The rational process is only a partial aid in the discovery of ways of existence; it is primarily a critical guide. The most crucial aid to such discoveries is the indispensable "experiment" of existing, and this may be done either by giving oneself to an idea or by imaginatively and empathically reliving an idea in terms of the poetic arts. The simple way of saying this is that in Kierkegaard, Nietzsche, and Camus we discover that lyricism is added to rationality as an effective means of philosophical discovery. The incongruity of this kind of philosophy with the Western philosophical tradition is a fascinating problem which will be taken up in Part Four. For the moment, however, these observations will serve to sum up for us some of the central ideas of Lyrical Existentialism, so that the remainder of our discussion of Albert Camus can be seen within this broader perspective. The relativistic viewpoint, the concern for struggle, and the lyrical-rational method which characterize this perspective are all found within the central word of Camus' philosophy: *revolt*.

If one is to sum up the thought of Albert Camus in one phrase, there is no better phrase for it than "philosophy of revolt." In using the word *revolt*, Camus is not referring to an idea, nor is he speaking of a social convulsion. Revolt is an event in human experience; it is a personal condition, a state of being. In characteristic fashion Camus begins with an experience, not with an idea. The experience of revolt is a real and primary event, an undeniable moment in human existence. It is from here, from existence, that Camus finds a living event; here is a concrete datum worthy of philosophical analysis.

A man who revolts does not only say no to something, he also says yes to something. In revolt a man has drawn a line, a final limit and frontier which may not be transgressed. This is the "no," this drawn line. But at the same time the rebel has emphatically said yes to what is within this frontier, something that must be prized and protected. The "no" of the rebel applies to something done to him or perhaps to something he will not do. But this "no" finds its justification and power from the "yes," which affirms some irreducible value within the rebel that must at all costs be maintained and protected. There is a value here, simply because it is this which has driven the individual into revolt against that which threatens him.

Moreover, in revolt this value, which once was only a part of the individual's life, now becomes his total being; he is driven to demand all or nothing for the sake of this value. This totality means that he is fully willing to risk and accept death for the sake of his value. And if this is so, then we see that the value affirmed by revolt is more general than the individual himself; it is "horizontally transcendent" to him as an individual; it is something which is common to him not as an individual but as a man. In revolt the rebel affirms a value which is common to all men.

As Camus describes it,[1] revolt reveals the complicity of all men. This is not an egocentric event; the rebel may very well revolt against his general social condition. Or revolt may come from some unoppressed individual, who in seeing oppression around him has identified his destiny with that of the oppressed. Thus revolt carries the individual away from himself toward all men, affirming the complicity of all men around a common value and against a common oppression. In revolt, a value is affirmed which all men possess—even the oppressor himself.

It is clear that the term "revolt" is the description of a relationship or, more precisely, a disrelationship. Two things are affirmed: the external oppressor, the internal value. Revolt is the human experience in which one is conscious of this conflict. It is a dialectical experience, giving a relative, immediate testimony to something about the world. The description of revolt is not a rational exercise; it cannot be, for revolt is

1. This entire discussion of the term revolt is taken from Albert Camus' essay, *"Remarque sur la révolte," L'Existence,* ed. Jean Grenier, Paris, Gallimard, 1945.

not an idea. It can only be described from within by immediate experience or from without by an empathic sensitivity. The lyrical method is apparent here, even as are the previously mentioned traits of relativity and conflict. But it is equally clear that the personal event of revolt does not reveal a precise value. This is to say that when Camus says that the rebel affirms a value, he is not implying that he affirms a specific moral value. The specific value affirmed by the rebel is as variable as is the specific oppression against which the rebel revolts. What is important for Camus is that revolt (1) is an undeniably real human experience, (2) that it affirms a value, and (3) that this value is transcendent to the individual himself and thus is a value common to all men. The discovery of complicity, of commonality and unity is what is essential here: there are revolts in which men are drawn out of their own solipsistic shells and are joined with other men. The value is relative, but what is centrally important is that there are values which proceed from individuals and which bind them together in a common action. The individual is not alone before the absurdity of the world and the oppression of society; he has a solidarity with the men about him. The experience of revolt reveals something meaningful about human existence itself.

Revolt is not revolution. Whereas revolt is a primary human experience, revolution is the attempt to translate a clear idea into history. Revolt is an experience which continually and imperatively moves toward an indefinite and never-static idea. Revolution *begins* with a clear idea and seeks to make history conform to this idea. The dream of revolution is to create a society which is definitively stable; the idea is there, it is only a matter of making history fit it. But the curious fact is that such a definitive revolution never has and never will take place. What happens is that before the revolutionary idea has been fully developed over history, this history has so changed that it has moved beyond the situation which the revolutionary idea was intended to correct. History never remains still for the ideas of men, and so the revolution miscarries. The pathos and the tragedy of revolution are that once it has taken place, a new revolution is needed to take its place, attempting once more to make the human condition conform to an abstract formula. Thus, says Camus, we have not really had revolutions in these last two frenzied centuries; we have had only a progressive and never complete affirmation by man of himself.

But revolt and revolution do have one trait in common: both make a demand for justice and freedom. However, the abstract mold of revolutionary ideas always ends by destroying one at the expense of the other. In the desperate attempt to achieve absolute justice, a revolutionary regime will erase all vestiges of human freedom; or, in the effort to liberate all men from restrictions, another regime will see justice disappear as the strong and cunning freely forage over the weak and guileless. Justice and freedom are, as Camus sees them, antinomies: each can exist only to a relative degree in tension with the other; as soon as one is absolutized, the other is no longer possible. And because revolutions seek an absolute social stability, it is for this reason that they are destructive as well as unsuccessful. The abstract social machinery of revolution will always run counter to the personal experience of revolt. It is this primary event of revolt which plants the seeds of revolution; it is the impetus and justification for revolutionary action. Whereas revolt is basic, revolution is a later ideology and plan of action, and, as such, it inevitably betrays the value which the basic event of revolt brought into being: the solidarity of men. The active complicity of men is the value affirmed by revolt, and revolutions fail when by violence, by falsehood, and by enforced silence, this complicity is destroyed. At this point, the primary value of revolt has been betrayed, and revolt runs against the tyranny of a revolutionary regime: it is necessary to revolt again against this new oppression. And so it is.

Rather than being a sociological term, revolt is presented to us as an essential dimension of human experience. This is a crucial experience in which a man says no to his condition and says yes to his complicity with others. The external oppressor may be a power, or a regime, or a man; it does not matter which. What does matter is that this oppression has awakened a response within the individual which drives him into lucid, passionate action. In face of this external threat, the individual has found something irreducible within him, something which he must defend and preserve. This value and the lucid, passionate activity which defends it is the very nature of revolt's contribution to individual experience. It must be maintained and can never be relaxed. What Camus is saying is that revolt is a way of existence whose value is maintained only so long as this tense, conscious struggle is maintained. There is no peace or completion at the end of this: there *is* no end. Revolutions may move toward an end; this is their goal: a final stability, a static Utopian peace. But such ideas are illusions, and such regimes are failures. What is beneath this social turmoil, and what must at all costs be maintained, is a condition of the individual who makes up this society. Camus has thrust himself into the thorniest and most explosive fact of modern times, social revolution, and within this frenzy he has found a meaning and focus: the individual. All things point to the individual; it was only a matter of finding his place and significance within the cacophony of contemporary history.

The attentive reader has, no doubt, made the somewhat surprising discovery that what Camus depicts as revolt is precisely the same dialectical consciousness which is at the heart of Kierkegaard's and Nietzsche's way of thinking. Camus is, indeed, concerned with social-historical problems, but it is the peculiar nature of his genius that his thinking shoots through the welter of social history and roots the meaning of this history in the one thing that can give history its meaning: the individual. Through Camus we learn that the insights of Lyrical Existentialism have immediate and incisive relevance to the problems of social-political morality. The incisive quality of this way of thinking is that Camus will never let us delude ourselves with the meaningless abstractions: society, history, the state, etc.; he forces us out of this "abstracted" state of mind, reminding us of the individual lives which are at stake in any such discussion. These abstractions are the deceptive and sometimes dangerous terms which exist only because there are individuals. They never have and never can give meaning to an individual life; on the contrary, it is the lives of individuals which give whatever meaning there is to these terms. Once this proper perspective is reversed, then the individual and his authentic meaning are perverted; and Camus is profoundly aware of the fact that political history of the past two centuries has consisted largely of just such a reversal. He insists upon the obvious and half-forgotten truth that the terms "state" and "society," which so dominate modern thought, can never give the individual a meaning for *his own* life; such abstractions only take away what little meaning he does have. Even though one may assent to the truth of this contention, most contemporary thinkers —political as well as philosophical—should be struck by the profound difficulties they must feel in attempting to think in these terms. To the extent that they experience such difficulties, they are giving tacit consent to Camus' belief that some of their ways of thinking are not only invalid but are dangerous.

Revolt is a way of existing which involves a tense, dialectical consciousness of what the individual is and of what the world is. It does not move toward a goal or cessation; it is its own goal, and, as such, it must be constantly reaffirmed. The experience of revolt is nothing more than an individual's lucid and passionate awareness of his uniqueness and difference in face of an environing world which is a threat to this uniqueness. In revolt the rebel discovers a meaning to his life which is not his alone, but which draws him outward to other men who commonly possess this meaning. In this experience there is a foundation for both love and respect among men; barriers have been broken down, and solidarity is a fact. And out of this general value of solidarity, revolt creates specific values for society. Social values are themselves temporary and functional; as soon as they live past their function they are worthless. But from whence shall new values be gained? There is but one answer: from men in revolt, in tense, lucid struggle against new conditions which have begun to oppress them. Revolution cannot adapt to new conditions, and this is its monolithic limitation. But the very nature of revolt is to respond and react to new environmental conditions in terms of its passionate effort to maintain unity and discourse among men. This is its single value, and it creates specific values out of this passion. For a society to be healthy, men must themselves be healthy: they must be in revolt. But this does not suggest that individuals train themselves to be constantly destructive and negativistic, roaming the streets in anarchistic gangs and disrupting parliaments with time bombs and pamphlets.

This would seem to be the surface meaning of "revolt," and we must guard against misunderstanding Camus on this crucial point. Revolt is first and foremost an individual experience, it is a quiet passion burning within a man. It is a constant state of wake, a lucid vigil in which the individual knows his own importance and responsibility for what transpires in the world. He has not surrendered to society and its traditions; he stands apart from them, intensely aware of their relative, temporary value, and is constantly molding, changing, correcting, amending these traditions in order that men may not be cut off from one another by the barriers of injustice and bondage. The rebel revolts in favor of the individual: not only himself, not only some individuals, but in favor of all individuals. This is the solidarity he seeks and affirms, and any power, or regime, or man which breaks this solidarity is the oppressor who must be revolted against either in the quietness of criticism or, if necessary, the fury of combat.

Even though this description of revolt has been framed in a sociopolitical context, it will become clear subsequently that this "essential dimension of human experience," revolt, is, as a way of existence, the matrix for all human creativity, not only in social values but also in all of art, the art of living as well as the fine arts. All things proceed from the individual, and they proceed from the individual who is, as Camus describes it, in revolt. The important thing is that in the experience of revolt, the individual has set himself off against his environment and has discovered that within himself there is a unique value which only he can guarantee, only he can thrust into the world. In revolt, the individual finds his justification as an individual.

This particular description of revolt can be carried no farther. The further investigation of this experience waits upon an actual encounter with it in the palpable history of men and the fictitious history of drama. Camus has provided both of these in abundance. *The State of Siege*[2] is a fictitious history; it is a drama, elucidating how oppression may come and how revolt may arise in the hearts of men. *The State of Siege* is not an exceptionally good play: this is primarily because it is an allegorical drama; one might call it a morality play of revolt.

The place of this drama is the Spanish city of Cadiz, and this walled city has abruptly found itself stricken with the plague and imprisoned within its own ramparts. Except that, in this case, the plague is not an amorphous, frightening disease: it is personified as a man. The Plague himself has personally declared a state of siege over the unfortunate city. His is a reign of death; he controls death, and, henceforth, the citizens will no longer die willy-nilly as was their former custom; death is now organized. People shall die according to a prearranged and reasonable plan. The Plague has made an invaluable contribution to the life of Cadiz; he has brought order out of chaos. "I bring you silence, order, and absolute justice. I do not ask that you thank me for this, inasmuch as what I am doing for you is quite natural. However I do require your active cooperation."[3] The reign commences; logic and order are brought into the lives of men. Men shall no longer die arbitrarily; their names are now drawn up on a list, and a priority system of mortality is brought into effect. This is, as has been said, an

2. Albert Camus, *L'Etat de siège*, Paris, Gallimard, 1948.
3. *Ibid.*, p. 95.

allegorical play, and the immediate application of the allegory to totalitarian regimes is both obvious and intentional.

The various moments in this drama need not detain us. The tyranny of the Plague is lowered upon the people until they can bear it no longer. The "no" is spoken, and revolt begins. It finds its first voice in the central figure, Diego:

> I have come to understand your system quite well. You have given them pain, and hunger, and separation to distract them from their revolt. You exhaust them, swallow up their time and their strength, so that they will have neither the leisure nor force for fury. Don't worry, they are really cowed! They are alone in spite of their mass, as I too am alone. Each of us is alone because of the cowardice of others. . . . Don't laugh, don't laugh, fool. You are defeated, I tell you. In the midst of your most evident victories, you are already defeated, because there is in man . . . a force which you shall not reduce, a lucid madness, mixed with fear, unknowing and yet victorious for all times.[4]

These words are not a description of revolt, they are evidence of it, taken from a moment of human drama. Diego's speech gives full recognition to the finitude of men: they can be cowed and exhausted and manipulated *but only within certain limits*. Once this limit has been passed, then the oppressor is faced with a rebel, with an awakened, passionate individual ready to die in the defense of what he feels is irreducible within him. There is no way to manipulate this "lucid madness, mixed with fear and courage" which is called revolt.

4. *Ibid.,* pp. 175-6.

This speech from *The State of Siege* is similar to many of the remarks made by Camus in a series of four letters, assembled and published under the title *Letters to a German Friend.*[5] These were open letters published separately and clandestinely during the German occupation of France. They were addressed by Camus to a German former friend, an intellectual who, like Camus, was an unbeliever, seeing no higher meaning to this world, yet attempting to adjust to this fact. The adjustment made by the German was to embrace the tribal madness of the Nazi party. It is in the light of such a situation that Camus writes—this compounded with the irony that a man who was on the side of the defeated would address such letters to one of the presumed victors. Like the play, these letters are instructive in telling us what it is that revolt discovers which gives meaning to human existence, despite the higher absurdity of the world.

I continue to believe that this world has no higher meaning. But I know that something within it has meaning, and this is man, because he is the only being who demands it. This world has at least the truth of man, and our job is to prove his case even against destiny itself. And there isn't much to argue this case on other than man himself, and it is he that must be saved if any meaning of life is to be saved. Your smile and disdain say to me: "What does it mean to save man?" But I say to you with all my heart that it does not mean to mutilate him, and it means to give him a chance at the justice which he alone is capable of conceiving.[6]

5. Albert Camus, *Lettres à un ami allemand*, Paris, Gallimard, 1945.
6. *Ibid.*, pp. 78-9.

This is not philosophy; this is a lyrical plea. And in this plea we find the insight that, no matter how meaningless the world, men themselves bear a meaning which must be defended and preserved.

Another passage from these letters suggests the way in which revolt is imprecise in its demands and defines its movement largely in terms of what it revolts against. In replying to his German friend, Camus is like Meursault in seeming to have empty hands but in possessing a certainty that he is right and that what is proposed to him seeks to destroy his one certainty:

> What is truth? you have asked. Yes, that *is* a sore point, but at least we know what falsehood is: it is precisely this that you have taught us. What is spirit? We know its opposite: murder. What is man? But there I can stop you, for we know what man is. He is that force which, in the end, always holds off tyrants and gods. . . . If nothing at all was meaningful, then yours would be the true way. But there is something which does still have meaning.[7]

Camus here is replying to Martha, to Caligula, to all those in this contemporary world who have been struck by the absurdity of this world but who have not been able to go beyond this vision. Revolt has gone beyond this vision, because it has turned its attention away from an outer world which does not answer man's demands and has looked at the abiding and meaningful source of these demands: the individual himself.

Most probably there is a need at this point in our discussion of revolt to reply to a question that should

7. *Ibid.*, p. 42.

be troubling the Reader. The question is somewhat the following: "You say that for Camus this event of revolt is an experience in which the essential value of the individual is discovered; but is it not the case that this kind of revolt and its discovery of solidarity among men is precisely what Nietzsche scorns as 'the revolt of the masses,' a revolt which is not the affirmative action of the noble man but, rather, is the negative reaction of the sickly individual who seeks comfort in numbers?"

Offhand this looks to be a fundamental contradiction between Nietzsche and Camus, a contradiction which seems to strike at the very heart of any attempt to identify them under the common banner of Lyrical Existentialism. The solution of this apparently clear-cut contradiction is not far to seek, and it is found not so much in rethinking Camus' ideas as it is in calling to mind our discussion of Nietzsche. The clarification of this issue can lead us to an even better understanding of the concept of revolt. The simple fact is that there is no contradiction here. What Camus means by revolt is precisely what Nietzche is describing in the Dionysian-Apollonian experience. The essence of the Dionysian state of mind, as seen by Nietzsche, is that in this "intoxicated" moment all barriers of individuality were broken down with an affirmation of the oneness of all human creatures. This is the same lucid madness which Camus attributes to the rebel in his revolt against the oppression which plagues him. And Nietzsche, in the Apollonian forms of the tragic stage, states that an external focus has been given for this inner Dionysian passion. This external form is nothing more than the spectacle of human suffering, of the oppression to which all men are subject in this world, and which, in the Dionysian-Apollonian synthesis, is transcended in the triumphant affirmation of one's own life and of the world in which one must live. For Camus, the lucid madness of revolt finds its external focus in the oppressor, him who has threatened the ultimate limits of one's individuality and/or the world which stands mute and threatening before the individual's desire for meaning and duration. And, even as the Dionysian-Apollonian experience leads to a higher acceptance of the world and its society, so also does revolt lead to that acceptance which, as with Meursault, opens itself to the "tender indifference of the world." With none of the Lyrical Existentialists is there any suggestion of a mass feeling in this central experience, there is nothing but antipathy to the idea of relaxing and letting large groups of people carry the burden of one's responsibility. Quite the contrary. What is at stake in this description of revolt or Dionysian-Apollonian experience or tragicomic consciousness is a particular way of existence for the individual consciousness. In this way of existing the individual not only has an ultimate perspective of what the world signifies but also of what he, as an individual, signifies. He not only accepts the world on new terms but he accepts his own nature on new terms, and in this acceptance he has affirmed a common status for all men as well as for himself.

For all three Lyrical Existentialists, this way of existing is in no wise social, it is categorically individual, but its implications concern all men as individuals. Expressed in Camusian terms, this way of existence involves the acceptance of the human condition. We find this feeling of complicity with all men both in Camus and Nietzsche, and we find it as well in Kierkegaard, who, in his discussion of Religiousness A, points out the fellow-feeling involved in this way of existing; this is a sympathy for "man qua man" based on the knowledge that all men have it within them to relate themselves to that "eternal" which is within them.[8]

So then, the contradiction between Nietzsche and Camus is only apparent; as a misunderstanding, it is the product of Nietzsche's audacious unconcern for system and consistency in his random explosions of thought. Nietzsche, as well as his two colleagues, centers his concern on a conscious way of existing which is dialectical; there is both a "yes" and a "no" in this consciousness. It is true that the noble man is a yea-sayer, but this is only half of the story: he is also a "great despiser," and this rounds out the Nietzschean dialectic. The Nietzschean individual is in tense, competitive struggle with his world, molding both this world and himself into a stubborn image of his own uniqueness and inner sovereignty. Such an individual is, in Camus' terms, in revolt. And in this revolt there occurs a feeling of solidarity and complicity with all those who have experienced this same revolt. This is a hidden community, a quiet, implicit aristocracy which is founded not in the world but in individuals. It is precisely this kind of aristocracy that is referred to by Camus when he says "we rebels"; it is the same thing which Nietzsche points to when he says "we free spirits"; and it is this very same secret community that is addressed by Kierkegaard when he reaches out in his writings to "that individual whom with joy and gratitude I call *my* reader."

Within the dialectic of revolt the individual makes discovery of a value which is more general than his own person. Camus has said that this rebellious consciousness strikes into the world with an affirmation of justice and solidarity, or, put in its negative sense, with a negation of injustice and solitude; that is to say, with a movement against whatever force or forces

8. Kierkegaard, *Postscript, op. cit.*, pp. 518-19.

make the individual undergo meaningless suffering and stifling silence and division. Absurdity in society as well as absurdity in the world is cause for revolt. But this revolt gives rise to a third demand on the part of the rebel: it is the demand for freedom. The play *The State of Siege* suggests this affirmation of freedom only in a minor way; the problem of justice/injustice is the central concern. But in another work, *The Fall*, Camus has succeeded in suggesting in a much more poignant way all these demands made by the individual upon his world. Freedom, justice, and solidarity are the themes flowing through this remarkable literary work, but they are presented to us in their "existential incarnation," and in such a form we encounter them in all their complexity and difficulty. As has been said, all things point to and proceed from the individual; *The Fall* presents us with an individual, and in him we have a veritable case study of the demands which Camus describes as latent within all individuals. Our task has been to ferret out the understanding which Camus has of the individual, his uniqueness, and his nature. The tortured personage of Jean-Baptiste Clamence will perhaps serve as the best exemplification of this uniqueness and its problems. What we shall find is not a simple affirmation of clear-cut values, but rather an anxious groping within three basic moral-religious categories: freedom/slavery, judgment/forgiveness, solidarity/solitude, and out of these categories there arises a fourth, a dialectical consciousness which is the summary of these other three: innocence/guilt.

The Fall[9] is a masterful short work. It has both complexity and depth, traits which will insure its importance as one of the more enduring literary testimonies of this century. It is not a novel but a narrative, and

9. Albert Camus, *La Chute*, Paris, Gallimard, 1956.

the narrator is the singular figure of Jean-Baptiste Clamence, a formerly successful trial lawyer in Paris, who now lives out his days in a wretched Amsterdam bar that bears the incongruous and exotic name, Mexico City. Clamence sits among thieves, pimps, and prostitutes, occasionally dispensing legal advice but primarily concerned with practicing the curious profession of judge-penitent. The narrative of this judge-penitent is largely an explanation of why he has forsaken Paris and his former success for the sake of exile in a hopeless and sordid corner of humanity. Why is it that he has fallen from his earlier paradise and now sits far from Eden in a condition which seems voluntary rather than imposed? Clamence explains this to us by recounting his past life and the events involved in his fall.

The enormous number of similarities and complementary ideas among the Lyrical Existentialists should no longer be a surprise to the Reader, and so we can take almost as a matter of course the somewhat curious fact that both Søren Kierkegaard and Friedrich Nietzsche were well aware of such sickly and tormented creatures as Clamence and have even given us descriptions of Clamence. The reason for this coincidence is not surprising: Clamence represents the type of man who is stopped at midstream between an old life which was blithely "aesthetic" and "bovine" and a new life which is inwardly oriented in self-affirmation and freedom. In reacting against one way of existing, he is not quite capable of embracing what he knows is a better way of existing, and so he remains fixed in a limbo of anxiety and compromise and longing. The Lyrical Existentialists have recognized this Clamencelike state of mind to be typical of modern men; in an age which is transitional and in-between, it is understandable that there will be individuals who are incapable or fearful of existing in terms of the existential admonition which they see as modern man's only possibility of moral health. Nietzsche describes Clamence in the following way:

> What is noble? What does the word "noble" still mean to us today? How does the noble man reveal himself, how can he be recognized under these heavily veiled skies of incipient plebianism which render everything opaque and leaden? It is not his actions which will reveal his identity—actions are always ambiguous, always unfathomaable—nor can "works" reveal him. Among artists and scholars one can find in this day and time enough of those who reveal in their works the impulsion of a deep yearning for nobility; but it is precisely this need *for* nobility which is radically different from the needs of the noble soul itself and is actually the clear and dangerous sign of this lack.[1]

Nietzsche draws a sharp line between the existence that is noble and the existence that is not noble but needs and yearns for this nobility. Clamence is in precisely this transitional state of recognizing what he needs to be but of remaining incapable of being it.

One hundred years before the fictional appearance of Clamence, Kierkegaard had already described him in a much more penetrating way than did Nietzsche. In Kierkegaard's mind Clamence is a man in despair, and it is in discussing different degrees of despair that he comes to Clamence's state of mind which is "despair about the eternal or over oneself":

> Despair over the earthly or over something earthly is really despair also about the eternal

1. Nietzsche, *Jenseits von Gut und Böse, op. cit.*, VII, Sec. 287.

and over oneself, in so far as it is despair, for this is the formula for all despair. . . . The despairer understands that it is weakness to take the earthly so much to heart, that it is weakness to despair. But then, instead of veering sharply away from despair to faith, humbling himself before God for his weakness, he is more deeply absorbed in despair and despairs over his weakness. Therewith the whole point of view is inverted, he becomes now more clearly conscious of his despair, recognizing that he is in despair about the eternal, he despairs over himself that he could be weak enough to ascribe to the earthly such great importance, which now becomes his despairing expression for the fact that he has lost the eternal and himself.[2]

The above words as well as those of Nietzsche are slightly different ways of describing the same Lyrical Existentialist viewpoint: the description is of one who cannot fully embrace the dialectical existence which his intelligence indicates to him; he perceives that the world is insufficient, that he should refuse it, yet he unfortunately takes "the earthly so much to heart" that he cannot refuse it; yet he longs for and knows his need for the eternal, for himself, for the noble existence, but he cannot free himself so that he can exist in this manner. This situation then doubles back upon him, becoming a despair over himself for being in such a situation of despair. This is the state of mind we find in Clamence: a man who knows what he must be, and yet knows that he can never be what he must be. Clamence is in despair, he has given up hope, and it is in seeing *what* he has given up hope in, that we shall have Camus' most piercing insights into the

2. Kierkegaard, *The Sickness Unto Death, op. cit.*, pp. 97-8.

unique values which are buried in the hearts of men.

Jean-Baptiste Clamence fell when he discovered his duplicity; this is to say that the eventual moment arrived when he recognized that the suave, easygoing, urbane life he had patterned for himself was in no way an expression of his inner nature. The duplicity he discovered was that between Clamence-as-he-functions-in-society and Clamence-as-he-is-to-himself. He discovered the inner-outer dialectic, which Nietzsche and Kierkegaard have claimed is the most elementary and yet most important fact which an individual can learn about his existence. Clamence reacted to this discovery, but his reaction was less than heroic; caught in a "reflective grief," he arrived at a stalemate of poignancy, melancholy, and hopelessness, which endures to the end of his narrative.

Imagine an eminently successful trial lawyer, blessed with high intelligence, great eloquence, noble character, and infectious charm and good looks. These were given to Clamence without the asking. He specialized in "noble cases," a type of work which further ennobled him and gave him enormous satisfaction. No matter which way he turned or what he set his mind to, Clamence was successful, professionally, socially, privately. It was a success which was natural; he did not need to strive or worry for it. It was an effortless, satisfying life which he had never needed to learn. And he was modestly aware that such happiness and accomplishment were so fortuitous in one man that it was if he had been picked out and graced by some power greater than he. In short, Clamence felt himself to be a whole man, with no divisions, or torments, or uncertainties within him. As he expresses it, he was in "direct contact with life," no intermediary stood between himself and his world; without soul-searching, really without even decision, words and deeds poured forth from him as virtuous and high-minded as they were effective.

This is the first stage in his chronicle, the Eden into which he, like Adam, was born, whole, innocent, and perfect. The second stage begins with a curious and tragic incident which occurred late at night in the middle of a rainy, desolate Paris. The story is simple: after an evening's amour with his mistress, he is returning home on foot and, while crossing over the Pont Royal, notices a young woman, alone, leaning over the railing; he passes by, and after he has reached the street, he hears a splash and cries of help; he does not move but only listens as the cries move downstream. Then there is silence. Clamence does not know why he did nothing; some thought of its being "too late, too far" crept through his mind. But this cry of distress, once it had torn into the consciousness of Clamence, remained embedded there. In the now silent night, that scream took voice in his heart and would never cease. On the bridges of Paris, Clamence the noble, the hero, the virtuous had found himself free, alone, and uncompelled before the needs of another, and he had done nothing. The significance of this was to come upon him only in time. Once the voice had lapsed into silence, Clamence walked on. Indeed, it *was* too late now. The moment was irrevocable and had to be lived with for the remainder of his days. He had begun his fall.

Like a great bird shot while in flight, Clamence continued his lofty existence for some time before falling. Three years after the bridge incident—now forgotten—he stood on another bridge, feeling a quiet triumph within himself for his continued successes. He heard laughter behind him, turned about but saw no one, then looked beneath the bridge but saw no boat passing. He could not find the source of the laughter. This curious event is the crucial moment in Clamence's narrative; it is the beginning of the end of his Eden. It is not only significant that laughter should have come while he was on a bridge, nor only that it should have rung out at the moment when Clamence felt complete satisfaction within himself, but more than this, the bodyless voice which came to his ears was, in effect, his *own* voice, the voice of that being who, three years earlier, quietly observed and remembered the moment when the noble Clamence stood motionless in the rain, doing nothing. As the laughter rang out, Clamence realized his own duplicity, the lie of his own life. He realized that his life was not perfect but, rather, was undercut by guilt. He had begun to judge himself, for he now knew that there was something within him to judge.

Clamence's fall was both tortured and frenetic. For the first time in his life he was self-conscious. Knowing that there was something within him to judge, he realized that others had been judging him every moment of his life. He had been oblivious to it. And it was judgment in any form which hurt; it hurts because one is aware of being split, of being one kind of being for the exterior eye and a contrary being for the confiding eye of one's inner consciousness. Unselfconscious, Clamence was whole: he totally identified himself with the noble figure which he cut through society. Self-conscious, Clamence was split: he was tortured with the knowledge that he was not that person which he should be and which people thought he was. His first reaction was an honest attempt to destroy that external illusion which others took to be the real man. This failed, however, because both he and others were too much in the habit of accepting and acting in terms of the accustomed Clamence. The duplicity and judgment thus remaining, he attempted a more radical escape: the emotional paralysis of debauchery. Through women and alcohol, Clamence sought to drown his senses until all vitality was gone, until the judgmental laughter within him and outside him could no longer be felt or even heard, until the anxiety of all tomorrows was quieted and he could look out with exhausted eyes upon the present moment and only upon this. But he soon discovered that even debauchery could not still that scream which was embedded in his consciousness. This guilt was inescapable, and its judgment was inevitable, and this solitude was unendurable. Clamence had to face up to his duplicity and find a way of living with it. This he did, and the solution he found was his stalemate with existence.

Clamence became a judge-penitent. But before going into the nature of this curious solution, it is much more important to take stock of those ultimate contradictions in which Clamence was caught. In these we see the essential nature of Clamence's anxiety and the central insights of Camus' story.

The basis of Clamence's anxiety is, of course, his feeling of duplicity. He knows that the external self which he displays to the world is neither real nor even important; he is struck with the relativity of all conduct in the world and, simultaneously, with the absoluteness of his self-conscious existence. He admits that "I have never really been able to believe that human affairs were serious. I had no idea what could be serious about them, but at least I knew that it had nothing to do with all this around me, which seemed to me to be nothing more than either an amusing or bothersome game." [3] And life was a game which Clamence played at; he discovered that from the beginning he had always been play acting. The incident on

3. Albert Camus, *La Chute, op. cit.,* p. 101.

the bridge finally brought this home to him; in that revelatory moment he saw that he had spent all his life fulfilling a role which had nothing to do with himself. The moment was revelatory, because he knew he was not play acting when he stood in the rain, motionless and unheeding, and, besides this, he realized that in that instant of isolation and freedom with no audience about, the noble Clamence ceased to exist and the actual Clamence asserted himself. This duplicity is what we have come to recognize as the religious state of dialectical consciousness of oneself and the world. But Clamence's curious situation is that he feels constantly accused by the noble image which he has held out to the world. Even though he knows that the noble image is relative and without serious importance, he still cannot forgive himself for having betrayed this image. There is always anxiety for one who has become dialectically conscious: the anxiety is that one longs for wholeness, a conformity of one's existence-in-the-world to one's inner consciousness. But in Clamence's case, rather than suffering because his external image has not been conformed to his inner conscious existence, he suffers instead because his inner conscious existence cannot be brought into accord with his external image. As Kierkegaard has said: "He despairs over himself that he could be weak enough to ascribe to the earthly such great importance. . . ."

This is the case of a man whose revolt has hung fire. Clamence is partially in revolt against his world and partially in revolt against certain imperatives which have now been revealed within him. His consciousness plays back and forth between these alternatives, and this is his anxiety. The depth of Camus' characterization of this man is seen in the fact that it is not simply that Clamence cannot make a final choice or that he will not make such a choice, but rather that the inability and unwillingness are somehow fused together in a single image of modern man's impotence and sickness. It is this very insight into the confusion of human motivation that lends greatness to Camus' characterization of the human condition. The more ancient tradition of Western morality would say that Clamence was morally culpable; the more recent tradition would say that he was paralyzed by social and psychological conditions which were external to any self-determination. Camus sees men as overwhelmingly finite in the second sense and yet pitifully and inescapably responsible in the former and more ancient sense. Clamence is neither to be blamed nor coolly appraised; he is to be pitied—and this would be in the sense that all pity involves a common identification of our own lives with the life of him who suffers. In Clamence we see ourselves, children of the mid-century, as unheroic, anxious, desperate creatures.

But duplicity is only a basic description of Clamence's anxiety; it remains for us to point out the specific contradictions inhering in this dialectic. Clamence makes one of them very clear when he says, "But on the bridges of Paris I, too, learned that I was afraid of freedom. So then, long live the master, whoever he may be, who will take the place of the laws of heaven." [4]

Here is the contradiction between freedom and slavery, and the anxiety is in this: Which is better: to live solely and courageously by one's own inner imperatives, assuming absolute moral responsibility for them, both before others and before oneself, or to live solely and abjectly in terms of an external system of values, for whose guarantee there are representatives

4. *Ibid.*, p. 157.

who assume full responsibility? This is the choice, and it is the familiar one between the free existence and the bovine, aesthetic existence.

The possibility of freedom and responsibility is the value which Clamence discovered within himself; it is freedom that he yearns for and yet is afraid of. He yearns for the ability to accept his inhuman action by the bridge, but he is afraid of the prodigious weight of responsibility which this places upon him and him alone with no one to assuage this or guarantee it or to buttress this lonely responsibility with an excusing, forgiving, absolving word. He would be absolutely alone with this burden, and it is more than he dares to bear. He is both afraid of and incapable of ". . . the holy innocence of those who forgive themselves." [5] He both cannot and will not follow the Nietzschean formula, whereby one surpasses and accepts one's sins by asserting, "Thus I have willed it!" This kind of assertion is farther than Clamence dares to go; he can see his problem and understand his choice, but he refuses to assert himself against the world, living solely in terms of his inner determination. The existential admonition stands just beyond his reach, urging him to break free. But he is both afraid and incapable of freedom. The existential admonition is not easy. And any man in Clamence's place must ask himself if he too would not be afraid of this freedom with the responsibility it entails.

Another way of looking at Clamence's anxiety is to notice how all of his conversation shuttles between the alternatives of forgiveness and judgment. He judges himself but cannot forgive himself; he judges others but does not forgive them; others judge him without forgiving him. What is involved in this dialectic? The answer is that we are again faced with the

5. *Ibid.,* p. 167.

difference between internal and external determination. The judge is one who demands conformity to an external law which either is of his own making or is a law which he represents. The judge is thus bound to his external law and asserts that all others must be bound by it. Forgiveness is the opposite of this, for the forgiver is one who denies that there is any external, absolute law either for himself or for any individual, and thus allows to any man the same free responsibility which he demands of himself. To forgive means to ignore the fiction of absolute laws and to assert the deeper morality of individual freedom and responsibility. The experience of forgiveness is without a doubt one of the ultimate revelations of the nature of existence, and theologians have too little pondered the fact that a forgiving God implies a lawless God who is anxious, free, and self-determining even as man is himself.

So then, freedom and forgiveness are different aspects of the same category of inward determination. And it follows that Clamence's anxiety over solidarity/solitariness is of the same nature. Clamence has come to realize that during the days of his Parisian paradise, he had never really known or loved a single individual. "I, I, I was the refrain of this blessed life of mine, and it could be heard in everything I said." [6] Clamence did not need or want others; he had his justification and his solace in the smooth-flowing external patterns with which he was identified. He was solitary, untouchable, and happy until that moment when he discovered that Clamence the virtuous lawyer and Clamence the self-conscious individual were not the same. Then it was that he came to understand what it meant to exist as an individual; in discovering his own confusion and suffering, he simultaneously

6. *Ibid.*, p. 58.

saw his identity with all other individuals who led an anxious, groping life even as he did. But Clamence could not follow up this discovery. He saw others as too much like himself: he perceived within him the vocation of judging and thus saw in others the danger of being judged by them. Because he could not be free, and because he could not forgive himself or others, he equally could not feel a oneness between himself and his fellow creatures. The value of solidarity beckoned within him, but Clamence would/could not respond.

The final expression of Clamence's anxiety—and perhaps the most searching expression for it—is in the dialectic innocence/guilt. These are wide-ranging terms, for they suggest the most general feeling which an individual has about himself and his world. A man who is guilty is one who is no longer free, he stands under judgment from something outside, and he is cut off from any positive relationship with his fellow men. The innocent man is the free man, the forgiving man, and the compassionate man: he is the man who finds the source for his existence within himself. And with this inner motivation he moves out into the world with a different face than the man whose existence is entangled in external values, fears, and commitments. The innocent man is whole: his existence in the world is the immediate expression of a confident, inner authority. Thus, he is happy. The guilty man is divided: his existence in the world is not the immediate expression of a confident, inner authority, rather it is the expression of an afflicted, confused consciousness which finds its sole anchorage in some person or system which supposedly has external authority. Thus, he is unhappy. He is attempting the impossible task of finding wholeness by conforming body and soul to a fixed nonexistential determinant, which is unlike his own self, which can never be himself, and which can never have the authority of himself. He will remain divided, unhappy, and in guilt.

Clamence is caught between these two modes of existence. He neither wants the life of guilt, nor can he bear the life of innocence. He stands between them, mediating the two in terms of despair and anxiety. His choice is to accept both and make do with both. His choice is to become a judge-penitent.

The nature of a judge-penitent is both simple and cynical: inasmuch as the vocation of judging eventually leads to judgment of oneself both by oneself and by others (thus penitence), it is better to begin by roundly judging oneself, thus earning the right to judge others as well as stimulating within them the act of self-judgment. In this way everyone is on the same plane. Not being able to attain forgiveness, Clamence settles for penitence. Unable to be free, he settles for universal entanglement. Unable to find solidarity, he settles for complicity. Unable to feel innocence, he mitigates his guilt by sharing it. This is the stalemate reached by Jean-Baptiste Clamence. He insists that it is the right way, the only way of existing, yet he knows and suffers from the knowledge that it is the wrong way. He has not escaped the laughter,[7] and he knows that he is ". . . a false prophet crying in the wilderness and refusing to come forth."[8] The heart of the matter is in his confession that

> My solution, of course, is not ideal. But isn't it true that when one doesn't like his own life, when one knows that it should be changed, there isn't any choice? What can you do to become another person? Impossible. You would have to stop

7. *Ibid.*, p. 164.
8. *Ibid.*, p. 169.

being anyone at all, at least once to forget oneself
in order to be someone else. But how?[9]

Clamence's "how?" goes unanswered for the simple
reason that there is no answer to the plea "How can I
be someone else?" Clamence is stuck with his history,
with his anxiety, and with the scream that cleaves to
his heart. He cannot escape these any more than he
can escape himself. He does not overcome his contradiction but, instead, shuttles back and forth between the demands of the world and the demands of
his inner nature, wallowing in a pathos which was
made for him and yet which he has made for himself.
Clamence is in despair over himself for being what
he is, and this is why he longs for an entirely different self with a different history. And Kierkegaard is
right in saying that this despair over himself is at the
same time the loss of "the eternal and himself." Both
are lost, because such despair forfeits the inner imperatives, the eternal which tugs at Clamence's consciousness. In his refusal to come forth, he has refused
the task of what Nietzsche calls stylizing oneself.
Clamence cannot trade his identity for that of another; this is not the solution to his problem. The only
solution is the effort of accepting himself more fully
and existing more intensely in terms of this conflict.
His guilt before the world could then become transformed into a self-imposed feeling of inadequacy,
which drives him to an ever-greater affirmation of
himself as against his world. It is not a question of
self-destruction but rather of self-surpassment.

But Clamence does not do this. Like Martha, like
Caligula, like so many others, he is caught midway
in the process of inward orientation. He has not fully
explored this discovery of duplicity within him;

9. *Ibid.*, p. 167.

rather, he is stunned by it and has devised a makeshift solution for it. In the end we can say of the judge-penitent what Caligula said of his pedagogy of the absurd: "My kind of freedom is not good."

But we cannot blame Clamence; we can only feel compassion for him, for he is the summary of the faults of the present age and thus a limping epitome of the modern individual: confused, anxious, desperate, and ineffective. In the middle of the twentieth century we have discovered a desert whose horizons give way to yet farther horizons, and we tread through an emptiness without definition, or limit, or providential guides. We err about in a desert without laws or paths, and all of us who, like Clamence, think we have found the way are like false prophets, who not simply will not but, unfortunately, cannot come forth from the desert.

John-the-Baptist Clamence, like all men, awaits the coming of a better time. He gazes at the white-feathered doves soaring above the stair-stepped roofs of his Amsterdam and awaits the moment when these bearers of peace and the holy spirit will finally descend and move in the midst of a troubled people. Clamence is waiting; the expected time will come, it *must* come—this is his certainty. He knows that freedom, and forgiveness, and solidarity, and innocence are necessary for men, simply because men cannot escape themselves. But the wings of innocence do not soar above us, they flutter within us. And we must learn to know them and accept them. They will not teach us to fly; this is impossible. But we may learn once more to lift our feet and dance. This is all that any man could ever hope for.

CHAPTER TWELVE

TO BE A MAN

LITERATURE is the imitation of reality, but from time to time in its history it focuses upon certain aspects of that reality and brings to light new dimensions in human existence that amount almost to a discovery of them. The great discovery of recent modern literature is human suffering, and this sustained concern for what is pathetic in human existence is the central characteristic of the great literary works of this century.

For a number of reasons, writers from Latin countries have been most sharply conscious of this dimension of human reality. Certainly, *Bread and Wine*, by the Italian writer Ignazio Silone, gives us an unrelieved mirroring of the pathetic. And in France there have been at least two great novels of pathos. One of these is André Malraux' *La Condition Humaine*, a work hardly to be equaled in its vision of what is unendurably painful and ultimately hopeless in human life. The other and equally great work is Albert Camus' *La Peste*. Few scenes in any literature can match the moment in this novel when a group of tired, anxious men stand vigil at the bedside of a small boy stricken with the plague and helplessly watch this frail and innocent body as, for hour upon hour, it is devoured with convulsive pain until at last, exhausted of all possibility for further suffering, it is quietly and pitilessly released into death. There is really no response to be made to such a scene; it is ultimate and irrevocable. No soothing word, no facile summary or slogan, can assuage or justify this suffering. It happened, it is a fact, and there is nothing but to live with it, a memory which cannot be dispelled or excused. "All that a man could gain from the struggle between the plague and life was knowledge and memory." [1] These are the resigned words of Dr. Rieux, the narrator of the unhappy story of the plague which afflicted the North African city of Oran. Rieux, after the death of the child, has but one feeling, which pushes its way through a body paralyzed with fatigue: "There are moments in this city when I no longer feel anything but my revolt." And when a priest suggests that, rather than revolting, Rieux should resign himself to the fact of suffering, and trust in the higher love of God, Rieux replies, "No, Father . . . I have a different kind of idea of love. And to my dying day I shall refuse to love this world where children are tortured." [2]

Human suffering is a fact in this world, an unjustifiable fact, and Rieux sees it as his task to struggle against this fact. The death of a child makes clear to us that Rieux is a man in revolt; he has recognized and accepted a bitter truth about his world, but this acceptance does not lead to resignation but rather to a rebellious consciousness of the need to struggle against a scheme of things in which suffering is meaningless. The soothing slogan or the invocation of a deity has no place in this struggle, for this would rob man of the only certainty he possesses: that this is a world in which men suffer, find unhappiness, and die. For the honest man, a reality, no matter how bitter, can never be traded for an illusion or hope, no matter how redemptive. Rieux must live in terms of what he

1. Albert Camus, *La Peste,* Paris, Gallimard, 1947, p. 238.
2. *Ibid.,* pp. 178-9.

knows and remembers, and to do this means to live in revolt.

There is a conversation in *The Plague* which is highly suggestive of what it means to live in revolt. In the midst of the ceaseless struggle against the plague, Rieux finds a moment of reprieve when he sits on a terrace overlooking Oran and speaks with his friend, Tarrou, a strange, secretive man, who has given himself, as much as has Rieux, in the struggle against the plague. Tarrou tells his friend that this is not his first encounter with the plague but only another chapter in a continuing battle with it. Plague takes many forms, whether it be in bacilli or in the hearts of men, and the task is to struggle against it both in society and within oneself, for, whatever form the plague may take, it always ends with the unjustifiable destruction of one's fellow men. To the extent that one assents to the plague, either in oneself or in the world, one has assented to the murder of others. Plague means one thing to Tarrou: needless suffering of the individual. And no matter what form it takes—in totalitarian regimes, in personal relationships, or in one's own motivation—it must be fought against without respite. By approving regimes, and laws, and principles, Tarrou has discovered that, indirectly, he has approved and sanctioned the death of others who have run counter to these principles. To that extent he, like all other men, is afflicted with the plague, and Tarrou has spent the latter part of his life in the attempt to rid himself of this inner pestilence and to harm no living creature.

"In the end," said Tarrou with simplicity, "what interests me is knowing how to become a saint."

"But you don't believe in God."

cance: the subjection of the individual to a meaning which not only is not his own but, moreover, is a lying substitute for a God that never existed.

We have no honest choice but to recognize the universe for the gigantic, insoucient arena that it is. But if the world and its history are meaningless, it does not follow that there is no meaning; the recognition of meaning is found by man in himself. The very anxiety with which he gazes at the empty heavens is testimony to his realization that there is a meaningful demand within the human creature which does not find its response in the world. In the present age the task is to remain faithful to this meaningful demand; the task is to cultivate it. There is no other way of doing this than by a difficult and sustained attention to what we feel gives meaning and happiness to our existence. This is a groping, uncertain ascetic task. No one can guarantee its outcome, for the simple reason that its outcome depends upon the existing human being himself. It is, in the end, a question of creation, of giving form—in terms of habit, patterns of relations, and institutions—to these imperatives which press within us. At times this asceticism will blaspheme our old certitudes, but it is blasphemy in the service of a new meaning and a new God which is aborning. And during this difficult period of becoming there will be no pat answers, no easy solutions; every step of the way is a decision and an uncertainty. The tension cannot lapse; otherwise nothing would become, no creation would arrive. And, more importantly, one would cease being honestly and fully a man.

Camus has given us a poignant example of the groping, careful life of the rebel in his play, *Les Justes*.[5] Here we meet a group of young Russian

5. Albert Camus, *Les Justes*, Paris, Gallimard, 1950.

terrorists at the turn of the century, who are in revolt against the unalloyed misery of the Russian people and who hope to make one extreme and startling
protest against this by assassinating the Grand Duke
Serge. The intensity and dedication of this small
group is fervent; each has cut himself off from comfort, security, and even hope, and is ready to sacrifice
himself for the sake of a value which is far greater
than his own self. In short, they are a group of individuals in revolt, and the one member among them
who is most exemplary of this tense, controlled rebellion is Kaliayev, a young man who is nicknamed
"The Poet." Kaliayev is the one designated to throw a
bomb into the Grand Duke's carriage as he rides by.
But the carefully prepared assassination does not
come off. The carriage moves by and Kaliayev
makes no move. The reason: the Grand Duke is not
alone but is riding with his two young nephews. In
his refusal to throw the bomb, Kaliayev has drawn
a sharp line between the fanatical revolutionary, who
will sacrifice anyone for the sake of political efficiency, and the rebel, who is not slashing out blindly
against all that oppresses him but is limited in this
negative action by the very values which continue to
underlie and justify his protesting activity. One of
the terrorists, in summing up Kaliayev's reticence, explains that

> . . . he agrees to kill the Grand Duke, since his
> death can bring nearer the time when Russian
> children will no longer die of hunger. That in
> itself is not easy. But the death of the nephews
> of the Grand Duke will not prevent any children
> from dying of hunger. Even in destruction
> there is an order, there are limits.[6]

6. *Ibid.*, p. 73.

This is a clear instance of the manner in which the rebellious "no" is qualified by the "yes" which motivates the revolt. Between these two extremes the individual is caught, and it is only he who can mediate them. This is the inner tension in which the rebel is caught; there is no ready answer, no covering value which justifies anything and everything. There is only the necessity for action and the necessity for careful, uncertain choice before each action. The rebel finds his decisions painful not only because he has no external guide to rely on but also because, if he chooses wrongly, there is no one but himself to bear the responsibility and the guilt.

But the second time, the Grand Duke is alone in his carriage. The bomb is thrown and the assassination is successful. Kaliayev is arrested, tried, and sentenced to death. This is as it should be; it is the way Kaliayev intended it to be. One has the right to sacrifice another's life for an idea only if one is equally willing to sacrifice one's own life for it. The idea to which Kaliayev gave himself had significance only in so far as he guaranteed it with his whole being. For the rebel, turned terrorist, there is no other way to proceed, otherwise the value which one defends loses all significance. In revolt, if one must kill another fellow creature, then one has destroyed the demand for solidarity which was at the nascence of the revolt. There is not any justification for murder, nor can there be. But if the life of revolt leads one to the murder of another, then there is no alternative but for the rebel himself to die for the sake of his revolutionary idea. There is no other way. Kaliayev knew this, and he chose his one justification: death. In death, Kaliayev found happiness and completion.

In another place, Camus has spelled out the tortuous and groping way in which the rebellious heart must create and stand by its own decisions. In the short story, "The Guest," [7] we are at some remove from the frenzy of terrorism—on its borders, in fact—but the inner tension, for all its quietness, is nonetheless extreme. When a policeman delivers an Arab prisoner to a country schoolhouse in a desolate section of Algeria and requests that, because the police force is overextended in the face of terrorist raids, the schoolmaster himself should deliver the prisoner to the prison authorities, the schoolmaster rebels against being made to stand in judgment over another man and deliver him to punishment. He refuses to guarantee delivery of the prisoner, and he stands by this refusal. He will not force the young Arab to judgment, yet the man is a murderer, and he must in some way be held responsible for his crime. Once the policeman had departed, Daru, the schoolmaster, treats the Arab as a guest. He gives him supper, makes his bed, even puts away the pistol left him by the police agent. He sleeps next to the Arab, unarmed. The morning comes, he packs a lunch, motions the Arab to follow him. They walk for miles until a crest is reached on the mountain pass. Stretching off in one direction is the path to the prison; in another direction lies a trail leading to escape and sanctuary with other Arabs. Daru points the trails out to him, gives the Arab the lunch and a 1,000-franc note, then turns and walks back toward the school, leaving the young man to decide for himself which trail he shall take. Eventually, the Arab moves down the trail toward the prison.

From the point of view of Lyrical Existentialism, here is an individual who is existing fully as a man

7. Albert Camus, "L'Hôte," *L'Exil et le royaume*, Paris, Gallimard, 1957, pp. 101-24.

and has aided another to exist in the same way. Fully upon his own risk, Daru has defied the authorities in his handling of the prisoner, and the final irony of the story is that, upon returning to the schoolhouse, he finds an Arab terrorist note scrawled on the blackboard threatening revenge for having handed over their "brother." No situation could better suggest the manner in which the inner asceticism of the rebel places one at odds with the murderous absolutes of legalism on one hand and fanaticism on the other. True, Daru defied the authorities of legalism and thus served the Arab cause, but simultaneously he was instrumental in serving the authorities and thus incurred the wrath of the terrorists. To say that he served both sides and yet defied both sides is to say that he was actually concerned about neither. Daru's sole concern was with his own integrity and with the inviolable integrity of the Arab. Judged externally, his action is paradoxical; judged internally, his action is irreproachable. This isolated action, in the midst of warring ideologies and static policies, suddenly interjects the force of sanity and humanity into an otherwise hopeless and unhappy moment in history.

Like the schoolmaster, Camus has, from the beginning, been deeply concerned to interject a voice of sanity into the clamorous political and social struggles which have marked this century's character. The voluminous essays, as well as his plays and novels, have been a powerful and effective testimony to this concern. And the extraordinary book, *L'Homme révolté*, is, in a general sense, the summary of his reflections on the tragedies and redemptive possibilities of modern European history. Camus asserts that the phenomenon of revolt has been the crucial human experience in the background of the upheavals of modern history. The great historical revolt of modern

times is against God; this is the God whom the oppressed peasants and burghers of Europe saw as the
justification for the church which threatens, the di-
vinely ruling monarchs who oppress and destroy, and
the laws and values which constrict and wither the
individual. In revolting against this Godhead of oppression, men were affirming a common need for a
world of solidarity, of innocence, of justice, and of
freedom.

But if the seeds of modern revolution were healthy,
the trees became gnarled and their fruit was bitter.
Revolt remains revolt only so long as it affirms as
much as it denies, only so long as it retains this tension between the two poles of its contradiction. This
is difficult to sustain, for it takes its toll in personal
patience and suffering. And it was not sustained. As
soon as one pole of the revolt was asserted at the
ultimate expense of the other, revolt was transformed
into something simpler and more murderous. At its
extreme, when a man puts forth an absolute negation,
the result is nihilism; and modern history has known
nihilism not only in its personal representatives but in
its politics and its art forms as well. At the other extreme, the absolute assertion of the values of revolt
has metamorphosed into a formalism which doggedly
asserts its values into the world with no concern for
their correspondence to any real situation. Between
these two pendulumlike extremes of nihilism and
formalism, recent history has left a trail of suffering
which has been as destructive in its moments of insouciance as it has in its more obvious moments of
rage. And out of this betrayal of revolt, philosophies, and art works, and political regimes have been
spawned which have not served the presumed values
of the individual but have ended by oppressing him
even more—this time in the name of absolute justice

or absolute freedom or an absolute conviction of the moment.[8]

Between these aberrations of a revolt gone wild, Camus seeks quietly, yet almost evangelically, to call men back to the difficult and ascetic life of revolt. Between bourgeois and revolutionary nihilism, between formal and negative art, between total mysticism and total engagement, there lies a middle possibility which is not a path or direction but is a way of existing. Camus does not point to a principle or an institution; he points to the individual, for everything depends upon him. There is no other place to start, and it is only here that all serious thought can terminate. But who is this creature, the existing individual? He is a creature whose measure is the dust of this earth of which he is made and to which he must return; and yet this creature has no measure, he is beyond calculation and understanding, because he is free. And in this freedom he finds his sovereignty, his responsibility, and his self. Man is neither dust, nor not-dust: he is both. And he must learn to live in terms of both, never denying one at the expense of the other. He can deny neither his finitude nor his eternality; both are part of his being as a man, and his sole, authentic task is to be just that: a man.

If the life of revolt is as much an affirmation as it is a negation, this is only a more personal way of expressing a more general insight into the nature of the world and of man. The personal imperative within the existential admonition is the distillate of modern man's discovery that his world is inescapable and real, and yet it is unacceptable and insufficient. It is insufficient,

8. The reader who desires more than a cursory glance at Camus' social-historical critique can consult my volume, *The Thought and Art of Albert Camus*, Chicago, Henry Regnery Company, 1958.

because men themselves are the only measure of their needs; but, at the same time, without the world, men would never know their needs or discover their measure.

There is a truth here that is simple yet all-transforming: men are wedded to their world with insoluble bonds. Freedom, and solidarity, and justice, and innocence will always be compromised, for to exist as a human being is to be compromised, anxious, and uncertain. There can be no absolutes, but, after all, it was never in the nature of human existence to wither for the lack of absolutes. To the contrary, human existence flourishes only in their absence. This is the marriage between men and their world, and Camus' task has been to urge us to accept this bond. Once the acceptance is made, the marriage feast will begin: this is the renaissance which Camus has awaited. It is, of course, true that the world is indifferent to men; but seen through the eyes of courage, this is a tender indifference, which softens the visage of the universe and lends it beauty. But, to round out the circle, it rings even truer to say that men are, after all, indifferent to the world; but this indifference also is softened. The individual who has become a man has not only learned to understand himself, but, as well, he has learned to look upon the world with tenderness, opening himself gratefully to its gifts.

Part Four

THE IRONIC CONSCIOUSNESS

*Life in the world alone leads to one re-
sult, meditation alone leads to another. So
have we heard from the wise.*

*They who devote themselves both to
life in the world and to meditation, by
life in the world overcome death and by
meditation achieve immortality.*

*To darkness are they doomed who
worship only the body, and to greater
darkness they who worship only the
spirit.*   from the *Isha Upanishad*

*He who sees the inaction that is in action,
and the action that is in inaction, is wise
indeed. Even when he is engaged in action he remains poised in the tranquillity
of the Atman.*   from the *Bhagavad-Gita*

*If one man conquer in battle a thousand
times a thousand men, and if another conquer himself, he is the greatest of con-
querors.*

*One's own self conquered is better than
all other people conquered; not even a
god could change into defeat the victory
of a man who has vanquished himself.*

        from the *Dhammapada*

CHAPTER THIRTEEN

THE IRONIC CONSCIOUSNESS

WE HAVE NOW HEARD the voices of three extraordinary modern thinkers, and the intention has not been solely to discover *what* these men have said, but, rather, *how* we can best understand what they have said, to see their thought as a whole piece in its integrity and in its full relevance. In understanding each man's thought as a whole, we have discovered a basic identity in the thought of Kierkegaard, Nietzsche, and Camus, an identity which merits their being considered as a single type of thinker, representing a single type of thought termed Lyrical Existentialism. In the wake of these three extensive essays, there should be little, if any, room for doubt in the Reader's mind as to the basic identity of these thinkers, and, during these final pages, it remains for us to bring together in a more precise manner the central ideas that have threaded their way through these essays. After this, some of the wider ramifications of these ideas can be suggested.

The term centrally descriptive of the identity of Kierkegaard, Nietzsche, and Camus is Lyrical Existentialist. This implies that each of these thinkers is preoccupied with the nature of the existing individual, with the problem of what man "is." And the burden of this preoccupation is their attempt to communicate a certain way of existing; this is their existential admonition. This admonition points to a subjective condition; it is not to be communicated by means of the traditional empirical and rational methods of phil-

osophical thought; rather, it must be communicated by
lyrical means. This is to say that existential facts cannot be communicated directly and explicitly but only
indirectly and implicitly by the suggestive, evocative
devices of poetry, or drama, or rhapsodic prose. Each
of these thinkers uses words and images which are
suggestive rather than indicative, deceptive rather than
explanatory. Their common voice is lyrical, because
they feel that words and concepts, in themselves, are
insufficient for a description of human existence. The
liberties they take with language are not the product
of a confusion or misunderstanding of the nature and
limitation of language. They know that words are
to be distrusted, not because they are too vague for
their task, but rather because they are much too
specific; they are static symbols of a static reality.
They know that individual existence is beyond the
grasp of words and concepts and can never be reduced to them. Only the world can be reduced to a
concept, not a man, for his existence is more complex
than the world's; his reality is dialectical. New tools
are required to describe this reality, and lyricism is
the added tool which can do more than can rational
analysis alone for this task. Analysis bids us look outward where the existing individual is not to be found;
the singing voice of lyricism draws us inward to become absorbed in the only existence we shall ever
directly encounter: ourself. Possessed with this existential preoccupation, all three men are character-
istically lyrical when expressing themselves. They
employ a means of expression that is singularly appropriate for what they wish to express. The term
"lyrical," with its immediate suggestion of the nonob-
jective experience of music, points to the subjective
source of this manner of philosophizing. So then,
"existential," so understood, and "lyrical," so under-

stood, imply and complement one another, and thus "Lyrical Existentialist" proves itself the most apt descriptive term for the kind of philosopher and way of philosophizing characteristic of Kierkegaard, Nietzsche, and Camus.

But if this be the most general description of the kind of philosopher these men *are* and of *how* they philosophize, it would still remain to be shown that *what* they affirm also shows the same basic identity. And this has been the central task of the preceding essays: the effort to show that a whole and integral interpretation of these thinkers reveals basic affirmations which they hold in common. These basic affirmations involve (1) a distinctive understanding of the environing world in which the individual exists, (2) a distinctive understanding of the self-conscious reality of the individual as a reality that is free in relation to this world, and, finally, (3) a distinctive existential admonition, indicating the way in which the individual should exist, given this understanding of the world's reality and this understanding of one's own individual reality.

It should be useful to give a résumé of these common affirmations, inasmuch as it is these that constitute the basic identity of the Lyrical Existentialists. In the first place, it was made clear that each of these thinkers is peculiarly modern in the way that he insists upon the sovereign and undeniable reality of the objective, sensuous world—all three insist that this is the one world given us to know, and that we cannot escape it to some other realm, either beyond or above it. But alongside this insistence that we are bound to this world and must take it absolutely seriously, there is the characteristic contention that this world is indifferent to and without meaning for the individual himself. The world is sovereign yet absurd, inescapable yet insufficient—this is the common attitude of the Lyrical Existentialists, an attitude which thus refuses the world as it is (from the honest recognition of the individual's own meaningful reality) but does not renounce it (from the honest recognition that there is no other world than this one).

But, in the second place, it is equally apparent how Kierkegaard, Nietzsche, and Camus assert the possibility of the free and sovereign reality of the self-conscious individual—a possibility which becomes an existential fact when the individual realizes the inability of the world to provide justification and meaning for himself. This recognition of the world's insufficiency is, simultaneously, the realization of the possibility of meaning and justification within the individual and by the individual. This is the experience of despair or revolt; it is the revelation of the individual's freedom and, thus, his responsibility for his own existence. In this experience, he has discovered the task of becoming something other than what he is; his task is to become more inward, more an individual, which is to say he must become freer, more responsible, more autonomous in relation to his world.

In the third place, it has become clear that in the light of these distinctive conceptions of the world and of the individual, the Lyrical Existentialists propose what is essentially the same existential admonition. Whether the admonition be that of infinite resignation, will to power, revolt, etc., the same way of existing is indicated: an existence of tension, conflict, and striving of the self-conscious individual with his ever-present and inescapable world. An existence such as this is never complete or static; it is always in process, always incomplete, an infinite task. Understanding the world and the individual in the way that they do, the Lyrical Existentialists contend that an authentic and honest existence is not that a man *be* something but, rather, that he *become* himself, i.e., that he become freer, more responsible, more autonomous, more in tension with his world.

The remarkable fact about the Lyrical Existentialists is the way in which they have fully accepted the disenchantment which has followed in the wake of modern science and critical reasoning, and yet they emerge unscathed by it. The unmasking of a mythless, inscrutable world and the discovery of the pathetic way in which men are manipulated by socioeconomic forces and by subconscious compulsions— these events have all but washed away the last traces of belief in a benevolent world and in a noble, freely determined mankind. Cynicism and bitterness are the consequences of this modern disillusionment, and the more science unveils, the more intense becomes this disillusionment in our traditional beliefs about ourselves and our world. Yet the striking thing is that these three men have pushed our modern insights out to their ultimate import, stressing both the absurdity of this world and the hopeless finitude of the individual, but they emerge from this with an impassioned reaffirmation of the importance of the existing individual. This is what is remarkable, and our last task is to attempt some explanation of how three such men can be so thoroughly modern in attitude and yet run absolutely counter to the main stream of cynical, nihilist, and escapist modes of thought.

The answer is not far to seek, for we have been confronted with it almost from the beginning moments of this study. What the Lyrical Existentialists have discovered, which sets them against the main stream of modern thought, is a sense of irony. There should be no misunderstanding here: irony has nothing to do with the comic. The comic is the awareness of contradiction in a situation which is external to oneself. Irony is quite otherwise. It is the awareness of a contradiction within oneself; it is the consciousness of existing in terms of a contradiction, and this contradiction is precisely the awareness, on one hand, of being a finite creature compelled by and subject to the demands of the world and, on the other hand, of being a free, responsible being who can never be compelled or subjected by any external force. The irony is that one *is* a contradiction, one exists dialectically.

The ironic consciousness was not far to seek, because it is, after all, the way of existing which all three of these men admonish us to discover. The existential admonition of the Lyrical Existentialists leads us to an ironic consciousness, and it is this which redeems the philosophy of these men from the cynicism of an unhappy age. The philosophical conviction that has been asserted all along by Kierkegaard, Nietzsche, and Camus is that there are two realities given in human experience: the reality of the world and the reality of our own unique individuality. But they make no effort to assert a dualism; rather, the genius of their way of thinking is that these two "reals" do not exist except as they are united within the self-conscious individual. It is quite irrelevant to speak in this instance either of monism or dualism: both are correct and neither is correct. Philosophical pigeonholes do not apply, because these men are not offering us the objective results of an exhaustive study of the physical universe and the human psyche. The sole focus of their concern is the arena of human consciousness itself, and in this arena they have found two realities which compete with one another and yet which are inescapably dependent upon one another. It is the consciousness of this inescapable competition that provides the irony of human existence, and it is the task of each man, through lyrical means, to suggest to us the presence of this ironic dialectic within the consciousness of all men. This is the philosophical conviction which motivates the Lyrical Existentialists to say, "You must become aware of this inner contradiction, for it is the truth about your existence; as long as you exist unaware of this contradiction, you are living a lie."

It is by means of an ironic consciousness that the Lyrical Existentialists have been enabled to embrace fully the disillusioning insights of a modern worldview and yet to riposte with an incredibly confident assertion of the paramount value of the individual, along with the related values of freedom, responsibility, and self-identity. It would seem that the traditions of Western humanism are somehow vindicated in this attitude, and yet there are more than a few thinkers who have glimpsed in the Lyrical Existentialists a disturbing tendency toward antitheism, antirationality, and amorality, which strikes deeply at the roots of Western civilization. There is no escaping the suspicion that an ironic consciousness is, in terms of two-thousand-odd years of Western culture, a subversive consciousness.

Even so, this nagging suspicion has not prevented many from claiming a rootage for existential thinking within Western culture. Not only Pascal and Augustine and Heraclitus, but even Thomas Aquinas, Hegel, and a host of other improbable candidates have been curiously ranked within a presumed age-old tradition of existentialism. But this attempt to root existential thought in the history of our culture is a failure, first of all because few historians of ideas seem to have any understanding of the ironic consciousness which is at the heart of all existential philosophy, and, secondly, even though it is always possible to find vague echoes of existential themes up and down the gamut of Western ideas, this is accounted for by the way in which men qua men always show certain similarities in thought; but there is no possibility of explaining away the emergence of existentialism in recent times as a dominant mode of thought. Existentialism is not a perennial theme within Western culture; indeed, scholars never suggested to themselves that there was any such theme until they were confronted with existential philosophy as a rather sudden phenomenon of modern times.

What I am suggesting is that the most significant event of the past century has been the steady dissolution of our Western cultural traditions in the face of a rebellion against this tradition. In the arts, in letters, and in many of the sciences, an intransigent revolt has appeared which has thrown itself blindly, at times, against a tradition of thought and morality that is felt to be bankrupt. This is a loss of confidence in the rational tradition of Greece and the religio-moral tradition of Judeo-Christendom that have structured our thinking and productivity for two millennia. Moving on the crest of this wave of dissolution is the philosophical attitude of existentialism, and, whether we like it or not, this philosophy is an authentic response to the problems of our age, even as modern art, poetry, drama, and the novel show the same exploratory and rebellious response to a decadent culture. To say that Western culture is decadent is to affirm that it no longer offers sufficient sustenance and justification for the lives of its most sensitive and thoughtful individuals. Something is lacking; there is need for some new insight or rationale, and the thought and art of the present moment give undeniable testimony to a groping, anxious search for something to fill the void.

To say that Western civilization is decadent should

not be a shocking or frightful revelation. The revolutionary character of the past century and a half has been ample testimony to this fact. It is hardly a serious choice between saying that either our traditions are bankrupt or else that recent history has unaccountably spawned a brood of malicious malcontents who have revolted against a perfectly sound culture; the latter choice is as marvelously naïve as it is widespread. It is rather a matter of facing up to the fact honestly, that we have exhausted the resources of our civilization and can no longer live productively in terms of it alone. This is not surprising, for we never should have entertained the thought that "culture" was synonymous with "Western culture," and that to lose the latter was to lose the former. No, it is no more than historical accident that at the roots of our civilization we have Greek and Jewish cultures which have become inextricably intertwined, and which formed us, motivated us, grew with us as we grew, and finally became surpassed. We happened to have inherited a double-rooted culture; it might have been quite otherwise, but in this case it wasn't. I really don't think that God planned the character of Western civilization; a culture is a product of the confusions and defeats of men. We should not be shocked, then, to realize that the culture of Western civilization developed insights which were limited and not universally absolute. The discovery of recent times is that our insights *are* limited and lacking, and the result of this has been a groping that has not yet reached its goal.

Within this ferment, Lyrical Existentialism has made a significant contribution which has not yet been fully understood. It, too, has been groping and has come up with little more than a certain insight into the nature of human existence. But the discovery of the ironic consciousness has an extraordinary importance for two very good reasons: One of these is that an affirmation about the nature of man is the necessary foundation for any developing world view; the second is that the central insights of Lyrical Existentialism, even though out of key with Western culture, have an essential identity with the types of thought character- istic of Indian philosophy. This second point is, of course, a fascinating matter for speculation. It is re- markable that these three thinkers, none of whom betrays any particular interest or knowledge of Indian philosophy, should have revolted against Western tra- dition and painfully groped their way toward a point of view which is largely identical with the insights of orthodox Hinduism, of primitive Indian Buddhism, and of the Zen Buddhism, which carries on this primi- tive tradition. The existential role of philosophy, the skeptical acceptance of the world, the emphasis upon the conscious life and an inner reality, the need for asceticism, the rejection of direct modes of moral- religious teaching, the concern to *live* a truth rather than knowing it—these and many other viewpoints of Indian philosophy are, simultaneously, the discoveries of the Lyrical Existentialists. And they are discover- ies, because they are indigenous to this moment in Western history; the irony is that after much anxious thought, Kierkegaard, Nietzsche, and Camus should have hit upon "new" insights which were existent at the very moment of the birth of Western civilization. It has taken this long for us to discover that our cul- tural insights were neither complete nor absolute; and now the viewpoint of Lyrical Existentialism has moved out beyond a failing culture and joined with the viewpoint of a quite ancient culture. In kicking over the traces of Hellenism (in its antirationalism and anti-idealism) and Judeo-Christianity (in its anti- theism and amorality), Lyrical Existentialism can—

perhaps for the first time in history—lay claim to being a cosmopolitan philosophy.

There is no need to dwell upon all the implications of these ideas. It is sufficient, I think, to suggest that, in this light, the groping and "unphilosophical" works of Kierkegaard and Nietzsche and Camus may become the most important milestones in modern philosophical history. These three men are the authentic spokesmen for an insight gradually emerging in the modern West. They are the fountainheads of this kind of thought and have spawned many disciples, but I will perhaps not be misunderstood at this point if I maintain that those modern thinkers that we entitle existentialists are those who, in varying ways, have tried to "Westernize" Lyrical Existentialism, by interpreting its insights either in Judaic-Christian terms or in Hellenistic terms. These attempts have, by and large, been unsuccessful, for they have sought to translate the insights of an emerging viewpoint back into the set traditions of an aging culture. Sartre, Heidegger, and others may be said to be "Hellenizers," and Marcel, Tillich, Jaspers, Bultmann, and still others have primarily attempted to "Judaize" and "Christianize" the vision of Lyrical Existentialism. At times, these existentialists have created the impression that Western philosophy and theology were experiencing a sudden rebirth, but, if the Reader has accepted the cultural theories outlined in this chapter, he will see that the existentialists have embodied contradictory insights in their works which prevent them from speaking effectively either to a traditional audience or to a groping one. The principal effects of their works have been to put the insights of Lyrical Existentialism into a more palatable form, so that in terms of traditional modes of thought we could "get our teeth into them"; the other effect has been to shore up our tradition with the fancied hope that new and unexpected vitality had been discovered in our cultural roots. But, as I have said, the error in this is basically the ineffective effort to translate an emerging, exotic viewpoint into an older and different cultural language.

The unique position of the Lyrical Existentialists is that they are not trying to shore up a flagging tradition; they do not have a vested interest in it, emotionally or intellectually, and hence they are not threatened by its dissolution. This accounts, then, for the peculiar optimism and confidence which they manifest as they preside over a painful age of uncertainty. There is a dominant joyfulness radiating through their works, that belies any suggestion that they harbor a bitterness over the disintegration of Western culture. Joyfulness is a peculiar human attitude for anyone who has comprehended the problems of the present age; bitterness, open or hidden, is more often the response to our situation. Surely bitterness is found today in the desperate and vindictive evangelism that infects many behavioral scientists, whether Marxist or deterministic, as they remorselessly seek ever more effective methods of controlling the thought and conduct of their fellow men. The Marxist and Freudian discoveries of men's rather pitiful finitude should have awakened an even greater compassion in these scientists for the limited and fragile existence of the individual; instead the reaction is often a scarcely veiled contempt for the human creature, a contempt which betrays the inescapable disappointment they feel toward a mankind that has not turned out to be as noble and free as was believed. This is a bitterness which has its roots in a cultural situation, and it is primarily a Judaic-Christian disappointment. The same disappointment is apparent in the dogged attempt of scientifically oriented philosophers to cling to a truncated and miserable Greek conviction in external standards of certitude. This takes the form of resolutely denying the reality and meaning of conscious experience and then reducing human reality and meaning to objectively demonstrable corroborations. The effect of this is to reduce man to the world, thus denying special significance to the human individual and, consequently, making an absurdity of any concern for men, their problems, and oneself. It is true, certainly, that the measure of man is the dust of this earth, but it is sad to observe the haste in which many philosophers seek to reduce their fellow men to dust, although oddly enough they do not always do so with themselves. But, again, there is shock and a bitterness underlying these attitudes, which is understandable even though it can never be justifiable.

These are examples of the way in which we have lost our understanding, our feeling for, and our confidence in the human individual, and, in the end, this means the loss of confidence in our own self. This suggests an inability on our part to accept emotionally as well as intellectually the discoveries we have made about the world and ourselves. We appear to be incapable of rising above this disappointment, of surpassing it and thus living with it in a new and productive way. We lack precisely that ironic consciousness which sees and accepts the pathetic limitations of our individual lives and yet sees these limitations as only relative, as facts which cannot ultimately threaten or destroy the freedom and integrity that we possess in face of the world.

The insights of Lyrical Existentialism are not yet complete or exhausted; most likely, this attitude is just beginning to bear its fruits. This is to say that we do not end with what Kierkegaard and Nietzsche and

Camus have told us; we begin with it, because the ironic consciousness that they hold out to us is a redemptive response to the ills of an age; for the individual life, it appears to be the one present possibility of accepting the total impact of the modern world view without, thereby, being destroyed by it as a healthy individual. The importance of these three thinkers for moral and religious philosophy is obvious; in a time when human thought must take place within a closed universe where the individual is faced with total immanence, Lyrical Existentialism offers the one possibility of asserting a special meaning for individual existence without making the error of asserting another world, either distinct from or mysteriously inclusive of the only world known by honest thought and research. The inner reality affirmed by these three men does not exist apart from the given world of finitude; rather, it exists only in this world as an integral part of the world as we know it. It is not possible to account for this inner reality without taking the world into account, and in the same way, this world and its history cannot be accounted for without reference to the free reality revealed within individual consciousness. Within this dialectic of existence, the ironic consciousness takes its stand, not as a way of knowing the nature of the world and man, but as a way of existing within the truth of this condition.

Ultimately, we must recognize that the ironic consciousness is not so much an admonition to us as it is a presaging of the inevitable adjustment which individuals will have to make to a freshly envisaged world. The Lyrical Existentialists have, in a sense, suffered in our stead and have arrived at the one response which they find to be meaningful. Our estimate of Kierkegaard, Nietzsche, and Camus must be, first of all, as men, and second, as thinkers. The authority of their thought finds its source in the passion of their lives. They have lived in terms of an ironic consciousness, and when they speak to us, this consciousness reveals itself not only in their ideas but in the vibrant lyricism that moves within the sound of their words. There is an undeniable health and force heard in the voices of these three men, a health that resides within the fact of honesty. This is the honesty that can gaze somberly at the pathos which is our lot, and at the same moment accept it and rise above it with a kind of laughter. Both pathos and laughter exist within the ironic consciousness, and when the two of these exist together, we have risen above both the comedy and tragedy of life and have found its joy.

BIBLIOGRAPHY

Kierkegaard

(in the original chronological order)

The Journals, trans. Alexander Dru, New York, Oxford University Press, 1938.

Either/Or, trans. David F. and Lillian M. Swenson and Walter Lowrie, Princeton, Princeton University Press, 1944.

Edifying Discourses, trans. David F. and Lillian M. Swenson, 4 vols., Minneapolis, Augsburg Publishing House, 1943-46.

Repetition, trans. Walter Lowrie, Princeton, Princeton University Press, 1941.

Fear and Trembling, trans. Walter Lowrie, Princeton, Princeton University Press, 1941.

Philosophical Fragments, trans. David F. Swenson, Princeton, Princeton University Press, 1936.

The Concept of Dread, trans. Walter Lowrie, Princeton, Princeton University Press, 1944.

Three Discourses on Imagined Occasions, trans. David F. Swenson, Minneapolis, Augsburg Publishing House, 1941.

Stages on Life's Way, trans. Walter Lowrie, Princeton, Princeton University Press, 1940.

Concluding Unscientific Postscript to the Philosophical Fragments, trans. David F. Swenson and Walter Lowrie, Princeton, Princeton University Press, 1941.

Works of Love, trans. David F. and Lillian M. Swenson, Princeton, Princeton University Press, 1946.

Christian Discourses, trans. Walter Lowrie, New York, Oxford University Press, 1939.

The Present Age, trans. Walter Dru and Walter Lowrie, New York, Oxford University Press, 1940.

The Sickness Unto Death, trans. Walter Lowrie, Princeton, Princeton University Press, 1941.

On Authority and Revelation, trans. Walter Lowrie, Princeton, Princeton University Press, 1955.

The Point of View, trans. Walter Lowrie, New York, Oxford University Press, 1939.

Training in Christianity, trans. Walter Lowrie, Princeton, Princeton University Press, 1944.

For Self-Examination and Judge For Yourselves!, trans. Walter Lowrie, Princeton, Princeton University Press, 1944.

Attack Upon Christendom, trans. Walter Lowrie, Princeton, Princeton University Press, 1944.

Nietzsche

Nietzsches Werke, Vols. I-IX, Stuttgart, Alfred Kroner Verlag, 1921.

Camus

(*in the original chronological order*)

L'Envers et l'Endroit, Algiers, Charlot, 1937; Paris, Gallimard, 1958.

Noces, Algiers, Charlot, 1938; Paris, Gallimard, 1947.

L'Etranger, Paris, Gallimard, 1942.

Le Mythe de Sisyphe, Paris, Gallimard, 1942.

Le Malentendu, suivi de Caligula, Paris, Gallimard, 1944.

Lettres à un ami allemand, Paris, Gallimard, 1945.

"*Remarque sur la révolte*," *L'Existence*, edited by Jean Grenier, Paris, Gallimard, 1945.

La Peste, Paris, Gallimard, 1947.

L'Etat de siège, Paris, Gallimard, 1948.

Actuelles, Paris, Gallimard, 1950.

Les Justes, Paris, Gallimard, 1950.

L'Homme révolté, Paris, Gallimard, 1951.

Actuelles II, Paris, Gallimard, 1953.

L'Eté, Paris, Gallimard, 1954.

La Chute, Paris, Gallimard, 1956.

L'Exil et le royaume, Paris, Gallimard, 1957.

Actuelles III, Paris, Gallimard, 1958.

Miscellaneous

Barth, Karl, *Church Dogmatics, IV, 1, The Doctrine of Reconciliation*, New York, Charles Scribner's Sons, 1957.

Collins, James, *The Mind of Kierkegaard*, Chicago, Henry Regnery Company, 1953.

Hanna, Thomas, *The Thought and Art of Albert Camus*, Chicago, Henry Regnery Company, 1958.

Jaspers, Karl, *Nietzsche: Einführung in das Verständis seines Philosophierens*, Berlin, Walter De Gruyter und Co., 1950.

Kaufmann, Walter, *Nietzsche: Philosopher, Psychologist, Antichrist*, New York, Meridian Books, 1956.

Lowrie, Walter, *Kierkegaard*, New York, Oxford University Press, 1938.

Sartre, Jean-Paul, *L'Etre et le néant*, Paris, Gallimard, 1943.

Thody, Philip, *Albert Camus: A Study of His Work*, London, Hamish Hamilton, 1957.

INDEX